DEAR FIONA

Letters from a Suspected Soviet Spy

FIONA FULLERTON

For my darling John,

with love

Fiona

Dear Fiona
Letters from a Suspected Soviet Spy
Fiona Fullerton

ISBN 978-1-904380-85-6 (Hardback)
ISBN 978-1-908162-15-1 (Adobe Ebook)
ISBN 978-1-908162-16-8 (Kindle/Epub Ebook)

Published 2012 by
Waterside Press Ltd.   **Telephone** +44(0)1256 882250
Sherfield Gables   **E-mail** enquiries@watersidepress.co.uk
Sherfield on Loddon   **Online catalogue** WatersidePress.co.uk
Hook, Hampshire
United Kingdom RG27 0JG

UK distributor Gardners Books, 1 Whittle Drive, Eastbourne, East Sussex, BN23 6QH.
Tel: +44 (0)1323 521777; sales@gardners.com; www.gardners.com

North American distributor International Specialized Book Services (ISBS), 920 NE 58th
Ave, Suite 300, Portland, Oregon, 97213-3786, USA. Tel: 1 800 944 6190 Fax 1 503 280
8832; orders@isbs.com; www.isbs.com

Cover design © 2012 Waterside Press. Prepared by www.gibgob.com from an original
concept by Fiona Fullerton and Martha Milliken. Photograph of Alex Alexandrowicz
taken from a flyer "Free Alex Now" advertising a comedy benefit night in 1993. All other
photos are from the author's private collection unless otherwise stated.

Cataloguing-In-Publication Data A catalogue record for this book can be obtained from
the British Library.

e-book *Dear Fiona* is available as an ebook and also to subscribers of Myilibrary and Daw-
sonera. See above for ISBN numbers and the formats they relate to.

Printed by MPG Books Group, Bodmin and King's Lynn.

DEAR FIONA

Letters from a Suspected Soviet Spy

FIONA FULLERTON

❄ WATERSIDE PRESS

Dear Fiona

Contents

Acknowledgements

I am indebted to the following people:

The editor of the *Lancashire Telegraph*
BBC Points West
The Koestler Trust
Lesley-Anne Hornbogen for typing-up Alex's handwritten letters with such speed, enthusiasm and efficiency.
Ross Slater for finding Alex and for being so gentle.
Professor David Wilson for letting me use quotes from some of his writings.
Bryan Gibson for permission to use extracts from *The Longest Injustice,* a book Alex Alexandrowicz co-wrote after his release from prison with David Wilson. That work includes Alex's '**Prison Chronicles**' — a manuscript he created telling of his life, arrest, trial, imprisonment and fight for justice.
Piers Martin for generously printing the proof copies.
Corinna Honan for her sound editorial advice.
All those who have given kind permission to use their photographs.
Alasdair Kirk for scanning all the archive material.
Martha Milliken for her help with the cover.
Janie and Mike Wilson for providing a retreat in France.
Karen Todner of Kaim Todner for her legal help to re-open Alex's case.
Edward Fitzgerald QC for supporting this book and Alex's fight for justice.

And to K, for returning my letters to me all those years ago. Without them, this book would not have been possible.

Fiona Fullerton
2012

About the Author

Fiona Fullerton was for 30 years a leading actress in theatre, television and films. She is now a property guru, journalist, interior designer and author of three books about investing in the property market. She lives in the Cotswolds with her husband and two children.

Alex Alexandrowicz's story is one of a disturbing miscarriage of justice. Alex's perseverance in exposing injustice in this case is admirable. Fiona Fullerton's book makes for compulsive reading and poses profound questions about the justice system here.

Edward Fitzgerald CBE QC

This book is dedicated to all those who have suffered a miscarriage of justice.

And to Rhea Paige Keogh, Alex's goddaughter.

Prologue

Sometimes, a true friend can come to you from the most extraordinary circumstances. And so it was with Alex.

In April 1976, I received a charming letter from prisoner 789959, Anthony Alexandrowicz who was in HM Prison Parkhurst (He is known to everyone as Alex). I was appearing weekly in a popular television series, so fan letters were not unusual, but it was the contents of this one that made me pay attention (coupled with the artistry of the sender's miniscule and meticulous handwriting). Anyone who pays you a massive compliment and then gives it a twist is worth getting to know, I reckoned. 'Your face could launch the US Navy and a couple of submarines,' he wrote, 'but my pal says just the US Navy.' I was intrigued.

I replied, briefly, but this first simple exchange led to a correspondence that lasted for 12 years. His letters to me were profoundly wise, humorous and comforting and he wrote and dedicated poems to me that were full of pathos and beauty. He could lift my spirits instantly with his witty descriptions of life inside, such as his account of lunch on Christmas Day.

> 'Heard no bells jingling. Only keys.
>
> I've just had my Christmas lunch. Yeah, we had turkey. All three hundred of us—a slice each. I held mine up to the light and I could see right through it.'

With his wise counsel and extraordinary intellect (aided by his voracious appetite for literature), Alex took on the role of mentor, always advising me to give that little bit extra, to seek perfection in everything, a practice he called 'The Realm of the Last Inch'. He supported me through a crumbling marriage that was causing enormous heartache and a roller-coaster career. He would research film roles for me in the prison library, whether it was about

Lady Jane Grey or Van Gogh's mistress, Rachel. 'She was partial to drinking gin,' he wrote, 'so she fairly quickly lost what remained of her prettiness.' The eternal pupil in me responded, enraptured, to my new tutor.

In return I was there for him during his interminable incarceration, giving him news of my nomadic existence as my career took me around the world. I would encourage him to stay out of trouble inside, knowing that misdemeanours usually meant a stint in solitary confinement. He began to depend on my letters—a lifeline to the outside world, but also a world so very different to anything he could imagine. He couldn't quite believe that I cared sufficiently to keep writing to him. 'By the way, you must get hundreds of letters every week … do you reply to every one?' he asked. 'It is a continuous case of wonderment to me, you know.'

So why did I keep writing? It's simple. Because I was lonely and something about his situation resonated with mine. More than that, I felt compelled to do so as if there was an invisible thread between us: in recognition of a kindred spirit, someone who really needed me.

Alex was born in Lancashire in 1953. His mother, Elsie, was from Cornwall and his father, Viktor, from Odessa in Ukraine. Viktor moved to the United Kingdom in the late-1940s and found work as a forklift truck driver at the Belling Cooker Factory in Burnley. He married Elsie in 1952 but he was a domineering and unkind man with a violent temper, which would erupt unexpectedly, leading to physical abuse raining down on Alex and his sister Susan, who was four years younger.

Viktor was also a secretive man with connections to the KGB during his time in the Soviet Union. The family lived in Nelson, Lancashire, otherwise known as 'Little Moscow' due to its burgeoning influx of Ukrainian émigrés in the aftermath of the Second World War.

Alex started running away from home at the age of 12 and was taken into care. He began to abscond from local authority homes, preferring to live rough. His first crime was stealing from a market stall, for which he was sent to approved school. There followed a series of petty thefts and he was sent to borstal for housebreaking.

In early 1970, Alex visited the Russian Embassy in London and had a meeting with a diplomat that may have been pivotal to the extraordinary story that was to unfold. He describes the visit in his 'Prison Chronicles':

'I had gone to the Soviet Embassy in an effort to find out the whereabouts of my grandparents (on my father's side). I was referred to an official who said he was a councillor. We went outside and sat on a bench. He had some sandwiches in a paper bag. I told him what I wanted and he said he would see what he could do.

He asked me some questions about my father and whether I was born in this country. What did I want to be when I left school? He seemed curious but not unpleasantly so. He gave me his name, Igor Laptev, and a phone number. I was to ring the number after a few weeks and ask for him by name, by which time, hopefully, he would have some news. I did not go back to the Embassy, nor did I telephone the man. I had lost the phone number anyway.'

Unfortunately for Alex, whilst he was talking to the Russian diplomat someone was taking covert photographs.

In October 1970 he was sentenced to 18 months imprisonment after he broke into the house of a police inspector! He was released from that sentence in September 1971.

Shortly afterwards, someone broke into a house in Avenham Lane, Preston. It was in the middle of the night and the intruder was carrying a knife. Two women, a mother and daughter, awoke to find a man in their bedroom and started screaming so loudly that they frightened him off. The mother received a knife wound in the scuffle but was released the following day from Preston Royal Infirmary.

Alex had been sleeping rough in an office block that night and was picked up by the police at around three o'clock in the morning. He was questioned about the burglary and kept awake for over 48 hours, denied access to a lawyer and given minimal food and water. The interview was not filmed or recorded (circumstances that today would be unthinkable). During the interview, two Special Branch officers entered the room and started asking Alex about his visit to the Russian Embassy. They showed him a photograph of himself sitting outside the building with Igor Laptev, who, it turned out, was the First Secretary there. Four days before Alex was arrested, Laptev had been expelled from the UK along with 104 other Russians, on spying charges.

Alex was put under enormous pressure to admit to the break-in at Avenham Lane and told that, if he did not own up to it, his father might also be deported. It was made clear to him that it would be 'better for everyone' if he, Alex, went to prison for a couple of years 'until things quietened down'.

So Alex 'confessed', signing the statement that was written for him by the police, despite the fact that the two victims had given a completely different description of their assailant. He was told he would be charged with aggravated burglary and grievous bodily harm. When he appeared in court in front of Mr Justice Cantley, still concerned about whether his father would be allowed to stay in the UK, he pleaded guilty and the judge sentenced him to life imprisonment on each count.

David Wilson, now Professor of Criminology at Birmingham City University, was one of Alex's prison governors and got to know him well. He sums up the situation as follows:

> 'By any standards a life sentence for aggravated burglary is unusual, and disproportionate to the harm Alex was accused of causing. Did he really pose that much danger to the public or the police or was the sentence a reflection of the danger that he might pose to the state? Did they believe that he was some sort of "sleeper", about to become activated by his Russian spymasters ... ? I am convinced that they believed he was a spy. The conclusion that he was a dangerous person who needed to be locked up for all those years doesn't hang true.'

Alex was eventually released in 1993—22 years after his arrest.

In 2011 and quite by chance I happened upon all of Alex's letters. I had been looking for some old documents in a cupboard under the stairs and found a sealed box full of ageing photos, diaries and scripts. There, at the bottom, were his letters and poems. They were in neat bundles, pages and pages of his inimitable handwriting. In a separate buff-coloured file were most of my letters to him. I couldn't believe it.

One of the reasons for writing this book is the fact that, on re-reading his letters, I found they contained an added poignancy and beauty with the passage of time. It was evident that we had formed a special bond and that I had underestimated the depth of our friendship, which had been unusual to say the least. With both sides of the story, a book was possible.

Sitting on the floor of my office at home, with tears rolling down my cheeks, I realised these letters contained precious information about a period of my life that I had chosen to erase from my memory. With maturity I could appreciate the profound wisdom of Alex's words and the agonising desperation of his ordeal. I also noticed the astonishing juxtaposition of our lives—polar opposites but with a strong connection.

As I read on, I became saddened that I had allowed the correspondence to fizzle out when I should have been supporting Alex and writing to him *more* frequently. This caused an enormous amount of guilt and anguish. I started to wonder what had happened in the intervening years and suddenly, despite the fact that we had never met, it was imperative to know what had become of Alex since his release and whether he was still alive. So I set about trying to find him.

This is a story not only about enduring friendship and mutual support but also about contrasting worlds and lifestyles. His life was often in total isolation in the segregation block whereas the people, glamour and chaos of life in show business surrounded mine. He was intensely private, whereas my life (however much I hated it) was being played out in public. I was nomadic but he was unable to move, kidnapped by a regime that sought to silence him. Frustratingly, the more he protested his innocence the lengthier his sentence became. As he wrote in one letter:

'At the moment we are living in completely different worlds, most of your world, which I have not visited recently, is beyond my comprehension, and I am sure the obverse is true; that you know very little about prison, its stresses, pressures, Catch-22s; its psychology and utter frustration; its impracticality.'

With both Alex's and my own original letters in my possession, I have edited them for this book. I have also chosen just a few of his many poems. In addition, some of the narrative comes from Alex's 'Prison Chronicles', a manuscript which he wrote whilst serving his sentence.

I realise this memoir contains many references to my career as an actress, but this is not an autobiography, so many of the projects with which I was involved receive only the merest mention. This is usually to clarify the chronology of events in relation to my correspondence with Alex.

At one point he wrote:

'My hope is that one day you will be able to count me as a friend—a very valuable thing, friendship, never to be taken lightly, a commodity to be regarded with the utmost trust and respect.

May we one day become friends, then.'

How extraordinarily prophetic that wish turned out to be.

How many bricks make a prison?
And how many bricks make a cell?
And who made the bricks in the first place?
Were they baked in the ovens of hell?
Well, I've counted the bricks in my cell
It's amazing how solid they are!
Freedom is just on the other side
How near and how so very far!

Alex Alexandrowicz

- 1 -

The First Letters

And who are the men in the prison?
What are their reactions to gaol?
Do social workers make progress?
Individual statistics are frail.
And frail is the whole prison system
For containment is all it can give,
Men locked away from their families
Men who may not have that long to live.

Alex 1976

My career as an actress started by accident, not design, when I was eleven-years-old. I was studying to be a ballet dancer at Elmhurst Ballet School in Camberley, Surrey when I was summoned by the headmistress and told that there was a gentleman to meet me. This meeting resulted in a lead role in 'Run Wild, Run Free', a gentle film about an autistic boy and his friendship with a girl, and her kestrel, who lived on the moors. The film was a vehicle for Mark Lester, the star of 'Oliver'.

Two years later, I was filming the epic 'Nicholas and Alexandra' playing the youngest daughter of Tsar Nicholas II, the doomed Anastasia. Before long I was being photographed by Lord Snowdon for the *Sunday Times* to go with an article entitled 'Faces of the Seventies' and by David Bailey for *Vogue*.

This led directly to the lead role in a musical film adaptation of 'Alice's Adventures in Wonderland'. With an all-star cast and music by John Barry, the film had its premiere in December 1972, attended by Her Majesty Queen

Elizabeth II. Most of 1973 was spent touring the world promoting the film and I finally left school that summer.

However, the transition from child to adult actress was proving difficult (I had decided by then that I wanted to act and not to be a ballerina) so I found myself working, temporarily, in an optician's in Wigmore Street just behind Oxford Circus. Lord Hailsham, one of our more prominent customers, would cycle to all his appointments. On arrival he would lean his bike against the railings outside and come into the showroom, huffing and puffing, with his bicycle clips still firmly attached to his ankles. 'Be a dear,' he would say to me, sitting behind the reception desk, 'and make sure nobody takes it upon themselves to divest me of that bike.' (The irony cannot be ignored that he was Lord Chancellor at the time and therefore indirectly responsible for Alex's imprisonment). In 1975, things took a positive turn and I was making the leap into adult roles, filming a BBC television series called 'Angels', about six female student nurses, just starting out on their training. The viewing figures showed that enough people loved it for a second series to be commissioned. By 1976 we were half-way through filming that series.

The rain was almost horizontal, stinging my cheeks as I ran from the underground station to the BBC rehearsal rooms in North Acton. The tall building that loomed in front of me had been my workplace for over a year now and everyone in the reception and security area knew me.

'Blimey, Fiona, you look like a drowned rat.'

'Thanks Bill. Is Erin in yet?'

'Yup. She's just gone up.' I jumped into the lift and pressed six. The building was a purpose-built block of enormous rehearsal rooms, for television programmes that were to be filmed at the Television Centre just down the road in White City. We would rehearse each episode for ten days and then record for two.

The first series of 'Angels' had been shown the previous year on BBC1 at prime time, once a week, and was a huge success. The fan mail flooded in and the six of us who played the students found ourselves at the centre of a million teenage fantasies.

Erin Geraghty was a delightful Irish actress with whom I bonded instantly. She showed me the ropes, as I was the 'new' girl in TV, having only ever been in films before. (Having five cameras pointing at me when I had only previously been used to one, was proving rather alarming.) 'Well, would you look at that,' she said, smiling. 'Only eight for you today.' She handed me a bundle of rather damp letters. Over lunch, I had a quick look at them and one of them in particular caught my eye.

Prison number 789959
HM Prison Parkhurst
Isle of Wight.
14. 4. 1976

Dear Fiona,

I recently wrote to the BBC requesting photographs of the cast in your series 'Angels'. Unfortunately though, I did not have much luck.

    I began watching 'Angels' from the very beginning and since then I have not missed an episode. It is very rare for me to watch one programme consistently because there are a lot of other things I'm in the habit of doing; such as reading, painting, writing, listening to commercial radio and counting the bricks in my cell wall. Oh, and I have a budgie that talks and he keeps getting his words mixed up.

    It's a picture of you I'd really like though. Your face could launch the US Navy and a couple of submarines, but my pal says just the US Navy.

Sincerely Yours

Anthony Alexandrowicz (Alex)

It made me smile mainly because of the cheeky twist he gave to the compliment at the end of the letter. But the most interesting thing about this letter was the immaculate, tiny handwriting and the fact that it was written on prison issue notepaper. Something made me send him six photos of all the cast members and not just one of me.

BBC Television Centre
London
26th May 1976

Dear Alex

Thank you for your lovely letter. I enclose here pictures of all the cast and hope that they help to brighten up your day. I'm glad you enjoy 'Angels' because we enjoy it too!

Yours Sincerely

Fiona Fullerton

HM Prison Parkhurst
Isle of Wight
27. 5. 76

Dear Fiona,

Woke up this morning and hit me head on the coffin lid. 'That's it,' I thought, 'gonna be one of those days.' Not much sun outside and too much water in the porridge. My two budgies zooming about like the Battle of Britain and the battery on my radio is down to ghost power.

Got ready for work, being asleep on my feet and all that, rolled up a smoke and went straight down to the censor's office to see if I'd got a letter. Yeah, says the censor, you got a letter. Things are picking up, I thought.

So I got the letter and opened it up and when I saw what was inside it I thought, well just look at that! Fantastic. She's answered my letter. And how! Twenty submarines and the Merchant Navy too! All these pictures, got them here in front of me and talk about 'brighten your day'. Brighten up another century without any trouble at all.

Most of the guys in here are crazy over one or another of you. Many of the screws are too. Say, I still don't know what colour your hair is; guess I'll ask a screw as most of them have colour televisions at home.

I wouldn't mind having a go at medical work when I get out of prison. It seems interesting, but I'd only do temporary work because most of my time would be taken up by writing. There's a couple of books waiting for publication, but this can't be done until I get released – and I don't know when that will be because I'm serving a life term. I should imagine that it will be within the next four years, as I have done five already.

Thank you once again for the photos you sent, Fiona. I hope, when you are not too busy, you will write again.

Meanwhile good luck and best wishes for your future.

Keep smiling and take care.

Alex

Telling me that he was serving a life sentence so early on in our correspondence was a considerable risk. How did he know that it wouldn't bother me that much? And come to think of it, why didn't it? I suppose I must have read something in those lines that intrigued me but his humour appealed to me too.

Alex's first night in Parkhurst was spent on the hospital wing. It had been horrendous. In his 'Prison Chronicles' he recalls that he couldn't sleep.

'There were too many animals mooing and bleating. On one side of me was a bloke who thought he was an owl and on the other side a monkey. It was my first meeting with mentally-ill prisoners.

The doctor saw me the next day and told me he was putting me on C-Wing. 'You'll like it on C-Wing,' he said.

Of the four separate wings, C-Wing stood out because it was understood to house psychotics and prisoners just back from Rampton and Broadmoor. It was controlled by psychiatrists. It housed a maximum of 20 or so cons, although it had enough empty cells to house a hundred. My first few days were spent adjusting to the regime but I wasn't bothered by any of the other men. They were complex men, each throwing many shadows.'

London
15th June 1976

Dear Alex,

Thank you so much for your last letter. I'm glad the photos gave you so much pleasure but the one of me was so terrible that I'm enclosing a couple more for you.

To answer your question, my hair is chestnut coloured, I have green eyes, I'm five foot four inches tall and have two legs!!

I was interested to hear that you write and would indeed be most honoured to receive a copy of your book. It is so nice to receive letters with a bit of personality too, instead of a curt demand for a photo.

What nationality are you? You have an unusual name. I'm British but in fact was born in Nigeria, West Africa. My father is an officer in the British Army, so consequently we have lived abroad most of the time. I love travelling – I'm a bit of a nomad really, having never lived in one place for more than three years.

Twenty submarines eh? <u>And</u> the Merchant Navy – I'm very flattered.

You have such beautiful handwriting. Did you cultivate that in prison?

Alex, I'm going to play Cinderella at the London Palladium over Christmas, isn't that exciting? I'm only 19-years-old, so I'm very pleased. It's a musical, so I'll be singing and dancing in it as well. I've always wanted to do a stage musical. When I was little, I wanted to be Julie Andrews.

Also, I'm getting married on July 10th in the Crypt Chapel of St Paul's Cathedral to a wonderful young man called Simon MacCorkindale – do think of us on that day.

Please write again, when you feel like it.

Best Wishes

Fiona Fullerton

Simon and I met at a charity cricket match at the Oval late in 1975 where the cast of 'Angels' had been asked to sell raffle tickets to the spectators.

He was a struggling actor, I discovered, who had appeared in small roles on TV and on the stage, but he had a healthy dose of ambition and drive. His dashing good looks and rich, mellifluous voice were reminiscent of the old-style movie stars. Public school educated and with a father retired from the air force, we seemed to have a lot in common. Within three weeks, he had asked me to marry him.

HM Prison Parkhurst
22. 6. 76

Dear Fiona,

Caramba! Thank you for the photographs. Oh boy, what a smile. If I was the Chancellor, Desperate Dennis [Healey], I'd have your face printed on all new currency notes, then fellas would really be able to kiss their money goodbye, wouldn't they?

My nationality? Oddly enough I'm British. My father is from a town in the Western Ukraine called Odessa. He came over here in 1951 on a Party-swap and met my mother, who is from Cornwall, the next year. They moved up North and I was born on the 8th February 1953 in Manchester, although I was brought up in the small industrial town of Nelson, near Burnley, NE Lancs. Terraced houses, mill chimneys and cobbled streets. Near where I come from is Haworth, where the Brontes lived, so the countryside has its own special blend of mystery and charm.

So your father is an officer in the forces? My father also, during the last war. He was a colonel in the Red Army but, unlike others, despised Stalin.

My grandfather was with the Tereck Cossacks in 1917 and my grandmother fought in both wars. They still live in Odessa to this day. Occasionally they come to England for brief visits and once, a long time ago, my father took me to Odessa to visit them. I remember my grandfather holding me above his head as everyone danced to the accordion. My grandmother in her best linen, snow white, and my aunts and uncles performing Cossack sabre dances with wine bottles balanced on their heads. When I get out of this place I'd like to visit them again.

The Home Office has given me permission to apply for Soviet citizenship and I believe it will be granted, for although I am serving life, it is for no capital offence so I should be freed around 1979. With luck. Then maybe I will marry and settle down somewhere instead of belting around the country on my 850 Triumph Bonnie.

I love travelling too. When I wanted to be on my own, I'd head for Cumberland and the Lake District. Keswick – have you ever been there Fiona? Derwentwater? Well worth a visit. Sometimes it's good to be a nomad.

As I cannot send you a photo, I am 6 feet 1 inch tall, eleven stone ten pounds, brown hair, moustache and beard, blue-grey eyes, a broken nose (would you believe that I walked into a lamp-post when I was nine? True though. Wallop!!) and a North East Lancashire accent.

So you are to be married on the tenth. I am very happy for you – for both of you – but especially for you. Will you be keeping your present name? I hope Simon is really going to look after you. He's the luckiest guy on God's earth and that is a fact. May he always treat you good and proper, may he always love you and be forever faithful and be a good husband. I want you both to be very happy together. Many congratulations and most definitely I will think of you on that day.

Then there's Cinderella at the Palladium. You'll knock 'em for six. This may be your first stage musical but there'll be lots more because you have what it takes. Never lose self-confidence – if you really believe, then you can do anything. You'll have the time of your life. Rave on!

Next month I'll be up in Strangeways, Manchester, for my annual visits from my family, so you can imagine I'll be looking forward to that very much. I should be back in Parkhurst by the beginning of August.

For now then, Das Vidaniya

Alex

Alex would often include poems in his letters to me, displaying an unusually creative dexterity, considering his isolation from the world outside. Some of them are heartbreakingly poignant, while others are humorous and tender. I have included an edited selection of poems in the order in which they came.

Swim

Tonight I will go for a swim
In the deep blue sea of the universe.
I will dive into endless fathoms
And laze amongst the shoals of constellations.

Passing a plane of astral bodies
I will give to them a message of tranquillity
Then, into the Zodiac I will go
To call upon my Heavenly house of Aquarius.

Astride a comet's fiery back
I shall laugh; and sing joyous refrains
of passion and love.
My heart shall leap and swell
As I gaze upon the endless beauty of
Celestial surroundings
Then I shall be set down upon
A star; where I may rest and think
Should I surface from my Moonlit Sonata?

Perhaps I would find it preferable to
Just lay back and sink...

Alex 1976

At this time Alex was transferred to Strangeways Prison in Manchester so that he could receive visits from his family who still lived in that part of the country. The journey to Manchester was a master class in high security travel for a Category-A prisoner. Alex seemed bemused to be at the centre of such an expensive and coordinated operation. He was put into a yellow prison van and handcuffed to a prison warder.

'Two other screws sat in the back and there were two more, a driver and a navigator up front. As soon as we left the gatehouse I saw flashing lights; it was a police motor waiting for us, to escort us to the ferry.

Inside, a metal screen separated the back of the van from the driver and navigator, the latter having control of a powerful police radio, which was left on constantly when the van was in use. The van was not allowed to stop. Rumour had it that a shooter was kept in a locked box under the rear seat. Should an A-man attempt an escape he would risk being shot and killed.

As we rolled off the ferry at Portsmouth, there were a further two police escorts waiting. With lights flashing and sirens blaring the whole lot of us set off for Manchester.

As each county boundary approached, a fresh set of police cars would be waiting to take over; the convoy making these changeovers without any reduction in speed.

It was 1976. The summer was long and unbearably hot and the inside of the A-van became like an oven. The police cars forged ahead, their lights and sirens carving a path through the traffic, and I'm sitting there thinking... Before Parkhurst there'd never been police escorts. So what had happened to change that?

I closed my eyes and focused back to 1971, when I'd been an ordinary kid, albeit a sometime petty thief who stole while on the run. I had read some of Franz Kafka's stories but they upset me. And then I'd think: "But this is England—not a police state somewhere in Eastern Europe. What's happening?"'

BBC Television Centre
London
7th July 1976

My Dear Alex,

Just a very quick note to thank you for your long, chatty letter and for the beautiful card you made for me. I was really thrilled to receive that and it has pride of place on the mantelpiece.

We are busy now with last minute preparations for the great day on Saturday, and as we will be in France for two weeks, I thought I'd better write now. This will be the most important day of my life and I'm so excited. Thank you for the little poem.

I will send you a photo. I hope you are well and can share a little of my happiness.

With Fond Regards

Fiona

Strangeways Prison
Manchester
16. 7.1976

Dear Fiona

See, told you the weather would stay fine for you! How about that then? Good job the wedding wasn't in Manchester though because it was teeming down on the tenth. I hope this letter finds you intensely happy in every way.

I got a visit today from my mother, she's been twice since I arrived here last Thursday, and it's been very nice seeing her again although on her first visit I was at a loss what to talk about.

At present I am teaching myself Esperanto, seems to be a popular language, and I feel okay right now because of my visits and the course keeps me busy, which results in each day passing quickly. I don't notice the time as much.

Well, my father is coming tomorrow; I haven't seen him in five years, my mother is coming on Sunday, then back to Parkhurst again. You know, I miss that place, some-how. I suppose it's because all my friends are there. Funny that. They're all cons but some are *decent* – most especially the more 'dangerous' ones.

Where Will the Path Go?

Where will the path I tread go through?
Between the spoken word and silence,
Where skies are overcast and blue,

And where warring wills reach balance;

Where dreams of satisfaction breathe,
Undisturbed by gnawing doubts,
Where fiery passions toss and seethe,
Amidst a wilful drinking bout.

Where timid and uncertain eyes
Discover truthfulness and troth,
Where clashing lightbeams compromise,
And thus unite the South and North.

There sleepless lights give blessed light
To my faithful fountain-pen,
Like someone dumb I have to write
To communicate with other men.

Battles, courage and despair,
Rising hope and gathering storms-
Like the universe I bear
Amazing states and startling forms.

Words. Silence. Words come again.
The two are always with me.
I'm powerful as a hurricane
And endless as the sea ....

Alex 1976

Just got supper, let's see – mug of tea and currant cake. Now for a scientific experiment ... behold! I take the cake between finger and thumb, I let go! Jesus. As I'm standing here it bounced. Bounced! Hold on, I'll try it again. Fascinating.

Well, I have to finish now. Take care of yourself Fiona. Please write again when you can.

Alex

Alex was having an uneasy time at Strangeways:

'Strangeways was wary of me. They put me down the block in a punishment cell but I was allowed to use my radio. The visits with my parents (one at a time because they had split up) were spoiled because on either side of the table sat two screws. We weren't able to say anything confidential, we were so conscious of the screws.

My dad always brought me two ounces of tobacco, which I smuggled in hidden in my boots. At nights the red light was left on and my clothing had to be put in a cardboard box which was left outside the cell.

After a month at Strangeways I was back in the Cat-A van, en route home to Parkhurst. When I got back I learned that there'd been an escape from the Special Security Block (SSB), which is a prison within a prison housing only a dozen or so prisoners who presented the gravest threat to society.

It was beautiful. Two cons, wire-cutters, through the fence, over the wall, in broad daylight under the noses of the screws. Both were recaptured but it was a turbo boost for morale.'

BBC Television Centre
London.
19th August 1976

Dear Alex,

I loved your last letter. I find you extremely interesting Alex, but unfortunately I won't be able to answer at such length, as I'm quite busy at the moment.

Well, the honeymoon in France was amazing but so HOT. Paris was everything I wanted it to be but we couldn't afford very much and, as I was permanently thirsty, Simon had to ration the orange squash 'cos it was sooooo expensive. He took me to the Opera House to see 'La Traviata' but we sat in the gods and I had a long dress on and nearly melted.

In Provence we stayed in a little hut on a farm and ate with the family, which was kind of tricky because my French is very basic. Simon's is quite good though. Did you see the papers?

I hope all is well with you now that you are back in Parkhurst. Can you enjoy the sunshine?

I'm glad you were able to see your parents. I'm sure it gave you strength.

Well, I'm busy recording my last episode of Angels and decorating our new flat! It seems to be covered in horrid woodchip wallpaper but S is a real handyman so he is steaming it off. He decorates other people's houses when he is out of work.

Sorry this is so short. I promise I'll write at length later.

Best Wishes, Fiona

The honeymoon in Paris was indeed marred by the exceptional heat. Nineteen-seventy-six was a scorching summer and I remember walking down the Champs-Elysées on the Sunday morning, looking for a cold drink, and stopping at one of the little green newspaper kiosks. There, to our astonishment, were all the British newspapers with our faces on the front of every one.

Parkhurst Prison
Isle of Wight
26. 8. 76

Hello Fiona,

I am always finding that life is something wonderful. I hope you get the same feeling. Please excuse me for writing so often, this is a new experience for me and I find it extremely pleasant, so I hope you don't get too bored.

My friend Taffy delighted me on my return here with all the newspaper cuttings of you and Simon. Wow! Every Sunday paper. And thank you for the wedding photograph – you look extremely beautiful and how happy you look. Now *I* am decorating! I have to find somewhere in the cell to stand this photograph!

You find me interesting? A lot of people from every walk of life have said they find me interesting and I am baffled. This copper once found me asleep, around two o'clock in the morning (I was about thirteen years old) in a telephone box at Kettering

Bus Station. He marched me up to the local cop-shop and reported to the inspector what he had found. The inspector looked at me and said, 'Interesting'. Oh wow, I thought. Then he took my snake-belt off me. Happens all the time.

Fiona, I know how busy you are so of course you cannot write me long letters! My hope is that one day you will be able to count me as a friend – a very valuable thing friendship, never to be taken lightly, a commodity to be regarded with the utmost trust and respect. May we one day become friends, then.

How's this for coincidence; soon it'll be Christmas and you'll be on stage in London and I might be on stage in Parkhurst. This year we're thinking of doing a concert. On C-Wing we have two guys playing mouth-organ, an accordionist, two drummers and a couple of guitars, but I think the Governor would like us to sing carols, perish the thought.

I remember once in Blackburn, a friend called Catweasle and myself decided to get dressed up and nip over to the local dance hall to listen to one of the touring Rock 'n' Roll bands there. So we get there and find two girls listening outside the doors, decent kids – not the usual back-street freaks – and we asked them if they'd like to go in with us. They'd like to, they said but they couldn't jive … In the end they took *us* to this place where it's ten bob to get in if you're wearing a tie. And – we had to waltz!! You can imagine two guys wearing drapes, luminous socks, bootlace ties and beetle-crushers – dancing the waltz. Funny thing though, I took my girlfriend there regularly afterwards – dressed in the approved fashion of course – and that's when I began acquiring a taste for classical music, and I was only around 17.

I'm still messing around with the Esperanto stuff, it isn't very hard if one knows how to roll ones 'r's like a Russian. By the way Fiona, do you know how to pronounce my surname? It is 'vich' with the emphasis on the last six letters that begin with the rolling 'r'. No Englishman has ever pronounced it properly. Have a try. Be the first. Make history!

But now I must finish, I'll have the light turned out in a few minutes.

Be Happy. Take Good Care of Yourself,

Alex.

Alex's letters from Parkhurst seemed to be so full of humour and indicated that he had settled into a rhythm and routine. I looked forward to receiving them but had no idea of the horrors he was enduring. He kept all that from me.

'The Topping Shed hadn't been used for a long time, but it still sent a shiver down the spine to stand in it. It was located near the end of the wing and was kept unlocked, so I was using it to store some mop buckets and brushes. Looking up the chute you could see the trap doors, now nailed shut, and at the bottom there were stone brackets to hold the stretcher in place. It was easily the coldest room in the prison and it didn't do to linger there.

C-Wing was the oldest of the Parkhurst wings. It had clearly been built to house women, as all the cell doorways were less than five feet six inches high. Originally Parkhurst was a holding prison, before its inmates were deported to Australia. The prison ship would anchor in the River Medina and the convicts would be taken there, by way of a tunnel connecting the prison with the riverbank. The tunnel is still said to exist, although both ends have been blocked up.

Some of the C-Wing men had been building their own tunnel; it started under the shower house and ran directly towards the outside wall, some 15 yards away. Unfortunately, quite by chance, a screw fell into it one day, so it had to be abandoned when it was only half finished.'

HM Prison Parkhurst
Isle-of-Wight
C-Wing
15. 9. 1976

Hey Fiona,

I've got problems with my beard, it grows all over the place and I can't straighten it out. I can't stick Brylcream on it and, promising though it sounds, I think plugging my finger into the A/C socket is a little extreme, though people say go ahead. Don't fancy lighting-up like Blackpool Illuminations. Do you have any suggestions?

You know, if man would stop to look, to <u>see</u> his actions, how very different this world of ours would be! Can you imagine what a wonderful place this would be if we had people that truly cared, to make our laws, and to rule with feeling, instead of greed and the lust for power! There would be no need for dreams, for life would be real for each and every one of us.

Well, Autumn is here, and trees are beginning to cast their coloured leaves, the days are now a paler shade of grey, colder now that the sun grows weak and nights seem to come sooner. There is of course consolation in a good book (I've nearly finished Margaret Mitchell's Gone With the Wind, a marvellous book, have you read it Fiona?) the writing of a letter, and also the fact that one seems to have more time for thought. I seem to have so many plans for future times!

It has been pouring down on the I.O.W. these past couple of days and everyone is happy and all the farmers have been bombing around and vegetation is thriving I love rain, Fiona; it really clears up the air. And I love thunder and lightning. It may sound strange but I used to walk on the moors around home when storms broke out and, when thunder and lightning came, I'd just stand still and yell at the sky, 'Come on, then. Here I am! – see if you can hit me!?', and I never got hit once. Tempting the Gods? Sure, why not? They must like me, hey? Yeah. Never had pneumonia, either.

It <u>is</u> carols we're doing at Christmas and a few pop songs thrown in. I'm on drums, not guitar, as we have two guitarists, but if things drag I'll hot up that beat. Begin with Hark! The Herald Angels Sing, and finish with a rave from the grave or a blast from the past. Here's a poem I wrote the other night. See what you think …

Evening in Lancashire *For Fiona*

Soulful cries … of grubby young children.
Angry shouts … of unemployed men.
Long rows … of grey terraced houses.
Soot-blackened brickwork … A solitary wren.

Raindrops bouncing … from cobblestones.
Curtains drawn in … many homes.
Streetlights … orange against darkening blue.
Lonely, up in the sky … an aircraft drones.

Twin beams of Light … a passing car.
An ambulance siren … is heard from afar,
Echoing over … tired backyards.

A tramp lies gazing ... at the North Star.

The wary cat will ... spit and hiss.
Watching mice play ... hit and miss.
Darkness unites ... lights go out.
Beneath the heavens, stars, beneath the gold moon
A tender goodnight kiss.

Alex 1976

The trouble with writing poems is that they take up so much space. Anyroad, lass, here I am always thinking of you and, though I don't believe in God, I offer a prayer each night to the planets asking them to guide and protect you and Simon always. Take good care of yourself, Fiona, keep on smiling and keep up the good work.

Will write again when I can.

Alex

Earlier in the year, knowing that I was about to be married, I had asked the BBC to release me from my contract on 'Angels'. I could have continued in the show for years but it is rather telling that I chose domestic bliss over my career. It was ultimately to cost me dearly.

London
24th September 1976

Dear Alex,

Forgive me for not writing for so long—I'm so lazy—but things have been rather hectic here recently. Thank you very much for your beautiful letters (what a shame I cannot match them in beauty) and especially for the poem. I'm extremely flattered and think it's absolutely lovely. How clever you are.

Guess what? I was asked to be a representative of the British Film Delegation at the Moscow Film and Arts Festival next week. Isn't that amazing? I was <u>so</u> excited. I've always wanted to visit Russia and this trip would be a four-day stay in Moscow with a visit to Leningrad too. How marvellous I thought – I was raring to go. Then it was all called off. Not the festival, just the British delegation, because the producer who was taking us out there, Stuart Lyons, is in the San Sebastian Film Festival and consequently unable to make the trip to Moscow. Very sad. I'm so disappointed. However, I'm told I might be able to go next year.

Our flat is looking much more homely now. We're nearly finished with all the painting and papering, so it's just finishing touches.

You must have missed Angels on the 13th as you don't mention it at all. It was a big episode for me, (including a ride on the back of a Harley down the motorway!!) and a lead into my final episode on the 27th. Hope you can see it.

Yes I have read Gone With the Wind. A truly wonderful book. In fact I lived in Atlanta for three years when my Dad was serving out there in the American Army, on an exchange appointment. Have you seen the film? Must go now. Many thanks again.

Love and Best Wishes

Fiona

HM Prison Parkhurst
28. 9. 1976

Hello, Princess, just received your letter. A-wop-bop-a-loo-bop-a-lop-BAM-BOOM!

I am glad you've got the work coming to an end at the flat – you must be exhausted with all that painting and decorating! On second thoughts, it must have been plenty of fun while it lasted.

Ah, Moscow. What a pity you were unable to go, Fiona! And you must have been so proud to have been chosen! What a let-down. But do look on the brighter side, there will always be next year. What you <u>must</u> see in Moscow is the Monument to the Space Conquerors.

Still no word from the Embassy, so, as soon as I get the go-ahead from the Home Office, I'm writing direct to Leonid Brezhnev. Funny isn't it – one hears such a lot about people wishing to come to the West from the Eastern Block but never the reverse … I'm going to see, though, if I can get swapped for one or both of the two Britons who were recently sentenced to seven and eight years respectively in Soviet labour camps. The way I see it I'm no earthly use to the U.K. – unless they want a revolution, similarly, the two Britons are no use to the Soviet Union. So a swap may be quite on the cards. But first I must get permission to write to Brezhnev before I put the question to the relative authorities.

Yes, groan, you guessed it, Fiona. Out of the present series of Angels I have seen only the first episode. I am down the chokey block doing a total of 68 days Solitary at present, and privileges such as TV and radio, etc. are not permitted. I have done 20 days, however, so there are only 48 to go. Last night there was thunder and lightning on a magnificent scale. Each peal was as though the whole sky was being ripped apart piece by piece. It must have been like that when Tchaikovsky composed his Overture to the '1812', when Holst created 'Mars'. It's the only type of weather one might call 'inspiring'. Do you like thunderstorms, Princess? I think one day I might record a good thunderstorm on a tape recorder, over-dub it with some organ music and you never know – may have a billion-seller on my hands.

I've been sewing mailbags and I'll tell you something, Fiona, sewing mailbags is a very good way of getting the hands blistered-up. Every time I do a bag the needle ends up in my thumb at least twice, it's a good job you can't hear the language I use on such occasions! Most colourful. They ought to give us an anti-tetanus injection with every bag. Ye gods. No, it's a painful experience having a needle slide into one's thumb, honest.

Enclosed is my latest poem for you.

The Soldier

The brave young solider hears no more
The rifle's clash nor the cannon's roar,

He feels no more the burning heat
And listens not, for enemy feet.

He answers not, the bugle's call
Or runs to join the charge.
No more a soldier of the war.
He's … Human fodder for the crow.

His blood has stained a distant land,
He lies in an Unknown Grave
Somewhere beneath a distant star,
For sure, we know not where
For there's a Sea of Crosses
Stretching out afar.
Every one a Soldier
Who gave himself to war

Alex 1976

Maybe not exactly the right sort of verse to write to a girl, but criticism is a valuable commodity to me and I think somehow you would make a nicer critic than most.

So long for now, Princess. All My Love,

Alex

By his own admission he was 'down the block' doing 68 days in solitary confinement. In his Chronicles he explains what happened:

'I was walking around the exercise yard with my friend Chilly when another con, Pete, came up to us and started talking about one of my mates who was having a bit of trouble. He was due out in a couple of months and saving up his wages to supplement his pension on release. Another con, M, had been threatening to do him in if he didn't buy him things from the canteen. Pete suggested that we should "have a word with M". I didn't like it. Pete had a lot to do with Ron and Reg (Kray) and I was thinking, if Pete's so tough, why doesn't he do his own dirty work.

He gave us an excuse about the screws watching him and in the event Chilly and I went round and laid into M.

We did the 68 days and both went back to C-Wing. It turned out that the whole thing had been a scam. Pete just wanted someone to beat up M, told us porkies, and Ron and Reg weren't involved at all.'

London.
November 11th, 1976 (In a Christmas card)

Dear Alex,

Haven't forgotten you! Thank you for your letters but since rehearsals have started my feet haven't touched the ground. Richard O'Sullivan is really funny (he's playing Buttons) and I've just been told that I'm going to have four little white ponies to pull my coach onto the stage. I'm singing some really good songs too. Hope you have as good a Christmas as you expect. Be good!

Yours,

F F

H M Prison Parkhurst
D-Wing
24. 11. 1976

Hello Princess

I don't know where you'll be as you read this but I'm gonna make you smile at least once in this letter, Fiona, so watch out.

I have your photo the large one that I like best – pinned on the wall where I can see it from most angles and I gotta say the angles don't matter much on account of you being so much dynamite you're gonna blow a hole through them bricks one of these days.

Anyway, as observed from above, I am no longer on C-Wing and over the past week I've been busy moving in. Been doing a bit of decorating (six pin-ups) and making a couple of new friends and generally getting the feel of the wing. When I'm banged-up (locked behind my door) I still do a spot of writing. Doing a university course on British Constitution. Writing a few letters. Composing a new jingle for Tetley's Tea Bags. Which will be okay if I can get Fats Domino to sing it.

Anyway, that's the way it goes. Speaking for myself, I'm going straight when I get out of this dump. In fact there'll be a clause in my Licence stating that I must do, 'cos I've been disallowed from breaking various laws. It's nice of them to show so much concern. Of course, though, my first priority when I get evicted is to jump on the first available Aeroflot from Gatwick, skim over to Moscow, thump out a few books, sink a few vodkas and get myself citizenized or whatever it's called. Then I can book a seat for the 1980 Olympics or get shot at or something.

And you're going to be busy this Christmas, hey? I'll be keeping my fingers crossed for you on your first night, Fiona, it always works. But I guess you don't need luck from anybody 'cos you have what it takes and you're bound to win all the coconuts and a lotta flowers and such. Anyroad, lass, take good care of yourself, Fiona. Keep on smiling.

Will write again when I can.

Alex

Princess

Around you every Night — the Elves;
When you are fast Asleep,
Cast their mystic Spells of Light;
Myriad Starbursts at your feet.

As approaches the magic Eleven-Hour

Clothed in silken Leaf-Lace;
The Elf-Prince once more Appears
To gaze into your Face.

On Bended Knee he steals
A Kiss upon your Lips.
Onto your hair a tiny Teardrop Spills
And trickles to your Fingertips.

Next Morn' when you Awaken
From depths of Blessed rest
Glance into your Looking-Glass
For sure, you're bathed with Beauty
No Mortal has Ever Possessed!

Alex 1976

Cinderella had opened on December 4th and I did indeed have four adorable little Shetland ponies pulling my gold carriage. It was like a dream come true. The cliché being, of course, that I had only just found my very own Prince Charming.

HM Prison Parkhurst
D-Wing
24. 12. 1976
Christmas Eve

Hello Fiona,

Heard you're giving a really smashing performance and I think that is fantastic, so much so that I thought I'd slam my congratulations in while you're not bogged-down in floral vegetation, or signing autograph books or saying nice things to un-nice humans 'cos convention demands.

Christmas Day

Heard no bells jingling. Only Keys. Not a bad breakfast: bowl of Alpen, bit of bacon, a cold plastic fried egg and a tinned tomato. This morning I was outside on the compound, freezing me fingers off, watching the 'Over 40's' football match, which ended 4-3 and was a complete shambles – but a good laugh. Also I smoked a cigar.

I've just had my Christmas lunch: turkey, etc. Yeah, we had a turkey. All three hundred of us – a slice each. I held mine up to the light and I could see right through it. Anyhow, to supplement this, there was a slice of cold ham, slice of pork, and a square inch block of stuffin'. Plus greens. An' a pudding the size of a Chinese teacup with ersatz rum sauce to cover it up. Two inches deep. So don't be fooled by the press reports that we're all getting slap-up cuisine 'cos we're not – and that's straight from the horse's mouth.

Stayed the afternoon in my cell listening to the radio and reading a book or two, but watched the TV this evening. Bruce Forsyth on the Generation Game closely followed by the Morecombe an' Wise show whereupon Angela Rippon released exclusive proof that she's got legs. That's all for today, Princess. Off to bed an' another day crossed from the calendar. Sweet dreams.

Boxing Day

Woke up with a bloody great headache, stabbed at the 'on' button on the HMV, got an earful of the 'Post Horn Gallup' stabbed at the 'off' button in deep disgust an' grabbed me greys 'cos they were shoutin' 'anymore f'breakfast!' Bowl of cornflakes an' a boiled egg. Pow! Got the cornflakes down alright, threw the egg at the wall, caught it on the rebound and it was just right for shelling.

Lunch was okay, the Yorkshire pud was palatable and looking pleased with itself so I risked it. I'll give it four for presentation.

This morning saw me again in my cell, but this afternoon I'm gonna watch (yet again) the 'Wizard of Oz'. I got plenty of time for this film. Now that I'm on D-Wing I have a few more pals. One of them comes from Atlanta, Georgia. He was in the State Penitentiary there – he says it's a large establishment, which visitors can't fail to miss upon driving into Atlanta.

Said something about the city standing on the boundary of two States. He's done Bird in San Quentin, too, and tells some very interesting stories about the place, some of them terrible but believable. Over here they're more subtle.

Oh, what festivities and merriment! Yo-ho-ho! You know something Fiona, I bet Father Christmas is crazy. Look at it this way, there's thousands of houses in Britain, and they all have a front door an' a back door – yet this guy comes in down the chimney. Highly illogical and irrational behaviour, to state the obvious.

Fiona, I hope you have had a really smashing Christmas with lots of fun and parties to go to. I wish I could have watched you playing 'Cinderella' – I heard you even had some royalty at your Charity Show. Even as I write this you must be on stage. I do hope everything is successful and that you're happy and always will be. Please write when you find time. Meanwhile, my love and best wishes to yourself and Simon.

Your Friend

Alex

As December 26th fell on a Sunday that year, I was resting at home with Simon and my parents. Christmas came and went in a blur as on the following day it was back to two shows a day. I was having a ball, but soon the mood backstage was about to change.

- 2 -

The Journey to Parkhurst

Three days before Christmas 1971, Alex arrived at Risley Remand Centre. He was just 18-years-old. So began his Kafkaesque nightmare and a lifelong struggle to clear his name.

'There it was, the high wall with the razor wire looped around the top … the great wooden doors sliding open and my heart racing in time with the car engine — and the gloom of the gatehouse as the doors closed behind, shutting out the daylight.

The realisation washed over me — *two life sentences* — like a dread tide until I was submerged by it. I was taken out of the taxi and escorted into the reception block, given prison clothing and a number — 789959.

Normally, a prison doctor would see a new inmate in reception, but I was told I was to be located in the hospital wing anyway, so there was no need.

I was taken into the ward, not into a single cell, they wanted to keep an eye on me, I realised that. All lifers are treated this way because the authorities expect a suicide bid. I was given a tot of medicine which made me sleepy. I fell asleep.

When the teas were being served, I was woken up. I had a few hours of consciousness where I had the opportunity to replay the day's events through my mind. Sentenced to two life sentences … What had happened? This was my life, not theirs. As far as I could figure it out, I'd been set up. What a fool! *I hadn't committed those crimes. I was innocent.* There was a curious sensation of abstraction as if it was somebody else — that this wasn't happening to me. How could it be happening to me? The drugs bit into me and I was gone again.'

Since Alex began his sentence he had been moved to six different establishments before arriving at the notorious Parkhurst Prison on the Isle of Wight. After leaving Risley, he was transferred first to Walton Gaol, Liverpool.

'The cell was not overly clean. It was relatively spacious; its walls rough brick with patches of paint peeling away. The last occupant had left his pin-ups on one of the walls, a frieze of naked women in different postures. There was a bucket in a corner that stank, the toilet, which needed emptying—another gift from the last occupant. I put down the bedroll I'd been carrying and sat down on the cot. I realised that there was no water jug or wash-basin and immediately felt thirsty and dirty.

I was hungry; my last meal had been a small bowl of porridge, before leaving Risley that same morning... God, that seemed like *days* ago.

I hand-rolled a cigarette from a few dog-ends. I hadn't any more tobacco. I went for a piss. The bucket had a couple of inches of urine in it and a turd, which was melting into liquid, stuck to the bottom. I directed a stream of urine onto the turd and then threw up. To stop the vomit from falling onto the cot I had to put my face over the bucket.'

It was here at Walton that Alex discovered he was a Category-A prisoner, the highest security level, usually given to murderers and rapists who pose a 'threat to society'. But Alex was neither of those. He insisted in all his interviews that he had been set up, that he was innocent of the crime. So why was he Category-A?

Shortly after arriving at Walton Prison, he had been transferred to the hospital section.

'I was having tremendous difficulty accepting my lot, because I knew that it was not deserved. By that time I'd been pretty well briefed about the life sentence and I knew that—unless something happened to put a halt to it—I was likely going to serve ten or maybe eleven years. The prospect of that was disturbing. Gone was my hope that the police would honour their side of the bargain and make sure I served a short sentence. Yet my father hadn't been deported. That was something.

The hospital was a large and relatively modern part of the prison, and the cells were large and well-aired. My cell had a big sash window that let in lots of sunshine. I listened a lot to Radio 2.

One day I went for a shower and one of the other men was in there. He had breasts like a woman and was apparently awaiting a sex change. It was made more incongruous because he was a big, burly geezer built like a heavyweight boxer. If he had the sex change he would still look the same and there was no way he could ever be mistaken for a woman. I watched him deteriorate into a zombie-like state, perhaps because of the drugs he was on. He would shuffle along in slow motion. I guess he was sent to a mental hospital eventually.

While in the hospital I was seen by Dr. Gray, from Grendon Prison in Buckinghamshire. He wanted me to go to Grendon because he was concerned that I may try to kill myself. I *had* thought about killing myself, that was true. The feelings I had were awful. I was upset for most of the time because I couldn't accept my sentence.

I agreed to Grendon because it represented a soft option. Its relaxed regime was well known.'

Soon after his twentieth birthday, thinking he was going to Grendon, Alex was transferred to Wakefield Prison in Yorkshire. An adult, high security prison, built in the Victorian era, it was a dark and shadowy place, holding around 400 inmates, two thirds of whom were serving life sentences for murder. He thought there had been some mistake.

'In the outside world it is very rare to meet a murderer. If there were a high-rise block of flats, containing 300 killers and social misfits, it would be a place to avoid at all costs. No ordinary person in his or her right mind would want anything to do with them. I observed that most murderers regarded themselves as superior to everyone else and took great pains to project an image of violence. A weak person didn't stand a chance and was the first to be singled out and persecuted.'

Shortly afterwards, Alex suffered a brutal attack by four men and retaliated by hitting one of the perpetrators over the head with a metal bar. He was never to be bothered by another prisoner again.

'When the attack came it was when I least expected it. I had gone to fetch a bowl of hot water for a wash. As I was putting the bowl on the table in my cell, I sensed someone behind me. I started to turn around but I was too late. I felt an arm go around my throat and the press of sharp metal at the side of my neck.

I felt someone else undoing my jeans and pulling them down. I knew then what was going to happen, but I couldn't believe it. There were four of them. All the while I was held around my neck with the knife at my throat. The pain I felt as each one raped me was excruciating. I couldn't see anything because I was held face down across the cot.

My mind was a million miles away and everything that was relevant just died.

The cell door slammed shut. I couldn't sleep that night. I knew that I wasn't going to survive. No way.

Out came the razor blade and I put it to my veins … the temptation to end everything there and then was so strong.

A couple of days later, I was told who was behind the attack and where to find him. I was given a metal tube. Outside his cell I heard voices. Very quietly I opened the cover on the spy-hole in his door and saw that he was having sex with one of the other cons. I waited down on a lower landing, then I went back and saw that he was alone. I pulled the metal tube from my jeans and pushed the cell door wide open.

I gave him a few whacks with the tube and the screams could be heard in every part of the prison. I felt disgusted with myself.

I left his cell and leaned on the landing rail as the screws piled up the stairs. They marched me down the block and I was sentenced to 56 days in solitary confinement.'

In 1974 Grendon Prison accepted Alex, despite the fact that he was a Category-A prisoner, but he didn't last long there. One of the fundamental requirements of a prisoner at Grendon is to accept and come to terms with their offence. Alex couldn't do that. He refused to admit to a crime he did not commit, even though he knew it would affect his chances of parole. At Grendon, he found the regime, of group therapy and remedial programmes, extremely difficult and after only two months asked to be transferred back to 'normal location' in an ordinary prison. To his surprise, he was told he'd have to wait for another three months.

'That was too long. I began to look for ways to get myself moved. I had to break the rules somehow. I removed all the metal handles from the mop buckets and bent them into a hook. Then I tore a bed-sheet into strips and wound them around my waist with the hook attached. When I was sure that a screw was looking my way, I legged it a couple of hundred yards towards a corner of the perimeter wall, stopped and waited for the screws to catch up. That was it.'

Alex explained to the prison governors why he'd done it and his request to be transferred was accepted. He was taken to Winchester Prison the next day to serve his punishment, initially "down the block", in solitary confinement. When that was completed, he was quickly transferred to Albany Prison on the Isle of Wight, after a particularly harrowing journey in the vehicle hold of the car ferry, handcuffed to the van's windows.

'Albany was a maximum security (or "dispersal") gaol, just across the road from the more notorious Parkhurst. I was greeted in the reception area by a con I'd known at Wakefield.

"Stone the crows, Alex. Welcome to Disneyland! You're going on A-Wing mate; I'll see you up there as soon as I can. Don't go into the TV room on the wing tonight Alex, 'cos the telly's goin' up."

I was escorted up to A-Wing and the principal officer called me into his office to read out the rules. This was the pep talk that all new arrivals were given.

"You'll find that this is a relaxed community. Very little trouble ..."

A deafening explosion rocked the telephone on his table. There was the sound of glass shattering and people yelling. A blue-shirted officer, breathing heavily, appeared at the office door.

"They've blown up the television sir."

I wasn't at Albany for very long. Somebody put my name up as being involved in some scam and I was ghosted out within only a few months of my arrival. I thought I was going back up North, so I was surprised when the journey lasted only five minutes. I'd been taken across the road — to Parkhurst. I didn't know it then but this was to be my home for the next six years. My introduction to Parkhurst was F2, its notorious hospital landing. There were maybe 20 or so cons on that landing and all were either on heavy drugs or waiting to be sent to Rampton or Broadmoor Special Hospitals. When I asked a screw why I had been put onto a medical landing, he replied, "So the doctor can have a look at you."

I didn't like the sound of that.'

- 3 -

Dear Alex

London
16th January 1977

Dear Alex,

Well, here we are. The beginning of another year. How are things in the
Isle of Wight? Windy?

The show is still great fun but I am getting very tired and the critics
were a bit lukewarm to say the least. I know I shouldn't take any notice
but I do. My favourite bit of the show is the transformation into the ballroom scene. I wish you could see it Alex. One minute I'm little Cinderella
with my ragged dress on and then – whooooooosh – there's lots of smoke
and I'm there in a big, white ballgown with sparkly shoes and a tiara
in my hair. It's magic. I have 40 seconds to do the change and a lovely
lady called Edna helps me. When I come down the steps I feel like a real
Princess.

We only had Christmas Day and Sunday off but it was a lovely break
and mummy did the Christmas lunch for us and Simon's family came
over too. You made me laugh about your see-through turkey. Did you
have bullet sprouts too? Yuk!

We always watch Morecombe and Wise on Christmas Day; it's a sort
of tradition isn't it? We all thought Angela Rippon was v. brave and my
Dad is a big fan of hers so he thought she was 'daring'!!

Simon is being wonderful and is teaching me about his favourite classical composers. One of them is Gabriel Fauré and he particularly likes his Requiem but I really adore the Pavane. I think you'd like it too. It is very haunting.

Well, it's Sunday so I'm going to have a rest. Bye for now.

Love Fiona

HM Prison Parkhurst
D-Wing
26. 1.1977

Dear Fiona

Thanks a ton for your very welcome letter, Princess – six fantastic pages! How about a smile? – wow! Do that again and you'll melt the snow from here to Vladivostok …

Lukewarm? The critics? You know, they're a funny lot – the critics. I reckon they ought to be banned, personally.

And what's all this? The Ballroom scene makes you feel like a real Princess? Now I'm going to tell you this – you find me one genuine one-carat Royal Princess who *is not* envious of you, our kid, and I'll eat me size ten simulated-leather boots. No, I'm serious.

I hope you are enjoying yourself – remember that one day you may return to the Palladium when it is completely empty, you'll sit in one of the seats near the stage and feel the quiet all around. Then you'll close your eyes and everything will come back: the stage will no longer be empty and the applause of the audience will echo all around and you'll think – gosh! I was up there on that stage receiving that applause! So, for your last few shows try all that much harder, our kid – you'll see: it'll pay off.

Hurricanes battered the Island last night and all the windows were rattling like Ernie's Gold Tops. This morning dawned calmer with a little rain – but I'd have preferred more of the Hurricane. Appropriately enough I'm at present reading 'The Tempest' by Willie Shakespeare. Pretty good.

The Judge that sent me down for life, Cantley, is really enjoying himself these days. He's presiding over the current IRA trial at the Old Bailey. Last time I saw him was at Lancaster Assizes. What interests me is that he always seems to preside over political trials ... They still say – and insist – that I got these two life sentences for GBH. Truth will come out one day.

When is your birthday, Fiona? – I won't tell anyone – honest. (I think you're a – can it be? – an Aquarian also). Take good care of yourself, Princess.

Write soon, Alex

Hiding his fluctuating emotions seemed to be a priority for Alex. Touchingly, he didn't want to burden me with them. I found this letter, and his words about returning to the Palladium, quite thought provoking. As the saying goes, 'Youth is wasted on the young' and I didn't realise at the time quite how lucky I was to be doing the things that I loved the most. Only three years older than me, Alex was becoming a sort of teacher and mentor; 'try all that much harder, our kid, and it'll pay off.' The truth was more prosaic. He writes:

'I was fast becoming an underwater swimmer. Submerged by the system, I was learning now not to drown. But in the doing of it I was becoming known as a bit of a non-conformist, and this fact hasn't earned me any friends in the Home Office.'

HM Prison Parkhurst
D-Wing
21. 2. 1977

Hello Fiona,

Up in the sky the clouds are whizzing past a bright sun at a fair old rate, and the cosmic rays are invisible against a beautiful background of duck-egg blue. The flight of a crow seems to knock it all out of perspective. Beauty and unbeauty. Forget the dictionary. I do.

Nice to see Ronnie Barker back with 'Porridge' again. I watched the first programme last night – somewhat amused to note he's reading 'GWTW'. Be even better to see you, though. When does 'Cinderella' finish, Fiona? March?

At present, on my desert island, my selection of eight records would be as follows; '1812', Tchaikovsky; 'Planets Suite', G. Holst. 'Milada', R. Korsakov. 'March Militiare', Chopin. 'Image', Debussy. 'Blue Danube ', Strauss. 'L'Arlésienne Suite ', Bizet; and. To remind me of you, Borodin's 'Unfinished Symphony'. Unfortunately, Princess, I have not yet heard Fauré but I surely hope to do so in the not too distant future. Then 'Pavane' will replace Borodin.

By the way, you must get thousands of letters every week – do you reply to everyone? Forgive my curiosity, but it really is a continuous case of wonderment to me, you know. And I can't understand it. I mean, if you only knew, it was fabulous and unbelievable when I got your first real letter. I mean, over the six years I've been scoffing porridge I've built up a list of around forty correspondents, many of them famous, a lot of them powerful politicians, all of them friends. But you, lass, you're something else again. Out of all those correspondents I look forward most of all to writing to you because, in some way, I can relate to you better than anyone else. And your replies are delightful to read. I mean that. If you're an astrologer you will doubtless know that your ruling planet is the Moon. Mine is the Sun. In astrological terms the Sun and Moon are natural counterparts of each other, maybe that explains something. Perhaps also because I concern myself primarily with writing – yourself with acting, maybe, one day, I'll be writing scripts and will be working with actors and actresses. What do you reckon?

Celebrated the twenty-fourth anniversary of my birthday with …. you guessed it – orange squash. One can pretend the stuff is Soyuz-fuel if the eyelids are screwed tightly together in the 'shut' position and the liquid is poured straight down without touching the tongue. What happens then is that one has a warm psychological glow in de tum. Really weird.

By the way, I've done a pencil portrait of you which is pretty good, though I do say so myself. I took it from one of your photos. It's staying in my cell, somehow I feel the pencil has given it life and, although it's black and white, I've called it 'Technicolour' because it captures your smile. I still feel sad, though, because they won't take a photo of me and let me send it to you. It doesn't make sense.

However, I enclose a picture of Angel Kunchev who could be my twin brother in every resemblance, except my nose is broken, his being straight.

Wow! Time really disappears. I'll stay out of trouble, work hard and be good – you do the same, right?

Take care, our kid, and follow your heart. My best regards to Simon.

Your Friend, Alex

Why wouldn't they let him have his photograph taken? It is still a mystery but only adds to the element of secrecy surrounding his incarceration. Meanwhile, Alex was making friends inside. There was Bill, who was 'old and frail but he'd been a right villain in his day'. Then there was Andy, who'd killed his baby daughter and was three years into a life sentence; Keith, who was something to do with the Salvation Army, but one day he took an overdose and died; Doug, who was a psychopath from up north in Yorkshire; and The Major, the largest character of them all.

'The Major was a tall geezer with an immense girth, a beer drinker's stomach. His flight deck was severely damaged, and this also affected his way of walking; it was the stagger of a man who's had too many ales.

He was given a short home leave and before he went, he came around the cells asking if any of us could tell him where to find a decent prostitute. One of the men told him they could be found walking on Brighton Pier in the afternoons. Of course that was a lie. But The Major took it seriously, went to Brighton and accosted a woman who was out for a walk along the pier. She screamed and a policeman came and took him away. His home leave was terminated and he was back on C-Wing the same day.'

London
15th March 1976

Dear Alex

Your collection of poems is quite brilliant and I shall treasure them. As for the picture of Angel Kunchev – do you really look like that? Wow. V. handsome. I shall answer some of your questions now:

The show is still going well but is getting slightly tedious now. Two shows a day for 14 weeks is taking its toll and we all need a break. I know this sounds very ungrateful – I'm at the London Palladium! – but I've lost a stone in weight and am physically drained. I'm irritable and constantly tired and I hate myself. Poor Simon is marvellous to put up with me like this. We close on March 26th. Phew!

My hair is slightly longer and curlier now because I have let it grow since Angels.

My birthday is on the 10th of October. So not an Aquarian as you suggested, but a Libran. I was born 10.10.56 and I'm the tenth grandchild.

You mentioned a pencil portrait you've done of me. Gosh – you are talented. It's a coincidence too, because an artist is doing a portrait of me right now as his official entry to the Royal Academy Summer Exhibition.

He is a friend of the general manager here at the Palladium. I haven't seen it yet as he is working off photos he took of me. But isn't that nice?

Simon is doing a couple of things on TV and continues to be a wonderful, loving husband. He's looking after me and picks me up every night after the show. Sometimes my Mum comes in to see me between shows to bring me something to eat!! Usually soup.

That's all for now. I'm sorry this is such a short boring letter, but with the monotony of the show, nothing much has happened.

Take care and be good.

Love from Fiona

The harsh reality of doing theatre is that it can become extremely monotonous, especially when you are performing twice a day. However, the atmosphere during the run was one of great camaraderie and everyone in the cast was kind to me (being the baby in the company), but a dark shadow was about to descend.

My parents, Bernard and Pamela Fullerton, started to receive anonymous phone calls from a woman who was threatening to kill me. The calls became more frequent so the police were called in and all calls to my parent's private number were screened. Simon was told of the threats but I was kept in the dark, as she was insisting that she 'would get me in the theatre'.

The stage-door man was informed and security was, apparently, stepped up. My poor mother was in a terrible state and Simon came to the stage door every night to take me home. Unfortunately, one night the theatre Tannoy rang out with my name, asking me to take a call backstage. The caller calmly told me that I wouldn't leave the stage alive that night. I dropped the phone and went as white as a sheet. I seem to remember being very confused because suddenly it was as if everyone was in on something from which I had been excluded. I started shaking, so the nurse gave me something to calm me down.

Somebody called the police and two plain-clothes officers arrived to have a chat and they told me the full story. Simon arrived. Management decided 'the show must go on' but the officers insisted on staying with me at all times. So, that night, standing in the wings, were two very handsome policemen, watching my every move. It was as though I had wandered onto the set of a Hitchcock movie. Everyone kept asking me if I was okay because the adrenalin was pumping so fast, it made me slightly giddy and hyper. It was all rather surreal. Needless to say, the show went without a hitch.

After the performance, I was told there would be no stage door 'meet and greet' the fans. Instead I was led down into the bowels of the Palladium and into a secret tunnel that runs under most of Great Marlborough Street, emerging in Ramillies Street, where I was bundled into Simon's Fiat 500. The real sadness for me is that I wasn't allowed to sign autographs and meet the public at the stage door again during that particular run, which is usually terrific fun and very rewarding. The policemen hung around for a few weeks, enjoying their stint in the wings watching all the beautiful girls in the chorus doing quick costume changes.

In the end, the general consensus of opinion was that it was probably the disgruntled girlfriend of a member of the crew, with whom I was always friendly.

It is interesting that I didn't tell Alex about this episode.

HM Prison Parkhurst
D-Wing
17. 3. 1977

My Dear Fiona

How wonderful to hear from you again! Even though you feel tired with the show dragging on in its final stages. Tell you something though, this is when the critics will really be watching you. So bear up lass and show them some spirit; you can do it.

But anyway, you're among the World's Best – Ludmila Tourischeva got the Order of Lenin for it. If it is any consolation I want you to know I think of you and if that knowledge gives you strength to persevere, then my thoughts are not in vain.

Meanwhile, get some solid grub down you, and have a listen to me national anthem, the '1812' – strength, both physical and spiritual, can come from hearing good music. Be happy.

In a month's time the manuscript of my new book will be ready. I think I'll be permitted to send you the first chapter and I'm looking forward to that, so stand by. There's a thesis I hope to publish also when I get out (our S.O. reckons in three years). It's a critical analysis: On The Dialectics of Plato, More, Hegel, Marx and Engels. (Yeah.) That took me ages to write but it's finished and I'm satisfied.

There's no reason to hate yourself, Princess, that is A1 self-destruction. Say to yourself: 'I feel fantastic and I've never felt better, hate myself indeed!' and you'll feel better – you'll see. Magic. And for God's sake, if you have any major worries tell Simon – remember that he wears your heart and you his.

Oh, by the way Fiona, you have yet another fan here at Parkhurst Ghetto – and he isn't a resident … our Welfare Officer, Mr Haworth. By sheer coincidence his little girl's birthday is also on October the 10th. We were having a talk today and he said he'd seen Simon in a TV play called 'Romance'. It was screened too late for us cons to watch. Decent bloke is Mr Haworth. Funny thing is he's from my home town, Nelson, which at first I thought was incredible.

Well, this missive is drawing to a close so I got to say take good care of yourself, Princess and my best regards to Simon.

Love as Always, Alex

HM Prison Parkhurst
D-Wing
2. 4. 1977

Hello Princess,

I nearly cried this afternoon when Red Rum took the Grand National. Boy – what a horse! What a gorgeous, lovely horse! And how sad for Ladbrokes. My only hope now is for Manchester United to win the F.A. Cup – if they don't there's some consolation that it will go to Liverpool FC, 'cause Man. Utd's gonna beat Leeds and Liverpool will win the match against Everton. If I'm wrong I'll eat my books (I probably shall, at any rate, seeing as they contain more nutritional value than the current offal).

Fiona, do you read 'Country Life' magazine? If so, never advertise in it … and pass that advice on to your friends. There are many subscribers to Country Life in here – but it goes by another sobriquet – 'Burglars Gazette'. Take heed. Oh, and never trust a Yale lock for security, use mortice locks with as many tumblers as possible in each.

So this lady Tory M.P. comes out with the following profound statement: 'Prisoners should be made to give blood and help repay their debt to Society'.

Dear lady MP, Obviously it has not been brought to your sensationalist attention that, up until recently, a great many people in penal institutions have held Blood Donor cards and regularly gave pints. This practice has now stopped because of the fact that the Blood Transfusion Service will <u>not accept prisoner's blood because it is deficient of vitamin content.</u>

So the Eurovision Song Contest is to be screened over here, after all. That is nice for Angela Rippon. Wish I could watch it but it's on too late for us lot.

Here is a poem I have grown to like; the first two lines of the last verse have always been familiar to me – imagine my delight at becoming fully acquainted with the complete poem! You may know of it yourself, already?

To Althea, from Prison (last verse)

Stone Walls do not a Prison make,
Nor Iron bars a Cage;
Minds innocent and quiet take
That for an Hermitage;

> If I have freedom in my love,
> And in my soul am free;
> Angels alone that soar above,
> Enjoy such Liberty
>
> *Richard Lovelace*

Do you know how your name is spelt in Russian, our kid? Here, I'll show you; Фиона. That is 'Fiona'. Саймон – Simon.

Please write soon. Alex

The show had been so all-consuming that I hadn't written to Alex since March. We finished just before Easter and then I began filming in Scotland a small documentary about Scottish cashmere, directed by the legendary photographer Terence Donovan. Terence liked to boast that he 'taught Fiona how to swear', as the air was often blue. This gap in communication obviously caused Alex great concern.

HM Prison Parkhurst
D-Wing
23. 5. 1977

Dear Fiona

Hope you are well and happy.

Guess I've said something to offend. If so, not intentional. Sorry. I'll figure it out eventually and put it right. Better still, don't give up writing – tell me the trouble and leave it to me to put right. I'm okay. Missing hearing from you. That's all. Listen, Princess, take care of yourself, keep being beautiful and nice to know.

Wishing you great success in work, health, and fighting spirit!

Yours, As Ever Alex

I could never have imagined how much my letters brightened Alex's existence inside, or that the gap of a few months would cause him such misery. During this period he began to dwell on his situation and discussed it with his friend Nobby.

'I spent some time talking to Nobby about my arrest and the events leading from it. Nobby wasn't surprised at all.

"You're in need of a good solicitor, Alex—otherwise forget it. Do you have many people outside to take up your case?"

"No."

"It's important to stay in touch with the outside world. Drop a line to the Communist League. They could give your case publicity. You're a political prisoner."

"This country doesn't have political prisoners. I've heard them saying that on the wireless."

"That's to fool the public. If they're right, then you don't exist. Listen, I know about Special Branch and MI5; they operate against political targets. When an arrest is made they get the uniformed police to do it. You get sent to prison and then cease to exist, because the government says there are no political prisoners.

The Branch couldn't nick you, so they lay the burglary on you and the police nick you. You're inside … very satisfactory.

When were you sentenced Alex?"

"December seventy-one."

"Yeah. That fits. That was when they had the big scare on. Loads of embassy officials, Soviet diplomats, sent packing. You had direct contact with one of them Alex. That's what got them interested in you.'"

Alex's letters were always addressed to my agent's office and forwarded on to me from there. This was the usual procedure for fan mail and it always used to amaze me how the fans knew where to write. Some agents even screen letters before forwarding them. Today, the internet makes access even easier. Unfortunately, sometimes there was a small delay before they finally reached me.

London
3rd June 1977

Dear Alex,

How awful I felt when I received your last, little, sad epistle. How selfish of me to let you think you could, in any way, have offended me. That's the last thing you could do.

Well, after much delay, here I am. So very, very sorry but excuses will not do. Golly how time flies. Since the show finished I have put on a few pounds and feel much better. I look more human now.

No, I haven't read either 'Andersonville' or 'The Possessed' though I have read Dostoyevsky's 'The Idiot'. I prefer lighter books really (not being of great intelligence) and enjoy biographies very much indeed. They intrigue me. Classics like Dickens, Hardy, Wilde and Bronte I enjoy also and any romantic, historical novel will do!

I remember reading 'Desiree' after lights out, under the bedcovers at school. I've just finished David Niven's 'Bring on the Empty Horses' which is a good giggle.

I thought the Eurovision Song Contest was a minor disaster this year. Angela Rippon (wearing huge diamante earrings) made a couple of unfortunate ad-libs. It's probably just as well you didn't see it.

I bet you're pleased Man. Utd. won the cup then. I'm glad Liverpool won the European Cup too. I enjoy watching sport. Simon used to play a lot of rugby but has since given it up because it endangered his career. Now he's playing cricket, when he can, for the 'Stage Club' and I enjoy watching that and having a picnic on the grass, with the other wives.

At last the sunshine is here. London looks fantastic with a marvellous Jubilee atmosphere and decorations everywhere. The mall leading to Buckingham Palace is most impressive. We took a late night drive around London last night to see all the floodlit buildings and I thought our architecture was really very beautiful. I have been fortunate enough to visit many of the great cities in the world ... but somehow London has something else. I don't know what it is.

Maybe it's the vastly differing styles, the old/new architecture. Maybe it's the statues and the lakes. Maybe it's the fact that London has more parks, greenery and wildlife than any other city in the world. Maybe it's Harrods and Bond Street!! (Where I love to window-shop but never, never buy.) I don't know.

Have you ever read A A Milne's 'When We Were Very Young' and 'Now We Are Six'? They are children's books of poems and prose but they are very adult in a sort of way. I enjoyed them as a child but they give me just as much enjoyment now. Here is an example:

Solitude

I have a house where I go
When there's too many people,
I have a house where I go
Where no-one can be;
I have a house where I go
Where nobody ever says 'No'
Where no-one says anything—so
There is no-one but me.

A A Milne

All for now. Take care of yourself.

Love, Fiona

HM Prison — Parkhurst
D-Wing
13. 6. 1977

Dear Fiona

Thousands of grateful thanks for your wonderful letter, it was really marvellous to hear from you once again and I feel like I've just awoken from a grave somewhere in the Arctic Circle to the reality of a grave somewhere nearer the equator. You just don't know what effect you have on people! Well maybe you do.

Also, you can't know just how relieved I actually was upon receiving your letter – wow! Do you know how long it was before I decided to read it? Thirty minutes. Thirty minutes and two fags! Ce monde est plein de fous …

Anyway, I take note of your remark 'not being of great intelligence' – you're doing yourself an injustice there, Princess – how one can read and understand Dostoyevsky before the age of 20 and proclaim oneself 'not being of great intelligence' afterwards beats me. Sheesh!

I'm keeping out of trouble, like I promised, and I'm enclosing a letter from a friend of mine – a Probation Officer at Oxford Stalag – so you can have a little more insight. He reckons I have to grow-up a bit and although I agree with that, to an extent, I don't agree with him saying I have to use the people around me – god forbid! Everyone 'grows-up' and everyone dies growing-up. But, you know, Fiona, what really surprises me is that nearly all the cons in here are royalists and really think the Queen is something else. Personally, I hold nothing against the royal family except that I don't even know their last name.

Yes, I was ecstatic when Manchester United won the F.A. Cup! They ought to give Tommy Docherty an OBE and the management of England F.C.! And Liverpool did a right good job, too, taking the European Cup – that's two Cups for the North!

I used to play rugger once. It is a game we used to play at approved school – but with a difference. I'm just thinking back … I think you'll have heard of 'rollerball', yes? Well this 'game' we had to play at Approvie was called 'Murderball'. Christ, Fiona, I still get the creeps thinking of it. Thirty players – fifteen each side – and it was played just like rugby except one was permitted to use <u>any</u> means to gain possession of the ball. First time I played, it was on my first day at the lousy joint. Both sides lined up facing each other. The P. E. hands me the ball, blows the whistle and runs like merry hell. Right away I find myself lying on the ball, flat out on the deck, fifteen blokes on top of me, I was in a full nelson and one bloke had his fingers up my nose and another was belting away at my ribs …. Never again! Come to think of it that's where I left my back molar …

To be perfectly honest I'm bloody freezing so I'm going to get into bed, have a smoke, then carry on with this in the morning. 'Night.

Good morning, Princess! Slept like an unconscious log. Now, the place to feel the character of architectural structures is not London at all – try Stratford upon Avon,

Evesham and Broadway. I don't know what it is I most dislike about London – certainly a mixture of Centre Point, Subway Four (Piccadilly) and the Flying Squad. Friendliness in London, compared with Glasgow, Manchester and Salford, is virtually non-existent. To me there's more art and character in the design of a Burnley cotton mill, than is possessed by the Houses of Parliament and all the other aristocratic shacks put together. I think I can tell you what you find unique about London as opposed to the other great cities – in London *everyone* speaks English …? Uh-oh.

Still freezing. Course I like children's books but I'm restricted to Anthony Buckeridge's Jennings stories. A.A. Milne is someone I haven't yet had the privilege to read. The poem you enclosed, 'Solitude', now I really found that delightful.

Please take care and don't stop being happy, Princess.

Yours As Ever

Alex

I have always had a chip on my shoulder about my lack of a formal education and it is endearing here to see Alex try to assuage my insecurities about my 'lack of intelligence'. He was the first person to do so. My father used to tell everyone that I 'only went to school on a Wednesday afternoon' (based on the premise that I was hardly ever at school, due to filming) and my husband was quick to call me stupid.

London
4th August 1977

My Dearest Alex,

This will only be a short one I'm afraid as I'm feeling a bit mean, moody and miserable and I can't write letters when I'm depressed.

Well, we've been married over a year now. I had tears in my eyes when I opened your card Alex. A few people remembered our anniversary but your card was by far the most beautiful. Thank you, thank you. It touched my heart.

I'm reading all about Lady Jane Grey now because she is one of my favourite characters in all history. Such a tragic life she had. She was Queen for nine days only and lost her head seven months later at the age of 16. She was a victim of ruthless people trying to manipulate her for their own gain. I've been interested in her for some time now but find that all the books written about her have gone out of print, so this is making my research extremely difficult. I'd like one day to make a film about her.

I've started writing poetry Alex, thanks to your suggestion. It's not very good though. Maybe I'll enclose a poem next time.

Well, I must go to the launderette!! Such a glamorous life we actresses lead. Followed by a whizz round Tesco's with a wonky trolley.

Oh, don't you just love Carly Simon's new record 'Nobody Does it Better'? It's the theme to the new Bond film 'The Spy who Loved Me', which I have yet to see. It really grows on you.

Alex, you've mentioned being an 'A' man. What is that?

Must go, Love 'n' Things…

Fiona

P.S. The royal family's last name is Windsor, you nut.

HM Prison Parkhurst
D-Wing
8. 8. 1977

Dear Fiona

You ask what is an 'A-man'? Category-A is 'top security' classification for prisoners considered by the Home Office to be dangerous to society i.e. murderers, rapists, bombers, threats to the government, etc. (and likely to commit the same crime again). There are some 250 A-men in the total prison population of 42,000. And, yes,

I am one of the 250. I think, well I'm certain, that they've got me down as a 'threat to the government', a subversive element kind of thing.

To a Capitalist society, I, a Communist …

If you think, sometimes, whether I am a murderer, rapist or homicidal maniac let me put your mind at rest. No, Fiona, I am not any of those things and I loathe such people as much as you loathe them. Fiona, let me tell you this; this is from <u>me</u> to you; I do not intend, or advocate, harm or violence towards anyone. I favour a revolution, naturally – but not terrorism and violence as a means to revolution. I care about people, Fiona. I have only one enemy and that enemy is the enemy of the people; which is not necessarily a *physical* thing. It is so often a combination of many things i.e. pollution, thermonuclear power and the neutron bomb, for example. I favour international co-existence and positive steps to be taken in order for that state to materialise. In <u>no way</u> will I become a part of any scheme to intimidate others, and on that you have my word. There are much better things to do, as I'm sure you would agree. It may be that one day my views and outlook will change – ah, who knows? I look to the future and trust to circumstance.

So, it's Windsor is it? Ah. Next time you see her down the launderette send her my regards. Right now I must faze out. I'll bang out another letter in a fortnight. Take care Princess, stay happy and regards to Simon.

As Ever, Yours

Alex

I recall being unclear as to exactly what it was that Alex was supposed to have done, but it was reassuring to know that he was not a murderer, rapist or homicidal maniac! When my father asked me what Alex had done, I gave a vague answer about it being 'something political'.

Without asking, for it would never have occurred to me, Alex takes it upon himself to research the life of Lady Jane Grey for me. I had long been fascinated by her — and Anne Boleyn — as two young queens who both met a sticky end. Sadly, I was never to portray Jane, but a film of her life was made in 1986. However, in 1991 I did get to play Anne Boleyn in a grand theatrical production of Shakespeare's 'Henry VIII' opposite Keith Michell.

HM Prison Parkhurst
D-Wing
12. 8. 1977

Hello Princess

Hope you don't mind me writing again after so short a period. I have to work off all this excess energy or I will go barmy in stages. I hope and trust that this missive will find you in the 'un' mood; un-meanmoodyandmiserable.

Fiona I've this idea. One records the song of a lark, then human words are super-imposed plus maybe a minimum of flute or guitar and from this maybe five discs are cut and promptly despatched to the corresponding number of deejays who spin the plastic and – BLAM! – it's so hot it burns and everyone's going round like they've been hit on the head by a freak musical meteor storm and wondering 'Where's this new talent, man. I mean where's it at?' and while all these people are wandering about zapped out, the estimable but dubious membership of the Bird Watchers' Society would be buying up every disc they could focus their 10 x 50's on …. AND the disc is cut in luminous green plastic which actually – glows in the dark – are you ready for that? Luminous green! Anyway, it might turn out to be a lousy idea (but that's okay, surely, for a lousy idea is undoubtedly better than no idea at all …?)

On the subject of Lady Jane Grey, things are starting to happen. I wrote to Buckingham Palace earlier this week but the letter was stopped (for good enough reason, I should add). Anyhow here's what I have so far:

LADY JANE GREY: Progress Report

She was:	a.	Of the House of Tudor
	b.	Great-Uncle was Henry VIII
	c.	Great Grand-daughter of Henry VII
	d.	Married to Lord Guildford Dudley
	e.	Succeeded Edward VI as reigning monarch in July, 1553
	f.	She did, in fact, reign for 14 days
	g.	She was then imprisoned (by Mary, her Grannie!) until the 12th of February, 1554, when, aged 17, she was executed.

NOTES:

You'll have noted the last two points; reigned for 14 days, aged 17 when executed. I believe she became Queen aged 16½, Fiona. From what I make of it so far, Jane was the victim of a jealous grandmother (Mary) who wanted (and got) the throne for herself. Now Mary was queen when her grand-daughter was killed but I'm not quite sure whether she favoured the execution (Mary married Philip II of Spain – the execution might well have been instigated by <u>him</u> – we know how the Spaniards used to behave).

In fact I'm confident that Philip did a roaring import trade in thumb screws, etc. which found their way to the tower. He did, at least, bring a great deal of torture technological know-how with him from sunny Spain.

One thing about Strangeways – they have a <u>very</u> good library. I read a really belting book called 'Burr'; a novel by Gore Vidal. (Think I'll send him a few lines). Are you familiar with this author's work, Fiona? His last novel (previous to 'Burr') was 'Myra Breckinridge'. He has also written a few plays.

Strangeways is the only nick in this fair land that has a chain hanging outside the gates – and everyone has to pull it before they leave. I'm trying to give the joint a graphic description, but, boy, it's difficult! 1,600 cons in that place, our kid. 1,600 … in a nick designed and built for 700.

Tea! Got to get some tea. Will continue when I've supped up. Cheers, then, Princess. Aaaargh yuk … Half a pint of this would evacuate China. Create an international incident. If Typhoo put the T in Britain I shudder to imagine who put the T in Parkhurst (and I take note that it was left right to the end!) I bet they've got some clandestine government laboratory spending thousands a year writing up new formulas for our tea.

I like spelling words backwards like egabrag and skool. Now there's this place called Darton, which is famous for its hams, so I spelt Darton backwards and came up with a 'Lunchpack of notraD ham'. The Bells! The Bells! Fiona!

Anyway, Princess, Best Regards to Simon,

Love

Alex

Are You Real?

Are you real
Or a dream?
Or a morning star-
Shining but unseen
So close and yet so far...

The ray of love
Falls upon me
And then it dies...
I call you wonderful
Or gaze
Unable to believe my eyes.

Where are you now?
Where is my hope
To be with you?
My heart—an anxious chasm,
Is your captive too.

Are you real,
Or a dream?
Are you fire,
Or are you smoke?
Who will explain
Why you cannot happen again
If this earth can happen again.

A Prokofyev

I was overwhelmed by his enthusiastic research for Lady Jane Grey. In fact, Alex sent me pages of information about her, which I have edited here. (Although I'm sure she did only reign for nine days!)

In the summer of 1977 Simon was cast in a major movie adaptation of Agatha Christie's 'Death on the Nile'. He was thrilled and saw this as his big break. Suddenly things started to change. Simon fired his agent and signed with a bigger agency. He found a top-notch accountant who opened some off-shore accounts and he signed with the PR people who had been looking after me since I was a child. He was due to leave for Egypt mid-September.

HM Prison Parkhurst
D-Wing
17. 8. 1977

Elvis is dead … God, Fiona.

HM Prison Parkhurst
D-Wing
6. 9. 1977

Hello Princess

I sincerely hope that I find you happy and well, and that the world is treating you properly, as it should. The sun is shining brightly today and it is warm out, most of the men are just lying about while a few others play football and 'padder' tennis. I hope, too, that you and Simon are getting the most out of the weather – this is a Sunday to be out of doors and up in the fields and woods. I am reminded of Cumbria and the mountains of Scafell, Great Gable and Bowfell, The Old Man and Fairfield. That is a part of the world that is still clean and very beautiful. I would give anything to return; when I am released there is where I shall go. Have you been to Cumbria yet, Fiona? You would be thrilled with Keswick and Penrith, you know. There are a great many things of interest in the towns; in the country there are deer, if one knows where to look, and clear becks, terns and waterfalls. The best scenery in Britain.

I've terminated my affiliation with the Communist Party. I thought you'd like to know. I now support Albania and Tirana. I'm also honoured to be accepted as a candidate member for the Southampton cell of the C.L. (Communist League). I have to complete a probationary six months before full C.L. membership. During these six months I must complete a six-lesson correspondence course on social science (I am currently half-way through lesson two). Some of the questions are hard – some simple, for instance here is question 15: 'WHAT IS SURPLUS VALUE?' And my answer: *The economic exploitation of the worker, under capitalism, no matter what his wages may be, i.e. by the simple use of his labour power the worker produces a greater value than he is paid for by his capitalist bosses. So, we see the surplus value created (the capitalists promptly appropriate it – thus the worker in capitalist society is exploited)*… Probably wrong … (!)

No, that answer is correct, right enough. Fiona, tell me something? What is your opinion of British Communism? (Everyone is telling me; 'You'll come out of prison much quicker if you forget about Communism'.)

Really, I think it is only my political viewpoint that is <u>keeping</u> me inside – I should have been released years ago! And yet, I feel there is a <u>need</u> for me in here; maybe that is what makes me stick it out, I don't know. If the C.L. gives me membership I shall be making history – for, in British history, no-one has ever been *officially* given political status while in prison. So maybe my comrades think there is a need for me to remain, too.

Write soon.

Love Alex

London
23rd September 1977

My Dear Alex,

Well, my friend. What can I say? Your letters make me very happy. Your zaniness cheers me, your wit astounds me, your forthrightness scares me, your courage gives me strength. Your politics, however, I cannot fully understand and I must agree that they are probably the reason you are still inside.

You obviously have a great talent for writing and I just wish I could help you get your poems and book published. But I don't know how.

Don't worry though. They'll be published one day and you'll become very famous. Just wait and see. Sir John Betjeman – watch out!

Oh my god ... they're all dying. Presley – Bolan – Callas. I can't believe it. A whole era went with the amazing Elvis. I wept.

I'm all alone, Alex. Depressed, lonely and sad. I can't remember whether I ever mentioned to you that Simon was about to do a big movie. I didn't? Oh, well, he is and it's called 'Death on the Nile' (Agatha Christie.) He started filming about 10 days ago and yesterday he flew out to Egypt to do all the scenes around the pyramids, the Sphinx and the Nile, for six weeks. And I was left behind. However, I'll be joining him on Oct 8th so I can spend my birthday with him, and will probably be out there for two weeks. When he returns they continue filming at Pinewood Studios for nine weeks, so it's quite a long haul. They have many stars lined up in the film and Simon plays the part of Simon Doyle. If you can find the book do read it, it's a terrific story (If you like thrillers.) This is Simon's big break into movies, so he's naturally very excited and anxious about it.

Many, many thanks Alex for the research you've been doing on Lady Jane Grey. It has been extremely useful. We are now negotiating with Hester W Chapman's agents (as Miss Chapman is now dead) for the film rights of her book, as we feel hers is the most detailed and personal account of Jane's life and would like a script based on her book. As soon as this is done we can set about getting a film company interested in the idea. It could take years but we are hopeful.

I loved 'Are You Real' by Prokofyev. Very tender and says a lot about how one feels when one falls in love – and out again.

My portrait wasn't chosen for the Royal Academy Exhibition but seems to have been a great success regardless. I liked it very much. It is a very large canvas and I'm leaning to one side in a very stark, white shirt, thus leaving an enormous area of nothing, which is filled with grey swirly clouds. The artist achieved an incredible effect in the eyes, which really makes them look out at you and follow you around. It is currently on view in an art gallery in Los Angeles.

Sorry about Strangeways and the Parkhurst tea. Shall I send you a teabag?

Well, summer came and went pretty quickly. About two days actually. I don't seem to have put my winter woollies away at all this year. In fact,

I'm sitting here now in two sweaters, with cold feet and the sniffles. Think I've got a cold coming. Do hope the sun is shining in Egypt. Anyway, I feel much happier now. I've just had a pizza and coke for my supper and watched a bit of TV. Writing letters always cheers me up. It's like talking to someone. Being an only child, I should be used to being alone. But when you've been with someone for so long, suddenly being without him takes a little getting used to.

No poetry yet. I must build up my confidence before I send you any. It's all terrible at the moment.

Well, I'd better go and water the plants. They're all looking a bit thirsty. Don't laugh, but it's the launderette again tomorrow and the doctor's on Monday to have four injections for Egypt. Poor me. Think I'll recuperate in bed all Tuesday and read.

Be good. Once again thank you for all your letters.

Cheers – Fiona

HM Prison Parkhurst
D-Wing
30. 9. 1977

Hello, Dreamy.

Wow! Can you pass on good vibes or can you? I'm here to testify you can do it with ease. I never fail to experience a feeling of wonderment …

Am I zany? Oh. Wow. Fiona – I never knew that, you've got me worried. Anyway, if I do all that for you – you'll never know what you do for me. With a friend like you, Princess, who needs fresh air?

I'm all alone, too, Princess. Lonely – yeah, sad – yep. I do know how you must feel at times then, you see. The world out there can't help much – organized chaos, with everyone running around in circles and finding little, if any, time for the rest of mankind or the beauties of nature. And no-one really knowing just what they're chasing after, blind to the hurt they inflict upon the feelings of others, ignoring common courtesies. It's all wrong, Fiona. Is this why we're sad? A contributory factor without doubt.

You must be missing Simon terribly. It is fantastic news about the film! I am really pleased for you both – you must be proud as anything of your Simon! A big break indeed – but he must have simply <u>tons</u> of talent and drive. And Egypt must be something to look forward to.

Fiona – did you <u>really</u> like that poem of Prokofyev? I think he is a truly great master; his verse is so simple and yet carries a whole world of meaning. Andrei Prokofyev is, by the way, a Bulgarian.

I'm a vegetarian now. I've gone completely off eating meat. Now it's grated carrots and cheese every day and a tub of yoghurt four times a year. Wizard. Really appetizing. Yeah. God I'm starving. Also there's a rumour in the air that we're going to have a pay rise soon (our last pay rise was exactly a year ago when we all got 11 pence). The coming rise is said to amount to a staggering <u>40</u> pence! How about that? I'll believe it when I see it.

Best cure for the sniffles is a glass of 'Red Star' Russian Export – which is genuine vodka – and a box of matches. One swirls the matches in the liquid – then the red ends are bitten off with each sip of vodka. This cocktail is also a great cure for loneliness – just think of all those nice firemen ….

How quiet it is. Nothing stirring and the only sound coming creakingly from my pen. How strange it is to remember that the first letter I ever wrote to you, I found difficult. Now, when I write to you, Princess, the words come easy, and I find no difficulty at all – just a natural flow. It speaks a great deal for your ability to bring out such naturalness in others.

I reckon it's tough for any two people in love to be separated from each other – but it could also be a good thing, in that it helps preserve independence. It <u>does</u> help to be alone now and then, for it gives one time to ease up, think, and look forward with double pleasure to being together once again.

Gosh I'm tired. Read anything good, recently? I've just re-read 'Dr. Zhivago' and am scouting around for something else already. I have my eye on a book by Leon Uris called 'Armageddon'. Looks promising.

Off to bed now, Princess. Take Care of Yourself.

Alex

One year into the marriage and I was already feeling depressed. The transition from the warmth of a loving family straight to a tiny flat with an absent husband was proving a difficult one, particularly as, at that time, I didn't have a network of girlfriends to call on. Being an only child I had always found making friends really hard, partly due to my army childhood, moving home every three years, and partly to my early career as a child in the movies.

The trip to Egypt to celebrate my twenty-first birthday was not a great success. Simon seemed preoccupied (I discovered subsequently that he was having an affair) and I felt very vulnerable. However, being guided into secret tombs and singing loudly inside one of the pyramids, with barely a soul in sight, are memories that shall stay with me.

When Simon returned home, he seemed to have changed. Alarm bells started to ring, making me feel even more insecure.

Meanwhile, Alex was still desperately trying to keep his head above water.

'One day I heard that the Kray twins were being moved out of the special security block (SSB). The whisper was that they were coming onto C-Wing. And so they did.

Everyone was banged up one day after lunch, and when the doors were opened Ron and Reg had already moved in. Ron knocked on my cell door and introduced himself. He was my next-door neighbour.

"Haven't you got a record player?" he asked.

"Nah. It's broken."

"Right. Hang about a minute." He disappeared into his cell and came back with a large Dansette record player.

"You can use this for a while. You haven't any records have you?"

And he was gone again. When he returned he had a large pile of Tammy Yuro LPs.

"Use these for as long as you like. If I want them, I'll let you know."

I never did play anything on that Dansette; I wasn't going to scratch any records man...'

HM Prison Parkhurst
A-Wing
28. 11. 1977

Hello Princess

Only me. How's things with you? See any camels? Looks like Sadat missed seeing you. And, listen – is Simon enjoying making his picture (there certainly does seem to be a distinguished cast! Peter Ustinov, yet! David Niven, Bette Davis and Maggie Smith. Must have been hot, filming out there, though).

Did I tell you that I'd gone on a vegetarian diet? Yeah. I lasted a month. That month was one that I shall never forget. Yuk. Nut patties, soya bean sausage, raw carrot … Miserable. Felt like a squirrel. Storing up for the winter. Never again.

Before I was nicked peculiar things were happening down the Soviet Embassy. Special Branch was watching Soviet Trade and Cultural delegations to this country, most intently, because it had leaked out that the Russians planned to sabotage Britain's major cities. Ten officers of the Soviet Military Intelligence were given deportation notices. Bang – kicked out. Over a hundred others went with them. [Alex then listed 74 by name]. All of them were, and still are, officers of the Soviet Committee for State Security (Komitet Gosudarstvennoye Bezhopasnoski – KGB). No doubt you will recall them being expelled by the government back to the USSR in 1971.

So what's new? Frank Longford is coming to see me next month, 16th December. He's not the ideal person to have around, but I want my release sometime in the near future, Fiona, and if he can help, then by _all_ means. If he can get me an appeal to the House of Lords I would have a chance of a re-trial. And, should _that_ happen, I'd walk out of court, free. Everyone in here – the cons _and_ the screws _and_ four prison governors – says I should not be in prison now. I agree, I agree. Conclusively.

You know I work making curtains – well I almost sewed my fingers together yesterday. My fault. Sitting day-dreaming, thinking of my Triumph Bonneville, revving the sewing-machine … needle through a finger. Oooooh! Still, it gave everybody a laugh. Cretins.

Well, you've been my best friend over the past couple of years, Fiona. Straight. Maybe without your realizing, kid, you've kept me out of trouble. No-one else. You've made me happy – I only hope I've given you a few smiles now and then. Ha. If there is anything I can do for you in the future – I will do it gladly. Maybe one day you will need a true friend, who knows?

Remember

Alex

Neither High, Nor Very Far

Neither high, nor very far,
Neither emperor, nor King,
You are only a little milestone,
Which stands at the edge of the highway.
To people passing by
You point the right direction,
And stop them from getting lost.
You tell them of the distance
For which they still must journey.
Your service is not a small one
And people will always remember you.

Alex 1977

My life was slowly starting to unravel as Simon began to shut me out of his new life. He was becoming very secretive and played on my insecurities. There were a lot of tears and harsh words but to the media we were turning into a golden couple. I couldn't confide in anyone. Not even Alex. Not yet.

I started filming a series called 'Dick Barton Special Agent', playing the archetypal damsel in distress. It turned out to be one of the most appalling television projects I was ever involved in! However, it co-starred the beautiful actress Cassandra Harris, who was married with two children. In the make-up chair every morning she would tell me about a young man who was in love with her and how she didn't know what to do. She eventually married him. His name was Pierce Brosnan.

For Alex,
Best wishes from
Fiona Fullerton

'All the submarines have been launched'.

The first photo Fiona sent Alex in 1976, which stayed with him for 17 years, through 12 prisons.

'Angel Kunchev, who could be my twin brother'.

Because the authorities wouldn't let him have
his photograph taken, Alex sent a picture of
Bulgarian revolutionary Kunchev.

'I slept with the borrowed diamonds under my pillow'.
With Roger Moore at the Royal premiere of 'A View to a Kill' 1985.

'Enkhuizen is like a model village. Cobbled streets, sweet little canals, thousands of tulips'.
With husband Simon MacCorkindale in Holland 1978.

Free Alex Now!
Campaign poster for a
1991 club night starring
Steve Coogan.

FREE ALEX NOW!

A CLUB NIGHT AND CABARET
TO SUPPORT THE CAMPAIGN FOR THE RELEASE OF
ANTHONY ALEXANDROWICZ - PRISONER 789959

■FROM 7PM

SU ANDI
JOHNNY DANGEROUSLY
DAVE GORMAN
BILL McCOID
MRS. MERTON
HENRY NORMAL
DARREN POYZER
KEV SEISAY
LEMN SISSAY

With special guest appearance From 'Saturday Zoo' by
STEVE COOGAN as PAUL CALF

■11PM - 2PM
CLUB NIGHT WITH
THE FAMILY FOUNDATION
& GUEST DJ'S STEVE MORAN AND DANNY BAXTER

WED 9th JUNE
at JABEZ CLEGG

2 Portsmouth Street, Manchester. 061-272 8612 (Opposite Manchester University & Academy Venue)

TICKETS: £5.00 ADVANCE, £6.00 DOOR FROM: JABEZ CLEGG - 061-272 8612,
HMV MANCHESTER - 061-834 2810, PICCADILLY BOX OFFICE - 061-839 0858

Alex's father Viktor with
his sister Susan c. 1961.

Alex with his mother Elsie c. 1956.

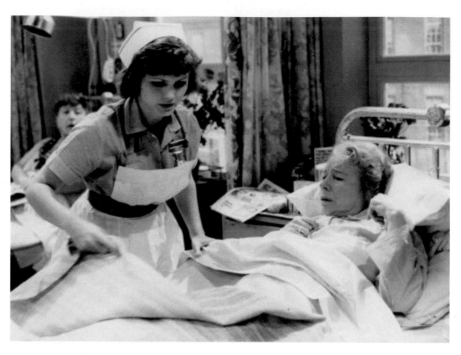

'I said to myself "Try writing to her". I never expected a response'.

As student nurse Patricia Rutherford in 'Angels' 1976. (Courtesy BBC)

'You know of my lifelong interest in Anastasia? What a coincidence this is'.

As Anastasia (far right) in 'Nicholas and Alexandra' 1970. (Courtesy Colombia Pictures)

Alex's pencil drawing of a British Railways Standard Class 9F Locomotive,
which he gave to Eric Cullen.

With his exceptional handwriting, Alex could eventually fit
the entire Lord's Prayer onto a postage stamp four times.

'Thank you for the wedding photo. How happy you look'.
Married in the Crypt Chapel of St Paul's Cathedral, 10 July 1976.

Alex hands himself in to Grendon Prison, February 1991, after absconding from HMP Leyhill.

Alex tastes freedom in 1993 and starts a protest walk from Moss Side to London.

'Why is the show becoming known as Hamlet?'
As Guinevere in 'Camelot' 1982.

VISITING ORDER	No. 93
(VALID FOR 28 DAYS ONLY)	

H.M. Prison *PARKHURST*

21 JAN 1980

Reg. No. *789959* Name *ALEXANDROWICZ,*

has permission to be visited by *MISS F. FULLERTON,*

% 29-31 KINGS RD, CHELSEA, LONDON SW 3.

1. The visit to last only **30** minutes.
2. Visitors admitted only between the hours of 1-30 p.m. & 3-30 p.m.
3. No visit allowed on Sundays, Christmas Day, or Good Friday.
4. Such of the above-named friends as wish to visit, must all attend at the same time, and produce this order.
5. Attention is called to the Notice on the reverse of this form.

Governor.

Visit paid _____ Initials of Officer in charge _____
No. 252 (28008—26-3-62)

No. 252 (28008—26-3-62)

'Try to come, will you?' A visiting order, which remained unused.

'She was partial to drinking gin, so quickly lost her looks'. Fiona as Rachel, Van Gogh's mistress in 'Gaugin, The Savage'. (© Scope Features/Brian Moody)

Alex and Fiona with Eric Cullen—July 2012.

London
December 1977 (A Christmas card)

For my dear friend Alex.

Christmas Greetings.

With Much Love, Fiona

PS I promise I'll write soon. Thinking of you.

HM Prison Parkhurst
A-Wing
December 1977

My Very Dear friend.

Thank you, Fiona, for the lovely card and beautiful photograph that you sent to me; I shall always treasure these things. Words on paper can express only so much, which is often so little. My heart, alas, cannot hold a pen.

I'd love you to come and see me here, you know, Fiona, but in reality I know that if you agreed and the Home Office agreed, there would remain the biggest problem, I mean it would not do your image any good to be seen visiting this Black Hole under any circumstances. And that's why I've never asked you to visit me here. I mention that in passing only because you may have wondered.

The graffiti on the walls here is improving steadily. Take, for example, this burning phrase; 'Tomorrow has been cancelled owing to a lack of interest'! There must be an entirely new class of criminal coming in these days.

You must let me know when Dick Barton makes the screen, Princess, I don't want to miss you. Take care, our kid, be cheerful.

Regards to Simon.

Love Alex

Sonnet to My Friend

This Platonic pen filled with love
And tender gratitude
Will write words sweet and clear
To bring my friendship near to you.
My heart is but an inky flow
Pouring out to you on paper leaves
My spirit brings me closer still
With every gust of wind and gentle breeze.
The air, an unpolluted breath
Sighs devotion on its way,
Enveloping you and the world with
Joy and happy dedication.
Forever will I keep this love
For you, my friend, deep within me

Alex 1977

- 5 -
The Realm of the Last Inch

HM Prison Parkhurst
16. 1. 1979

My Dearest Friend,

How are things? I got your card at Christmas, Fiona – have my letters been getting to you alright? Please write soon … I'm so despondent my beard's falling out.

This lunchtime I was taken off Category-A!! After eight long years. This means that I could soon be going home to the free world in the near future. It scares me a bit, I must confess, to even think about it – so used have I become to believing that I would never be released! Now I have been moved from my top security cell to an excellent cell on the topmost landing. It has a large window. My writing table is beneath it so that at this moment I am able to look out at the seagulls and fat pigeons flying about seemingly so close that I could reach out and touch them. My world is suddenly full of relief and hope for the future, I see myself in those birds gliding here and there so free. This feeling is so great, Fiona – I can actually taste freedom, breathe it and hold it.

When I am at last free I vow that I shall never more set foot inside a prison's walls! Please write soon, my friend. You are my only true friend and I am longing to hear from you. Give Simon my finest regards. My love to you, take care of yourself.

Your Friend and Brother.

Alex

The palpable excitement in Alex's note led to a burst of creativity, for he enclosed three poems. Of which the first was a sonnet.

Sonnet to the Rose

Addicted is my mind to this; your scent
That with your blooming grows in its power
And becomes, from pauper, Queen of the Realm!
But more—watching you begin to flower.
At first a tiny, unambitious bud;
And then unfurling 'til at last displayed
In fragrant glory and with opened heart
You graciously accept my serenade!
To such a world of clumsiness and pain
And ugly manifestations of Cain …
What joy it is that I can see you thus!
Blushing pink and crimson … Ceres designed
To place upon your tender, fragile head
The power to intoxicate Mankind.

London
24th January 1979

Dearest Alex

I'm absolutely thrilled that you have been taken off Category-A. You've been so patient Alex and can now enjoy the various perks they have to offer. Well done! Big windows and seagulls, huh? Sounds okay to me.

I'm so sorry I haven't written for a while and I truly hope your beard is recovering! I'd hate to be responsible for hair-loss.

Simon disappeared off to Mexico on Jan 6th to make a film called Cabo Blanco with Charles Bronson, so I've been left with organizing builders and plumbers to finish off the house.

It's beautiful here in the snow and everything looks so serene and calm. It's so quiet here, away from the traffic that one could almost be living in the country.

For Christmas Simon gave me a beautiful, shiny, green Mini 1000 to bomb around London in. Trouble is, I haven't taken my test yet as I've had to postpone it twice already. I'm quite a good driver and hope to take my test within the next six weeks.

I seem happy at the moment as lots of exciting things are happening career-wise (I may be starting on a movie soon, fingers crossed), and I have my friend Beth living here with me, so she is good company for me. She's 19 and has just started a job in the city, so I'm giving her lots of corny advice!

Did I tell you that I'd had all my hair cut off? 'Fraid so! I took the plunge just before going on holiday and everyone says it suits me.

Simon doesn't return until the middle of March and I miss him desperately, but there's a chance I may be able to go to Mexico for a couple of weeks when I'm free of the builders. I'd love that.

Be good Alex and all the best for 1979.

Fondest Wishes

Fiona

Having a friend to stay was a great tonic and helped to keep the loneliness at bay. Our house in Ealing was coming along and I really enjoyed dealing with the builders, plumbers and carpenters that arrived daily. Having created a haven of Sanderson gorgeousness out of a woodchip nightmare at the previous flat, I was soon discovering the joy of interior design. Texture, colour and mood became my new buzzwords and the art of creating a welcoming home gave me great pleasure. It is hardly surprising therefore that property became my next career.

HM Prison Parkhurst

30. 1. 1979

My Dearest Friend.

<u>Great</u> to hear from you! Your letter's full of enthusiasm, which is wonderfully infectious, I'm delighted at your prospects for a new film role – I do hope that you get the part. It will do you good, too, to be involved in something that demands your best.

Dick Barton is <u>awful</u>, I only watch it to see you and it's obvious that you're the only one holding that comic-strip together. (I think the way Dick Barton licks his lips after almost every sentence is disgusting.)

Some good news and some bad news. Good news is a friend of mine, Vivien Heilbron, wants to show some of my poems to John McGrath – a fellow poet and socialist – so it looks like I may be getting something in print at last; probably '77/78' which is dedicated to you. Also, it seems, the Free Alex Campaign's beginning – some newspapers have expressed interest in my case and the General Secretary of the Workers Revolutionary Party is now fully informed on what happened to me in '71. But whatever comes of it, I don't want you to get involved. Stay well clear, my friend.

Bad news is I've been informed that I may have to give evidence in a murder trial at Winchester in a couple of months' time. What happened was that one of the cons got himself killed. Another two cons and I found the body and the killer and I had to notify one of the screws. It was a mess. Anyway, what it boils down to is that I may have to go to the trial and give formal evidence that I found the body and reported it to the screw. That's all. But there are technical difficulties in that I cannot recognise a British 'Law' court and – obviously – cannot take the 'Oath'.

They say if I refuse to give evidence I will be given an extra three months imprisonment. Big deal! What shall I do? I'm in two minds. To go – or not to go? I've only been told that I <u>may</u> have to appear, but I'm sure an order will be given before the trial begins. What do you think, Fiona? You're my genius – shall I go and give evidence? No, forget that. Of course I must go.

See what a fool I am?

I wish I was on a desert island somewhere with a decent fishing rod. Away from all this. A bit of fishing, writing – and your letters, of course, and I would be reasonably happy until the Revolution. Viva, Princess! You might even convert me. You've already got me off Category-A with your advice – and hey, while I'm on the subject of advice – less of this giving your comrade, Beth, 'corny advice'! If she listens to you I doubt if she will go very far wrong, don't go underestimating yourself. The fact that the world is round, that there are stars in the night sky, that the sun shines and the birds sing, that wheat and rye whisper in the fields – the fact that all these things exist would not be real if Fiona did not exist to give them substantiality and purpose of being. Beth is indeed fortunate to have such a tutor!

I've got the 'flu'. Yippee. I love catching 'flu'. Something to do. It makes a change from being healthy. I saw the doctor on Friday and he's put me on vitamin capsules for 14 days, so if I survive I'll let you know.

I hate to ask you, but there's a couple of things I <u>desperately</u> need – can you get them for me? Item; 2 bars Astral soap, 1 tube Macleans toothpaste. I'm allowed to have them sent in, so it's ok at this end. And a watch, just a cheap one – we're allowed manual wind or automatic – but <u>not</u> anything with batteries or quartz. If you can manage that it would come in very handy for me. (At present I borrow a friend's watch whenever I have to time my courses and essays).

What I'm really praying for is a move from here to Grendon as soon as possible; this place is giving me the creeps. This is my fifth year at Parkhurst and I've had enough, I want to live in a normal prison instead of this dustbin. I've lost something in the last few years, our kid, and I want to get it back before it's too late. I feel as though I'm sitting on a time bomb and it's about to go up. I notice men in here getting angrier day by day and it is creating an atmosphere – I don't know, maybe I'm becoming paranoid at last. But I want out of here bad. I think I'll write a petition to the Secretary of State and ask him to speed up my move to Grendon – though I doubt it will do any good, we don't get on very well together as I think I've mentioned before.

Fiona, should anything happen to me in here, if I have a heart attack or something, will you promise me one thing? I ask you because I really feel you're the closest friend I have, and because I trust you more than anyone; find me a grave somewhere peaceful and a stone, with the words, 'Alex Revolutionary'. Would you do that, please? No cremation. There's two sides to everything – a bright side and a black side, and it's only that I look at the black side and must acknowledge it exists and therefore must be practical about it so please don't be alarmed. My dearest friend – can I rely upon you for this?

Please, please forgive me for such a morbid letter, perhaps this mood will soon leave me and my fears will prove groundless.

You are the finest person I have ever known in my life, Princess, and I will be your devoted friend forever.

Your Friend and Brother.

Alex

Good Luck, Good Luck.

The real reason behind Alex's bout of 'flu was a spontaneous, unplanned stint on the roof of Parkhurst. It was a peaceful demonstration but his mate Steve had persuaded him to do it on one of the coldest nights of the year. They sat up there shivering to death while a couple of warders watched them from a sentry box with a blazing brazier.

After a while, just before midnight, they decided to call it a day and climbed down the drainpipe.

'We were taken straight down the block and the next day we were weighed-off by the governor. We both got three days and spent the whole of it asleep. So what about my reasons for going on the roof? I guess it was the prospect of not being banged up in the cell for a while; I'd forgotten what it was like to stay out in the open air for any length of time. It was the first time I'd ever seen the stars — the sky was full of them. Also the silence was beautiful because there is never any of it on the wing. Although I caught 'flu I valued the experience and it caused no trouble.'

However, his dark mood in the second half of this letter was caused by a rising anxiety due to a planned political demonstration that was to take place on the roof. Alex had declined to get involved but could feel that the prison was about to implode. Most of the demonstrators were IRA men and this time Alex feared for his life.

'When the rooftop protest went down a few days later, it went down with a vengeance. It was the roof on A and D-Wing and the men decided to go up from the inside. The operation went without a hitch; half a dozen men shimmied up a rope through a skylight and onto the roof. Thus began the most costly and damaging demonstration Parkhurst had ever seen in the whole of its history. From my cell on B-Wing I could see the men on the roof opposite removing the slates and felt a profound sadness that fellow human beings are driven to such lengths. If one of them slipped on that sloping roof it would mean instant death.

That same evening a fire engine came into the prison and hoses were connected to the hydrants. The water was aimed at the men on the roof—S caught a jet across the chest and almost toppled off the roof with the force of it.

On the sixth day there were no slates left and all the cons from A and D-Wings had already been relocated. They were to remain unoccupied for many years. As for the protesters, they were moved from Parkhurst, separated, and given severe punishment.'

London
1st February 1979

Dear Alex,

I'll do what you asked but I don't think you need worry about it just yet.

I'm so sorry that things are not good for you at present – hang on in there and I'm sure the phase will pass. It's probably the grotty weather and everyone hitting a low ebb at the same time.

You <u>must</u> give evidence. You, unfortunately, must always do whatever is asked of you if you want to see the outside world again. What harm can it do to just stand up there and relate the real events? Anyway, a trip to Winchester will break up the monotony of the day, won't it?! (By the way, I lived near Winchester for a while when I was seven or eight and it was the first place I ever saw snow!)

Just going to buy your goodies for you. A watch will follow when I can find a suitable one. In the meantime, keep your bearded chin up.

Take care – be good (please).

Fondest Love, Fiona

Shortly after delivering my little lecture about giving evidence, I bought a watch that I hoped matched his requirements, wrapped it up with some soap and toothpaste and posted it that weekend when I was visiting my parents. With Simon away I would visit Dorset every weekend and always felt more relaxed and calm when I was in the countryside walking my dog, Sunday.

Blandford Forum, Dorset.
3rd February 1979

Dearest Alex,

Here is the watch you requested. I do hope it's suitable for what you wanted and doesn't let you down.

I'm spending this weekend in Dorset with Mum, Dad and Sunday and the sun has been shining brilliantly. It's so beautiful here that I'm determined to have a cottage in Dorset somewhere soon.

I've just been offered a small role in a film called 'In Search of Eden'. It's all about the painter Gaugin and his friendship with Van Gogh. I play a French whore, Rachel, who lived in a brothel in Arles. How about that for a change of character? I'm looking forward to filming in Paris and Arles in March sometime. It will be a welcome change from all the boring ingénue roles I usually play.

I've been researching all I can on Gaugin. He and Van Gogh lived together (and fought constantly) in Arles before Gaugin moved to Tahiti. He died in 1903, quite a young man. Rachel was Van Gogh's 'special friend' and was, allegedly, given his ear after he cut it off in a rage!

I'm off to Mexico soon, so will write when I return. Be good.

As Ever,

Fiona

HM Prison Parkhurst

7. 2. 1979

My Dearest Friend.

Fiona, I'm deeply grateful for your understanding, you are the greatest friend that I have ever had and this I will never be able to forget. I don't wish to say more, words are inadequate.

As for this 'phase', yes, it is passing, my friend, just as you said. As I was writing my last letter things here were looking very black, the atmosphere was electric and there was talk of a riot – it looked as though Parkhurst was going to go up. In a place like Parkhurst one doesn't get caught up in a riot and walk out of it afterwards, which I hope serves to explain the cause of my morbid anxiety. Thank Christ nothing came of it and the screws managed to keep everything under control. A riot is something I can do without – as my promise to you to stay out of trouble holds good – yet the situation is like the 'Guy' on the bonfire … it's all happening around him and there's no way he's going to escape untouched by the flames.

I'm immensely relieved to read you received the poems. Certainly you must keep them! If it was not for you I'd have given up writing poetry long, long ago, Fiona. As time goes by, so the standard of my writing will improve; and every book that I write will be; 'For Fiona'.

Well, your first package arrived on Monday and the watch (<u>precisely</u> what I need) yesterday. Again, words cannot express how I feel. But if anyone ever wants to get this watch off my wrist they'll have to resort to surgery! It's from you and every time I glance at it, it will remind me of you.

Dorset is certainly a beautiful county, but a cottage there? You know what you want? I'll tell you – a TENT! The way you get around, you'll soon have the Arabs out of business.

Fiona, I think 'In Search of Eden's' producer has his facts wrong about Rachel. She was a destitute kid with two children and a mother to support.

She had a part-time job in a workhouse, doing washing or something, but the pay was very low so she had to resort to selling herself. She was partial to drinking gin – so she fairly quickly lost what remained of her prettiness.

Van Gogh had just received his monthly allowance from his brother – the latter a successful art dealer – and had, as usual, given most of it away, but not before renting a small pension in the town. Almost flat broke he decided to spend the last of his money on a meal for himself. He went to a café and was given a table. After a few minutes he became aware of a woman sitting alone nearby (Rachel), obviously short of a penny or two; shabbily dressed, hair all over the place. Yet Van Gogh saw her through a painter's eye and it dawned on him that here was what he had been looking for – a model! (He'd been looking for models to pose for him – nude, beware! – for some time but the prettier girls charged exorbitant fees that he could not meet). He shared his meal with her and propositioned her about modelling for him. The initial terms were, he'd pay her a small sum (I _think_ it was two francs) every week, for her to pose. She agreed and so became Van Gogh's _first nude study_.

She visited Van Gogh's apartment every day – after a while they made love together; and soon they said to hell with it and Rachel collected the children from Mamma's and moved in with him full time. The news got around and, consequently, Van Gogh was ridiculed and disowned (again!) by his father. Van Gogh began talking of marriage, but it was Rachel's mother who put a stop to that by telling her daughter that Vincent had sinister motives and was exploiting her and the children. (Of course, Rachel's mother was getting lonely and was becoming increasingly resentful of Van Gogh.) It was a great pity because living with Vincent had kept Rachel off the streets. Her appearance had changed for the better and the children were properly fed. But there we go. It ended.

There's no doubt that Rachel played a very important part in Van Gogh's life – so don't dismiss your role as a 'small' one. And remember, it's an unattractive woman you have to portray (!), if you want realism. And she definitely didn't meet Van Gogh in a brothel.

Vincent Van Gogh was also a Communist and perhaps the greatest Revolutionary the art world has ever known.

Love, Fiona, is something that exists that has never been properly defined, has it? A sequence of events, parallels, coincidences – all leading up to a moment in time, which culminates in an unshakeable belief and depth of feeling hitherto unexperienced? I fell in love with you the moment I saw you, and that love has grown into something so big, that now it is the love that a brother has for a sister; it is something that, if something happens to you, I also feel it; if anyone harms a hair on your head – that harm will not go unavenged. Whatever makes you happy, makes me happy. Whatever you do, makes me proud, Fiona. So many English people do not know what the word 'Friend' means – they use it so casually – with us it is a word to fight hard for, defend, keep and honour – above all, honour, and, if it is necessary, die proudly for! And there is much love in this world, Fiona.

Well, Fiona, I must close for the time being. In twenty-five minutes it'll be midnight and a second later I'll be 26. Born 26 years ago tomorrow. 50 years too late. Damn.

Am being good, OK? Keep your chin up, too. Take care of yourself and watch the tequila! Your Friend and Brother

Alex

This letter marked a huge turning point in our friendship. Firstly, the pupil/teacher dynamic, to which I always respond, became evident with his knowledge of Van Gogh's relationship with a girl called Rachel. I will never know if he rushed to the library and found the right book or if he already knew these facts, but either way, I was impressed and the research was invaluable.

Then there were his feelings — so eloquently expressed — and by referring to a 'sisterly' love, he cleverly bypassed the awkward fact that I was married.

However, my trip to Mexico was a disaster, with Simon making it quite clear that my presence was a nuisance. I didn't know it at the time but apparently he was having a torrid affair with a Mexican girl and everyone knew about it, so when I arrived, the rest of the cast found themselves in a tricky situation. I know what life is like on a film set and it can be very intimidating for 'outsiders'.

I also managed to contract a kidney infection and remember lying in the 30-degree heat covered in blankets. Another actor, not Simon, took me to the local doctor for some antibiotics.

London
26th February 1979 (In a birthday card with a picture of a corgi on the front)

Alex

Sorry to miss your birthday dear Alex but thank you so much for your letter and all the info about Rachel and Van Gogh. Very useful.

Mexico was terrific and Simon is well and happy. Met Charles Bronson and was surprised how small he is.

All chaos here as the carpet is being laid upstairs.

(The picture on the front is like my dog Sunday)

With Love, Fiona

Filming 'In Search of Eden' in Arles, France (the title was changed to 'Gaugin the Savage') was a frustrating experience, given all the research that Alex had sent me. Being an American TV movie, all the characters were cliché ridden and the script simplistic. I had one scene where Van Gogh presented Rachel with his freshly removed ear, to giggles all around the set. On our return to England, the actor playing Vincent was stopped and searched at Heathrow.

The BBC obviously forgave me for abandoning 'Angels', by casting me as Lisanka in Tolstoy's 'The Death of Ivan Ilyich'. Presented as a drama documentary, it looked at the faith of a man who feels he has lived his life without meaning. Once again I was back in whalebone corsets.

HM Prison Parkhurst
18. 3. 1979

Dear Fiona

Hello, Princess. Thanks a million for the lovely birthday card that you sent. I received only two cards this year so I'm additionally pleased. A card from you is worth a thousand sent by others! Yet I don't know that I deserve it. I've been in trouble again – not really serious trouble (though what is serious trouble I wonder?). I staged a rooftop protest with a pal a week ago last Friday, we weren't up for very long, only 10 hours, and it was very cold. We were quite fairly dealt with afterwards, receiving only 7 days punishment (we expected at least 21). I am extremely sorry, Fiona, I only hope you will forgive me for this infringement of my promise to you. In mitigation of my action I can only state that no damage was done to property nor was anyone hurt – it was a peaceful demo. Also, since I made my promise to you, this is the first time I've been in any kind of a fix and all I can say is that I am sorry, can you accept that?

I do hope you passed your driving test and got rid of the 'L' Plates from your Mini, I've been keeping my fingers crossed for you, see, so you must tell me whether or not this did help.

How's the decorating progressing? Have you got rid of the workmen yet? Remember, with painters, decorators, plumbers and the like, it isn't so much the installations you pay for but their time. Watch how much paint goes on … odds are if a wall needs three coats they'll put on two and charge for three. They're not all crooks, mind you. One thing about being in here is you learn all the tricks – which makes it simple to spot a con man. My mate, Chilly (he's out now, by the way, released last August) is a butcher and he used to explain how they work. Every butcher fiddles the customer at every opportunity – it's incredible. Yet they'll go out of their way to give a bit extra to pensioners. I'm particularly pleased that he's kept out of trouble, he's a decent guy but it doesn't take much for others to lead him off the rails.

I had a visit last Monday from Gillian, my Prison Visitor, who always asks about you and considers herself a great fan of yours. We had a talk about Solzhenitsyn and had two cups of real tea.

The teacups are something I can never get used to – they're so small I can only hold them between finger and thumb and I'm continually afraid of letting one drop and break. The ones we always use ourselves are great one-pint plastic mugs – and one can drop them on the concrete and play football with them and they never break. Good old nick issue. There's a lot of things I'll have to get used to again if I get out – like metal knives and forks, real food and decimal currency – it scares me just to think about it. Anyway. Don't forget to send a postcard from France, O.K.? Enjoy your work, Fiona, and don't get into any silly scrapes like me. Stay happy and beautiful.

With Love,

Your Friend and Brother

Alex

I didn't see this letter for quite some time due to my filming schedule, which had unexpectedly taken me to Los Angeles for re-shoots. It turned out that everything we had shot in France on the Van Gogh movie was out of focus and unusable. The cameraman was fired and sent for an eye-test. However, I now understand that any protracted gaps in communication would have caused anxiety and dread, especially as he had confessed to his rooftop protest, therefore leading to his suspicion that I may have felt let down and abandoned him.

> 'Most of the trouble caused in prison was down to guys getting "Dear John" letters. There was no love in prison, only brutalisation of the senses. Prisoners became desperate for word from their wives and girlfriends, for words of love, sympathy and understanding. For some men, letters to and from loved ones were the only things that got them through. Being sent to prison was a way of saying "Society's given up on you. Nobody wants to know anymore". To have one's wife or girlfriend saying the same compounded the trauma.'

Unwittingly, it seems that I had been cast in that role. He feared a Dear John letter more than anything, but I wasn't about to give up on Alex. Soon I would need him even more.

HM Prison Parkhurst
26. 3. 1979

My Dear Friend

Just a few lines to let you know I am not involved in any trouble and also to ask how things are with you. I think that by now you must be in Arles, so I don't know when this will reach you – probably on your return, but there's no harm in telling you that I'm wishing constantly that everything's going great for you. So I hope the sun stays bright and the sea warm and that the French Foreign Legion don't catch sight of you or they'll be out on strike too! You think I'm kidding?

Anyway, look after yourself, Princess, and don't work too hard. I must finish writing for the moment as I'm whacked and need an early night – hope you won't be too mad. But will write again at the earliest opportunity, promise. Best regards to Simon, your parents, Beth and Sunday.

As Always, Love, Peace,

Your Friend and Brother

Alex

On the back of this brief letter and dated a week later he wrote in italics:

Is Communism good or bad? And, if bad, what does that make me? But I cannot accept this – the basic principles of the Communist concept: 'Equality, Liberty, Fraternity' – that is not bad or evil. It is for the good of all. And yet it is no use to deny that in such places as the Soviet Union and Albania, China, Laos and Vietnam, in such places Communism represents, not the termination of wars, starvation, repression and terror – but quite the opposite, rather. Of course, the Party oligarchies in each of these states answer foreign and intellectual criticism with the stock reply that the people cannot expect a new society to occur overnight but that there has to be a period of transition, etc, and, although there is certainly some truth in that I have to question whether 60 years, or even half a century, of transition is not more than sufficient time to set up the foundations of our New Society – and when I am truly honest I have to accept that those foundations were completed long ago and we are now well into the building of the superstructure – and that the foundations were built rotten on threats, purges and tyranny. And so the superstructure too, the whole construction of our 'classless society' – this is contaminated by those rotten foundations on which it stands and on which it will surely collapse and die. Now I am not bad or evil, but Communism, as it exists today, is definitely the former if not the latter – so how can I justify my association with such a system? In the first place I know that all I want to bring about in this world is that which is Right and Just – yet I'm convinced that Imperialism and capitalism are not the mediums through which to attain this so I must look back to the very beginning of Communism to Christ, Plato, Moore, Engels and Marx to the fundamental dialectics of those whose ideas of 'Equality, Liberty, Fraternity' Communism is based. I need to find out just what has gone wrong – no one else is willing to give me the answer so I must look for it myself and, when I reach it, stand by it, and only then can I be proud to call myself Communist once more. Where I shall align myself in the meantime I do not know – but I want you to understand one thing, Fiona, and that is from now I renounce totally my belief and support for the direction Communism has pointed itself in the world today – from now I am no longer a Communist in the accepted sense.

This is a monolithic task I have set myself but I must dedicate my life to this end – even if I am to remain in prison, for I realise my destiny. I only wish that you will always remain my friend, for this means more to me than anything else. When times get dark I will need someone to turn to – and no-one understands me quite as much as you – in return, what? I don't know. But on the course that I have set myself it will be priceless to have a companion in spirit and in you I know I could not find anyone better or finer.

Ciao, Alex

With hindsight, I'm not sure if this lengthy statement was meant for the Home Office, the censors or for me. He was beginning to realise that compliance may be a way forward.

London
19th April 1979

Dearest Alex,

So glad you're not involved with the latest trouble. I think of you constantly and hope that you'll never do anything to let me down. I have such faith in you.

Well, I'm back from Paris from being a French whore and now I'm playing a Russian aristocrat for the BBC! Couldn't be more different. I'm playing Lisanka in Tolstoy's 'The Death of Ivan Ilyich'. My second Russian role. Isn't this a coincidence, considering?

Oh Alex, my friend, how I wish I could help … Simon is home now and our little house is finally finished, the daffodils are swaying in the garden and I'm working hard, so things couldn't be better really. (I'm doing an Otto Preminger film after the BBC Tolstoy.)

My father is always asking after you and is truly fascinated by our friendship. He thinks it's marvellous. (So do I.)

My driving test is on June 12th so keep your fingers crossed for me.

Much Love as Always,

Fiona

HM Prison Parkhurst
24/25 4 1979

To My Very Dear Friend

Hello, Green eyes! Welcome back again. And for the sensational pictures, your new hairstyle is <u>fab</u> – a lot like my own used to be – you look really great.

No, I will never do anything to let you down, Princess. Nothing could ever justify such a thing. Believe me in this. You say you have faith in me. Do you know what that <u>means</u> to me? If I betrayed that faith I might just as well find the nearest piece of rope that is long enough and hang myself – for my life would be worthless … because I'd be betraying myself.

Now this other role greatly intrigues me: 'Ivan Ilyich' and Lisa. Soon, you are going to end up with more of the Russian in you than I have! As for coincidence … you know of my lifelong interest in Anastasia. It was some time after I first wrote to you that you mentioned you'd actually portrayed her in 'Nicholas and Alexandra'. Now, what a coincidence <u>that</u> was!!

The Realm of the Last Inch

The job is almost finished, the goal almost attained, everything possible seems to have been achieved, every difficulty overcome – and yet the quality is just not there. The work needs more finish, perhaps further research. In that moment of weariness and self-satisfaction, the temptation is greatest to give up, not to strive for the peak of quality. This is the Realm of the Last Inch – here the work is very, very complex but it's also particularly valuable because it's done with the most perfect means. The Rule of the Last Inch is simply this – not to leave it undone. And not to put it off – because otherwise your mind loses touch with that realm. And not to mind how much time you spend on it, because the aim is not to finish the job quickly but to reach perfection. Yes?

It's an excellent rule to remember, for it applies to everything. Use it in your work and you'll never look backwards. I don't believe you're lazy anyway(!).

Next week I'll be writing to the European Commission for Human Rights regarding the Home Office's refusal to let me have my photograph taken – honestly I'm fuming about it – even in the Soviet gaols, prisoners may have their pictures taken to send to a friend or relative, and I want you to have a photo of me!

I won't have to appear at that trial, after all. The guy pleaded 'guilty' so there was no need for any witnesses. He got another life sentence, now he's got two – two life sentences, like me. Yet he's <u>murdered two people</u> and I got my two life sentences for GBH (which was a frame-up, at that).

I'll leave the ins and outs of it to my solicitor.

Do you know I'm the only person in any British gaol to be serving such a massive sentence for a non-capital offence <u>and</u> the youngest person in 70 years to have been treated in this way? The youngest, too, to have served over 7 years in Category-A? True. The judge was the one who tried the Balcombe St. siege men and he's due to try Jeremy Thorpe – a political judge is Judge Cantley, through and through.

As I've said before, if I got into an Appeals court I'd walk out free – but I've left it too late. Strangely enough I'm not bitter about it – so don't worry – I'll stay out of trouble for you. You say you wish you could help, but you're helping me just <u>as you are</u> and I can't ask for better help than that. Only be happy, Princess, and so will Alex. Okay? Any chance of a smile? – Wow! Take good care of yourself. Alright, Green Eyes? Best regards to Simon and Sunday.

Britain's democracy is no more and is doomed forever unless something is done to recognise the plight of political prisoners and prisoners of conscience who languish within her gaols. If the government is to be believed – then I, and many others, do not exist .... Alex GB

With hurt and alarm I am forced to note, in the wake of illusory liberalism, the growth of restrictions on ideological freedom, of striving to suppress information not controlled by the government .... Andrei Dimitrevich Sakhatov CCCP

All My Love to You.

For Ever – Your Friend and Brother.

Alex

'The Realm of the Last Inch' was so inspiring and seeking perfection an excellent rule to remember. However, my silence was only due to a hectic workload, finishing the Gaugin movie in Los Angeles, the Tolstoy project for the BBC and then starting on a film directed by Otto Preminger, the biggest bully ever to stride onto a film set. (It was a film adaptation of Graham Greene's *The Human Factor*). Alex would sometimes get news of me in the press.

HM Prison Parkhurst
4. 6. 1979

My Very Dear Friend

Not a lot has been happening here – how are things with you? I read a couple of weeks ago that you were back in France working on the Gaugin production; do you still have much to do? Remember the Rule of the Last Inch! I am getting along, still surviving, defying the laws of probability. I don't think I will know what to do if they ever let me out, Fiona, everything out there seems so totally strange and abstract from the life I've come to know!

I'm sorry, Princess – my mind is not very clear at the moment, it's difficult to think clearly. I'll tell you what; I'll enclose a copy of something I wrote about my case. The originals are in the hands of my solicitors. I'm sending these because I feel, as my closest friend, you have a definite right to know the particulars of what I am doing in prison.

Promise me one thing, though – let no-one else read them, yet <u>keep</u> them, somewhere safe, where they will not get damaged. Will you do this for me? I know you're the only person I can trust.

As Always, Stay Beautiful. All My love, Your Friend and Brother.

Alex

The documents I received must have been smuggled out somehow because of their inflammatory nature and made uncomfortable reading. It was the first time I was able to read about the details of Alex's case and to learn about the possible 'set-up'. I discussed it with Simon and my father, who suggested I might take some advice from his lawyer. Once again I failed to respond to Alex's letters because of work commitments. I wish now I had sent him something. Even two lines would have been better than nothing.

HM Prison Parkhurst
13. 6. 1979

My Very Dear Friend

Hello, Princess. Did my last letter reach you alright?

I'm becoming very lazy; reading books and watching the television, when my spare time could be much better utilised with a more constructive spirit. Time is so infinitely precious.

My thoughts mainly tend to be about my life in prison. To think about the world outside these walls is nothing but, what? a fantasy – like contemplating the way of things on a distant planet – unreal, not existing, alienable. So now I must begin to question myself. Can I really be so concerned about a society I am not a part of? And, if so, what am I doing but fantasizing?

A phrase springs to mind – it was written by a Soviet dissident in a letter to the outside world in, I think, 1969 – 'Having been buried, it's hard to prove you're alive – except perhaps if a miracle should happen and somebody dug up your grave before you died for good.' You, my friend, dug up my grave.

Not so long ago my solicitor wrote saying he needed certain documents relating to my 'trial' in 1971. These documents were transcripts of the prosecution's case against me at the time, and extraordinarily vital to the proceedings I am now entering upon and would be held today by the firm who 'defended' me at the trial. To these people I was advised to send a written authorisation for the documents to be released. I did this, but their reply to my present firm was; 'Dear Sirs. Thank you for your letter of the 29th instant. We do not retain files from 1971, and can be of no assistance to you in the matter.' What this means is that the events of my 'trial' in '71, and all documentation relating to it, have been <u>cut-off</u> from back-reference so that any legal investigation on my behalf will not be possible.

Before I sign off this time, Fiona, may I ask a favour? Could you manage to send in one of those radios I mentioned – you can be certain I'd pay you back for it eventually. It's Grundig 'Concert Boy' – only one thing; the shop must service it first to *remove (temporarily) <u>all</u> the wavebands, save L/W and M/W.* For in here we're only allowed to have Long and Medium waves, but when I go somewhere else I'll have the other wavebands replaced back. Could you do that? Big favour, I know, but in here there's no other way I can get around the problem.

Love Forever your Friend and Brother.

Alex

London
14th June 1979

My Dearest Friend Alex,

What can I say about the distressing documents and letters you've just sent me? I really can't believe that it happened to you. That they did that to YOU – my dear friend. My heart bleeds for you. What a severe injustice – something must be done. I'm so worried for you and want to help so much but am powerless to do so. Just pray that someone will hear your plea. Mr Sachs sounds as if he's going to get the ball rolling, so now you must have patience.

Of course I will keep those letters safe for you. If ever you need them, just say. Oh Alex, how can one chance meeting land you in all this? You are telling the truth, I trust you for that, but there are so many unanswered questions. Like, how does a list of Soviet names find its way into your cell, by chance? How can you be sentenced for a crime you did not commit? What sort of evidence can you possibly have given if you weren't even at the scene of the crime? I'm going to ask my lawyer a few things – I'm so incensed – but nothing heavy you understand. Just promise me to be good at all times.

I had to postpone my driving test yet again (3rd time) as I was suddenly whisked off to Los Angeles to do some more scenes on 'In Search of Eden'. They did a portrait sketch of me for the movie too. I like America but I wouldn't want to live there now. No style! However the filming went okay and Simon came with me to meet some 'useful' people. I start filming the Preminger movie 'The Human Factor' on Sunday 17th. Lovely Richard Attenborough is my father in the movie, which is based on a Graham Greene novel. Have you read it? (So now I hope to take my test mid-July.)

It's 5 am and I can't sleep. Will write very soon.

Yours as Ever, FF x

HM Prison Parkhurst
19. 6. 1979

My Very Dear Friend

How to begin this? I've just read your letter, which I got this afternoon, and although I can't shed tears I can still be hit by your words and feel the resulting shock long afterwards. Dear, dear Fiona – you have your own life to live. Live it! Don't entangle yourself with this thing – and don't consult lawyers … For me it is quite enough that *you know*. I am guilty of sending you those Photostats without considering before-hand that they may cause you distress or alarm upon reading them. I sent them primarily because I knew they would be safe with you and, secondly because, well, one cannot have a friend and not be entitled to know everything about him. I have kept from relating my case with anyone up until now … but I don't want you to do anything about it. One day, everything will come out, just as it did with Solzhenitsyn, but not just yet. But you keep those letters, for, sometime in the future, they will serve a purpose, a basis, do you see? As for the 'unanswered questions', I could write you reams of answers, and, eventually, one way or another, you <u>will</u> have the answers. Be that as it may, I get very embarrassed when asking for help, but this prison leaves absolutely no alternative whatsoever. So I hope I'll be excused.

Thank you for all your exciting news! Be sure I'll reply to that in my next letter! But for now I have to close, Green Eyes – cheer up, do not be concerned for me – I want you only to be happy for *yourself* … take care and stay beautiful as ever.

I Love You

Your Friend and Brother Always, Alex

PS I promise.

Morning Mountain Dew

Love is gentle, love is sweet
Love is tender, love is true;
Love is like the early morning
mountain dew.
Like the fragrance of the rose
And the summer wind that blows
Like the silver stars that shine
The whole night through.
As we ramble by day, through this lonely life we stray
It's better to have loved along the way,
Like the lark that lightly wings
And the joyful song she sings

Like the freshness of the early
morning mountain dew.

Alex 1979

Our garden at home was a source of enormous pleasure and both Simon and I could be quite particular about the planting. We decided to have a vegetable patch and I came home one day to find all these neat rows with little labels. At Parkhurst it seems Alex was doing a spot of gardening as well.

'I became friends with a mandatory lifer called Von, otherwise known, rather fondly, as The Mad German. Prisoners at Parkhurst were allowed plots of land to grow vegetables and Von secured a plot for us to plant a strawberry patch. The day came when the strawberries started to ripen. We slung a net over them to keep the birds off and then, one morning, we went down to the plot and found that all the red ones had gone…. Von put his head back and howled.

"It's the screws, it's got to be."

"Not necessarily. Could be the cons making it look like the screws."

"Anyway, if it is the screws they wouldn't admit it."

We never found the culprits.'

London

2nd August 1979

Dearest Alex, Hi again.

Many apologies for the long delay in replying but many things have happened recently, not least of which is that I passed my driving test FIRST TIME!! It's taken me 18 months to get round to it but I took it in Cambridge, where Simon's parents live, in my own green mini (have I told you I call it Kermit 'cos it reminds me of the green frog) and I couldn't believe how easy it was. Since then I've made two little journeys on my own, while Simon had a heart attack at home, and I feel quite confident. The main advantage to all this is that when Simon is away I can get about and there won't be any excuse for being lonely.

My little garden is looking quite pretty at the moment. Because of all this wretched rain, things seem to leap up at an incredible pace and we have to weed nearly every day and mow the lawn once a week. In the front we have roses and borders of little red, blue and white flowers – I'm hopeless with names. There's a hanging basket by the door and a tub with a huge rhododendron in it. There are various shrubs behind the borders which are still very small, but which hopefully will grow and spread to fill in the gaps. I keep saying we must 'fill in the gaps' and it gets on Simon's nerves. There are some geraniums too – you know, those bright red things – and with the pure white roses they look very striking. A bit like signal toothpaste!

Out at the back we have a little terrace with chairs on it, huge privet hedges on either side, a long area of lawn with a garage at the end, which is covered in honeysuckle, lilac and roses and a vegetable garden on the left. This is a bit of a disaster, as only the lettuces have been eaten so far. Everything else is being dreadfully slow.

The beans, carrots, spinach, radishes, tomatoes, leeks and courgettes will probably be great in November! I think it's all highly amusing. It was Simon's idea and I think he's very brave to even attempt it. However, it all looks very impressive even if we can't eat them.

Thank you for the beautiful anniversary card. We were both thrilled to receive it and appreciated its meaning very much. I hope the next three years will be as good. On the 10th we went to the Coliseum to see the Peking Opera, which was splendid.

Re something you said in your letter of 25.4.79 – I <u>am</u> lazy. Alas. But your Rule of the Last Inch is terrific and very true. The last supreme effort is what makes all the difference. I will apply it.

Now listen Alex, Ivan Ilyich was a dying man – you have life. Life is the most precious jewel. Last night on television I saw the end of Claude Lelouche's 'Life, Love, Death'. What a powerful movie. About a man's persecution as he faced the guillotine in France. That's what Ilyich was going through. He could see his own imminent death and just wanted to get on with it. He had no power.

If I haven't said so already, 'Morning Mountain Dew' is very beautiful Alex. I wish I knew how you did it. I suppose it's a gift. I am very proud to receive it, witness it, treasure it.

You must know by now that I don't share your political views. In fact, I'm extremely naïve about politics and really don't like getting involved in heated political discussions. But I don't think the things you say are helping your situation at all. Only aggravating it. Thank you for letting me read Doug's letter but it's none of my business what you did, do or will do, so I'll leave it at that. I'm just your friend. Always will be your friend. Just be good.

Simon is typing upstairs and it's driving me mad but it is marvellous that we are at home together.

Will you do something for me? Will you write me a silly poem about a carrot? You see, my nickname is Carrot (don't ask why!) and I'd love a carrot poem.

Fondest Love, Fiona X

Alex duly sat down and constructed a quite brilliant poem about a carrot (reproduced later in the chapter) and included it in his next letter, which was inexplicably withheld by the authorities. Maybe the censor thought it was some sort of sophisticated code. Having not received that letter, it led to a misunderstanding which resulted in a gap in our correspondence. Alex had been unwell once again and was sent to the hospital wing in F2. He describes the 'backcells' in which he found himself only once.

'In F2, in the padded, soundproof cells, prisoners are beaten up naked. Then they are injected with a Mickey Finn – usually paraldehyde – and when they wake up they find themselves in a canvas straightjacket. They will be kept in this condition until they beg forgiveness for whatever it is that they have said or done. Some are broken fairly quickly, while others take longer. Prisoners are forbidden to complain about prison conditions.

After a short period of time, the prisoner loses track of time. The atmosphere, hotly depressant, is silent day and night and because of the armoured glass bricks it is impossible to see outside.

After waking from the jab, the prisoner begins to shout that he needs to be let out to go to the toilet, but nobody comes. He cannot easily manoeuvre to the emergency bell-push because of the straightjacket, so the prisoner relieves himself on the floor. He yells in his loudest voice but nobody can hear him. He cannot sleep at night with the light burning through his eyelids.

When the "medical screws" come in they shout at the prisoner for answering the call of nature on the floor and slip another needle into him. Suffering from mental and physical exhaustion, the "doctor" comes in behind two screws and says, "Yes he looks alright. Let's see how he is tomorrow."

The prisoner doesn't get a chance to speak and the door is banged shut.'

HM Prison Parkhurst

27. 9. 1979

My Dearest Friend

Hello, Princess? It's only me creeping out of the shadows looking for daylight. I've just been hit over the skull with a migraine; the medics say if I go and bash my head against the window it'll take the pane away – I guess they think I'm shamming. How the hell does one sham a migraine. It's killing me. I've heard you're off to Paris again soon to launch a few French submarines for NATO; but I hope my letter gets to you before you go.

I've just got back from classes where I'm doing a Russian language course to brush-up on my grammar. It's a bit heavy going because there are two Irish guys in the same classroom studying Gaelic – and we're all using Linguaphones and getting on each other's nerves. I do two nights a week on the class and the rest of the time in my cell. I want to learn French next. Oui.

Are you in a good mood today? Can you possibly send that radio in, sister? I am just surviving the quiet nights but getting extremely bored in the process – I can't even sing because the walls echo sound and I'd wake everybody up. So I'm lying awake all night with nothing to do but think – and too much thinking leads to brooding and that ain't good. I'm a terrible singer, too.

Last night was freezing. I managed to get two extra blankets this afternoon from the stores and tonight I'm really going to dig-in. If <u>that</u> doesn't work I'll have to opt for a blood transfusion and a drip. Please write when you can, my friend. I'm keeping out of trouble still. Please take good care of yourself, and stay happy. Best Regards to Simon, your mum and dad, and Sunday.

All My Love, Peace, YF&B, Alex

It's quite clear that Alex would get news of my activities and movements from the press, as he knew I had been away. On this occasion I had been briefly in Paris and then did a stage play in Plymouth. I was also keen to clear up the mystery regarding the requested poem in my letter of August 2nd.

16th October 1979
London

Dear Alex,

Just a quick note to apologize for the long silence, but I've been in Plymouth for six weeks doing a play called 'I Am a Camera' which is the Christopher Isherwood story of Sally Bowles. I played Sally with green fingernails and all and had to down a raw egg every night (yuk!) but I loved every moment. Got great reviews and now thoroughly exhausted. Simon has been in America, again, but returns tomorrow for a week only. The house is wonderful to come home to.

Thank you for my beautiful birthday card. 23 aaaargh! I had a great day but feeling older every minute. It's sad that birthdays no longer hold the magic they had as a child.

By the way, I wrote a long, newsy letter a couple of months ago and you've made no mention of it. At the end I asked you to write a poem about a carrot. Did you ever receive that one?

The radio costs an absolute fortune, I'm afraid. £64.00 to be precise. I can't afford that Alex, is there a cheaper version? I'm so sorry.

My parents are moving to Winchester in November as Daddy has got a promotion. That'll be fun.

Will write again soon. Be good and keep warm.

Love,

Fiona

Simon's frequent forays to Los Angeles became a source of deep unhappiness for me. He felt his future lay there and didn't seem too perturbed when I couldn't accompany him, which made me wonder whether there was an added incentive to his wanting to be in LA. I wanted to stay in the UK for my career and during the production of 'I Am a Camera' I fell deeply in love with D, one of my co-stars. Whether it was a knee-jerk reaction to my feeling of abandonment or just an infatuation, I will never know, but he made me feel wanted and secure.

Of course I didn't tell Alex about this development, but during this play and for many weeks afterwards, I was the happiest I had been in ages.

HM Prison Parkhurst
22.10. 1979

My Very Dear Friend

Hello, Princess. Peace. It was absolutely great to hear from you again, and I'm immensely pleased and relieved that you're okay. Glad that you liked the card, too – I know that as time goes by, Birthday celebrations tend to lose much of their magic – and yet, when you think about it, they are signifying the really most important event of our lives, aren't they? Feeling older is also a good thing in many respects, too, although I suppose a girl feels it more keenly, though god knows why. Don't worry yourself about getting older, sister, for as times goes by you can only gain; in wisdom, things will change, inevitably, as will your understanding of life and people – and, as far as growing older physically is concerned, just as you are a beautiful girl so, too, will you become a beautiful woman. I know for sure, if I'm still around, I'll be sending you cards when you're eighty. You'll see!

Yes I <u>did</u> get your letter referring to a 'carrot' poem. As soon as I finished reading it I sat down and wrote the poem, then handed it in for posting. I remember quite distinctly. For some reason or other the letter must have been held back, though I wasn't informed of this. I felt very angry when you indicated it hadn't arrived, but I won't complain as you've told me to stay out of trouble.

Luckily, I still have the rough draft of the poem, so it will go with this letter by 'recorded delivery' – incidentally, when I receive a letter from you I shall always, without fail, reply, at most within 7 days. So this way you will always know if a letter goes astray.

Did I mention that I was writing to the Director of Public Prosecutions about my case? Well, I did – but he wrote back to the governor that he wasn't in a position to do anything. Nix Karosch.

I've just had a book sent in that I've always wanted to read, it's called '1984' by George Orwell – have you read it yourself? If you haven't, I'll post it on to you chop chop.

All my love to you. Keep warm yourself! Your Friend and Brother.

Alex

Carrot at the Ball
А. Александрович 1979
For Fiona

From the vegetable plot on Mid-Summer Night
We hear of the strangest scene
Involving King Edward Potato and his Runner Bean Queen.

Evidently, a Mid-Summer Ball in their name
Was proclaimed from the greenhouse cucumber frame,

And 'twas rumoured the Strawberry Prince would appear
To dance for a while, until midnight drew near.
Well, of course the Misses Sprout, Cabbage and Lettuce
At once made adjustments to their billowing dresses
And took dancing instruction from the Blackberry Bush
(who was charging ten pea at the height of the rush!)
'Of course *we* can't go dancing—on account of our bunions,
And we'd make the Prince weep'—sadly stated the onions.
'I think, perhaps, the Sweet Corn', contributed the cress,
'will make an impression with her style and finesse' ...
'But,—who will provide the music?' demanded Mrs. Pea –
Who was Second-in-Charge of the Ball Committee.
Lady Celery paused—trying to smooth out a pleat –
'Why not contact the neighbours ... and hire a *Beet?*'
As the date of the function drew increasingly nigh
The spirit of the occasion was reportedly high,
And everywhere nothing but chaos was seen
Until everything was perfect for the King and the Queen ...
Nothing short of the finest would do,
The drinks were of nectar and carafes of dew
Sparkling vermilions, emeralds and whites,
Reflected from cascades of bright fairy lights.
Folks travelled miles to descend on the plot;
A mole from a hole and a Stoned Apricot,
Damsons, Cherries, a Plum and a Pear, -
And, in a long white coat, a contrary old Hare
Who, peering through a monocle, his eyebrows an arch
Cried; 'I've walked eighty miles since the beginning of March ...'
'New boots,' said Lord Turnip, 'I must have new boots
For, bless me—will you look—I'm growing four extra roots!'
And so, as the sun came down upon the land,
And the Moon gave the sign to strike up the band,
The Royal Delegation chose partners to dance
Declaring 'Open', the Ball, with great circumstance.
Of course, the great question of everyone there

Was; who would be partnered by King Edward's Heir?
And every young lady—the ones who were 'Free'—
Was particularly anxious it was going to be she …
But the Prince passed Miss Sweet Corn, Miss Bean and Miss Pear,
With a glance that ignored all but one who was there,
Through rows of Knight Currants in splendid array
And ranks of Horseradish Guards on display;
He came before Carrot, bowing low with a smile,
Requested permission to waltz for a while.
No happier couple at the Ball could be seen,
She became his Princess
And, later, his Queen.

Alex 1979

This amazingly clever poem, written in his tiny, perfect, handwriting, has given me such pleasure over the years and I was totally thrilled when I received it. At the time, its brilliance and lustrous wordplay seemed extraordinary given the circumstances in which it was written. It also proved that Alex could write poetry in a very different vein and could well have had a future as a writer of children's stories and poems.

HM Prison Parkhurst

5. 11. 1979

My Dear Friend

Hello, nomad! Hope you are okay and bright as ever. I'm pretty shattered at the moment; we've been shifting things around in the workshop all morning to make way for a massive new cutters table. When it arrived it took ten of us to move it and must have weighed all of a quarter of a ton, which is heavy enough. Sure, I end up getting a ½ inch splinter of wood in my hand, so I ran true to form. One of my workmates, Kojack, got hold of a needle and spent nearly 20 minutes digging the damn thing out – by the time he was finished I was beginning to wish he'd left it where it was, next thing I know I'll be down with blood poisoning. I'm trying to avoid the Hospital Wing.

I've been taken off sewing curtains and now I'm on 'hooking' – placing the hooks in the tapes. It's very much better than my last job because I'm not sitting down all the time and am able to move around a bit. I've been told I must get myself in shape because I haven't been well lately what with one thing and another, including 'flu' and sinus trouble; it seems I'm particularly prone to 'flu' as I keep catching it every couple of months. (It's OK though – I haven't been breathing on this letter, I'm keeping it at arm's length away).

Also, last week, I got a letter from the Probation Service in Oxford; they want to know why I want to live there if I get out. I think I'll leave answering until later in the week when I can get my head together, I'll have to write a really sensible letter for a change. (Like, I want to join the Boat Race or something.)

I've just eaten lunch; boiled rice and stew. The rice went down like a pile of bricks tipped out of a Wimpey dumper. So it'll be heartburn this afternoon, I wouldn't wonder. What I'd give for a steak or a newspaper full of cod and chips. Wow. Do such things still exist? I often wonder.

Stay cool, stay beautiful.

All My Love

Alex

London
19th November 1979

Dearest Alex,

I thought the poem was <u>absolutely</u> fabulous and Simon was thrilled when I showed it to him. 'Carrot' is now famous and I shall treasure that poem. You <u>are</u> clever! A million thank yous.

We've just returned from Paris where Simon and I attended a film festival. S. dashed back to the States again and will return next week.

I'm on a mad pre-Christmas diet, as I can't afford to put on any more weight.

You sound busy – which is good – but do look after yourself. Sorry about the splinter. Ouch!

Thinking of you often.

Your Friend,

Fiona.

HM Prison Parkhurst
22. 11. 1979

My Dearest Friend

I'm really delighted that you thought so much of the poem, Fiona, I was terribly anxious of what you would make of it – particularly as it was the first poem you asked me to write especially for you. I hope you will be happy to know that your response makes everything worthwhile for me. Please let me know if you should, at any time, like anything else done, for there is nothing I would not do for you, and doing things for you would always give me the greatest happiness and pleasure. I really mean what I say. I owe you the greatest possible allegiance and devotion for helping and supporting me through these black years.

Your Friend and Brother

Alex

I Am Coming With You

There is a breath, a whisper,
touching my cheek — only to disappear
for a short time, then returning stronger

with a great power, bending the trees
this way and that with clattering leaves
   Where have you been? Where do you go?
   Take me. I will go with you …

There is a laugh, from across the meadow,
rising and falling and fading into nothing
until, drawing nearer, I find your flow
and a chorus of sparkling melody
fills up the whole world with magic
   Where have you been? Where do you go?
   Take me. I will go with you …

Here I perceive a certain fragrance
carried to me on the wings of an idyllic breeze
from somewhere elusive, yet near,
where flowers defend a Kingdom
and roses open their hearts to the sun
   Where have you been? Where do you go?
   Take me. I will go with you …

As I watch you, dew of the morning,
extending from your first cool drop,
far across a sea of grass in the moonlight
into a carpet of a million diamonds bright!
I watch as the sunrise washes over you
   Where have you been? Where do you go?
   Take me. I will go with you …

And I can taste you, Freedom,
blowing whistling through the hedgerows
and flowing with the silver river to the shore;
scented by the Kings and Queens of all flowers
and more priceless than a million gems
   Oh, yes; I know where you have been

And I know where you go.
Wait! I am coming with you …

For My Friend, Fiona — Alex 1979

At around this time Alex made friends with a young man called Andy whose life had a tragic conclusion years later when they were at Grendon Prison:

'During my first year at Parkhurst I became fairly friendly with a guy on C-Wing called Andy. He came from a small place not far from Nelson, where I was brought up. This formed the basis of our friendship. He had married a foreign girl, who worked as an air hostess and he loved her very much. They had a child and the future seemed very optimistic. But after a while his wife turned against him and threatened to leave, taking the child with her. Andy found he was unable to bear the prospect. He killed the child and was sentenced to life. Child killers are not well tolerated in prison and he was dreading the knowledge becoming known. There are some heavy cons on the wing who would certainly have done him harm.

Eventually the word got out as to what Andy had done and he was attacked in the prison library. He was transferred to the hospital on F2.'

HM Prison Parkhurst
7. 12. 1979

My Dearest Friend

Hope everything is OK with you and that you're not starving yourself too much before Christmas! As you see from above I'm still here at Parkhurst. I doubt I'll be moving to any other place until the New Year, and it doesn't look like it will be Gartree Prison anymore – otherwise I would be there by now – so, it looks as though they're planning a surprise for me and another Magical Mystery Tour. Should be interesting, if nothing else.

On the positive side of things I've been backtracking through my book 'The Candlestick Kid', re-writing whole paragraphs and correcting grammatical errors. One of the things that surprised me was the realization of just how much work I put into it – it's enormous. That's if nothing is edited out (wishful thinking!). I hope I see it published, Fiona, and that you are the first to read it, this means a lot to me.

Take good care of yourself, Princess, and be happy over Christmas! I'll be thinking of you.

As Always, Love From

Alex

London
10th December 1979 (In a Christmas card)

My Dearest Alex,

Thinking of you and hoping the turkey isn't too thin. Keep warm and be good. A magical mystery tour awaits! Fingers crossed.

My Fondest Love,

Fiona X

The mystery concerning Alex's transfer to another prison was far from magical as it made him highly anxious about the destination. Surely it couldn't be to another maximum security dispersal gaol.

Meanwhile, Christmas was another joint effort for the Fullertons and the MacCorkindales and this time it was the turn of Simon's family to play host at their home in Cambridge. It was a rather jolly affair with lots of mad games, laughter and a surfeit of my mother-in-law's excellent mince pies. We seemed really happy. Simon and I returned to London and attended an incredibly glamorous, if slightly louche, New Year's Eve party to herald in the new decade. And what a decade THAT turned out to be!

- 4 -
Getting Through the Night

The Greatest Gift

The greatest gift that I possess
Being a con and no better
Is the faithful girl who stands by me
Replying to every letter.

I write, sometimes senselessly
Conveying mood and temper,
Knowing that she'll understand
The sincerity of this sender.

At times I really marvel
Why she bothers to write back,
My words are mostly routine
She really must have something
Other people lack.

Alex 1978

London
15th January 1978

My Dearest Alex,

How miserable I am when I don't write to you. I <u>must</u> do this more often!
Instant cheeriness.

I've just been re-reading some of your old letters and poems. You really
are exceedingly clever, Alex.

A lot has happened since I last wrote to you, which perhaps explains
why I haven't put pen to paper for a while. Apologies. I've been to
Egypt – had my 21st birthday there (which was pretty uneventful) – started
filming a new TV series called 'Dick Barton – Special Agent' (we've just
finished after 7 weeks) prepared, rehearsed and produced our (Simon and
me) first professional theatre production as producers, 'Relatively Speaking' at the local theatre for one week only – spent Christmas in Cambridge
with the in-laws and started rehearsals for a show on January 9th. Phew!!

The new show I'm doing is called 'Something's Afoot' and is a musical comedy Agatha Christie spoof set in the 1930s. It was on in London
recently and we are taking it to Hong Kong next week to perform in the
HK Hilton for two weeks. The Hilton apparently has a dinky little theatre
in their ballroom and we are staying there too, so it's all rather convenient.

We have a super cast of quite big names, including Virginia McKenna
and George Cole, all doing the short engagement because of the attraction
of Hong Kong. I must say, I'm looking forward to going there and the
experience of doing another musical will be very good for me. I play the
lead role and have eight musical numbers and am the last to be murdered!
Hurrah!

How was Christmas for you? I remember last year you made me laugh
by telling me about your see-through slice of turkey! I hope it wasn't quite
so see-through this year.

Maybe 1978 will be a good year for you. There's always hope. Maybe a
retrial is in store for you after all. Who knows? Was Lord Longford able to
help? Anyway, keep smiling dear friend.

1977 was a pretty rotten year for me. I should be grateful for all that I have, but I was unhappy for a great deal of the year and emotionally insecure. Now I am trying to put that to rights and am determined to make 1978 a good year – a turning point.

How's this for good graffiti then? 'Please do not adjust your mind: there is a fault in reality'. Simon told me that one.

I do have 'Lord of the Rings' but have never read it. It looks so frighteningly huge and lengthy, but I will now read it on your commendation.

I'm very tired now and ought to get some sleep before rehearsals tomorrow. Will send you a post-card from Hong Kong. Take care and be good.

Love, Fiona

At the time Alex had been unwell for a while and found himself back in the hospital which was located on Parkhurst's F-Wing.

'F2 is located in F-Wing in the prison hospital and is the most evil place to be found in any British penal slum. There are around sixteen cells on this ground floor landing; they stand in two rows of eight facing each other. Between these rows of cells is a central passageway, with a black and white stone floor, which is always kept spotlessly clean.

There is a barred gate set into one side of the landing, which is always kept locked. It opens onto a short, dark passage and at the end there are two cell doors. Upon going through one of these doors one is immediately brought up against a second door, heavily reinforced with iron studs and strips of steel. There is a reinforced spy-hole at eye level. Step through this door (most prisoners are *carried* through it) and you will find yourself standing in a small concrete box. On the floor there is a concrete bed, six feet long and three feet wide, raised a couple of inches from the ground, covered by coarse, evil-smelling padding.

There are glass bricks set into the wall and this constitutes the 'window'—though one cannot see the sky through it, merely a vague suggestion of light. The air comes via a special ventilation system and the heavily protected light bulb burns day and night. The box is quite soundproof. The box next door is identical. We call these the "backcells".'

Hospital
HM Prison Parkhurst
30. 1. 1978

Hello Fiona,

I must apologise for the crumpled writing-paper (this is how it was issued to me, so I gotta use it). Pretend you've just found it among the Dead Sea Scrolls.

Countless thanks for your recent letter, it lifted me from the depths of dejection – I'm in the hospital at present recovering from an attack of chronic depression (of <u>all</u> things!), so your letter arrived at the most opportune moment. Looks like we've both been hit by emotional stresses, one way and another. It happens to everyone sometime, though, so let's hope that's our share over and done with. (At one stage I thought I was going to die and go to hell – but it didn't worry me unduly because I've heard there's been a Revolution down there. They've deposed the Devil and elected a vicar as President; and now they're putting the fire out). Viva!

You need never fear the future, Princess. People say that beauty is only skin deep – very true. But your beauty is not merely skin deep; it is there, too, in your heart and in your spirit and in the things you do and say. As you grow older you will take all that with you – and everyone you meet will wonder what it was that hit them …

How about this saying I recently discovered: 'The sun, with all those planets revolving around it and dependent upon it, can still ripen a bunch of grapes as if it had nothing else in the universe to do'. The quotation is from Galileo. There's a very wise message there.

Fiona – I have a fantastic new idea about the manufacture of one-armed-bandit machines. I could make them <u>myself</u>. And they would all have this great <u>new</u> <u>original</u> <u>feature</u> – they wouldn't pay out! Can you imagine …!! The player puts a shilling in the slot, pulls the lever, busts the banco, and nothing pays out! Oh boy. Immaculate. Of course, the player then gets good and mad and gives the machine a flying karate kick – whack! Now, my machines would all have an inbuilt vocal amp. device, which would activate whenever the machine receives a sudden jolt (similar to a pin-table's 'tilt' mechanism). Once this happens, the device would let out a scream of <u>pure</u> <u>agony</u>. So when the player lets fly with that kick and a whack, all that comes out is the scream: AAAAAAAAAAAAAAAARRRGHHH!!! This way, the player gets satisfaction for losing all those shillings. Yeah?

Yes, we <u>did</u> get another see-through turkey this year, as it happens, because they gave us hen instead, geriatric hen. As I was chewing on it the Albanian army fired a fifty-gun salute and all the angels wept in heaven. Oh, Fiona – what I'd give for a real plate of sausages and mustard! I'd give anything! Anything! And a cup of coffee! The Bells, Fiona, the Bells! Seriously, though, it was your card that really made my Christmas a nice one. Thanks.

I received a letter from my MP the other day. He says he is taking my case up with the Home Office again, so I'll let you know what happens. But no – I really doubt that I'll get a re-trial now. Still, I'm surprised how many people are behind me, you know. Only a fortnight ago I had a letter from a comrade, Sue Slipman, President of the National Union of Students, who offered to help if she could. That's the old Party loyalty showing through with a vengeance.

That piece of graffiti that Simon told you about really made me laugh. <u>Very</u> good. Which reminds me – have you not tried your hand at writing verse yet? I'm positive you'd really enjoy it; once you rid yourself of the initial awkwardness and establish your own style. Do have a go.

I'm sure you will enjoy 'Lord of the Rings'– there's a Princess in it just like you! An utterly fascinating book – full of magic – you won't regret reading it (it was written for you).

Yours as Ever

Alex

Come Sweet Night

Come, Sweet Night, and kiss my eyes,
Sit by my bed and wipe my brow,
Cool me with your soothing breath;
Come, Sweet Night, come to me now.
Lay your blanket of darkness upon me,
A constellation of stars at my head,
Bind a bandage of moonbeam around me
To stop up the wounds where I bled.
Hold my hand, lest I tremble,

And all my noble dreams keep.

Soon we shall fly together into the sky

Come, Sweet Night, sing me to sleep.

Alex 1978

London (On Hong Kong Hilton Hotel notepaper)
15th March 1978

Dear Alex,

Please excuse the funny paper, it's the nearest to hand and here to prove I really <u>did</u> go to Hong Kong. Thank you for your last amusing letter, Alex. I like the one-armed bandit idea very much (maybe we could apply it to Public Telephones as well, as I have lost a fortune to the wretched GPO when their crummy machines insist on getting jammed!!) and I loved the Russian 'flu gag about the vodka and the firemen. I might try it!

I do hope you are better now Alex. Do they really put you in hospital for chronic depression or was there something else? I do hope you haven't misbehaved Alex. I like to think, in my selfish way, that I'm doing you some good (in a very minor, tiny way) so please be good – for me.

I love to write to you and it's so rewarding to receive your long, chatty, zany letters.

Well, now, about Hong Kong. I don't know where to begin. It is the most fascinating, beautiful, mysterious city I have ever visited; overcrowded and noisy but still fascinating. In a month we did everything (almost) and saw everything and were treated superbly. There is the romantic green Star Ferry, with its hard wooden seats, that shuttles between HK Island and Kowloon, which is on the mainland.

In quiet alleyways you can hear the click-click of old men playing mah-jong. We went sailing on junks (boats), san-pans, luxury yachts and the Wan-Fu brigantine; shopping in the market in Stanley; took tea in the Repulse Bay Hotel – v. Somerset Maughan; visited the Zoological Gardens; took the Peak Tram to the top of the peak on the island, scary;

had lunch at the Royal Hong Kong Jockey Club; sunbathed by the pool and of course, went shopping in Kowloon (You can have a suit made in 24hours!). The weather was warm so it was really pleasant for sight-seeing.

Because we had celebrities like Virginia McKenna amongst us, the rich, society people in Hong Kong (including the Governor) were only too delighted to host big parties for us, take us out on boat trips and to the races. We were very spoiled. We saw much more than a tourist could, in a way. It was tremendous. Cantonese food is quite the best I've ever tasted and I <u>love</u> using chop-sticks! Charlie Fung's 'Tong Fuk Store' was my favourite eating joint there.

The hotel was most luxurious and we went dancing in the nightclub every night after the show, which was a great success (luckily). I enjoyed it so much and as I was on stage longer than anyone else, I found it most rewarding. Being a musical, I had a lot of singing and dancing to do and I <u>loved</u> it. I hope to get the chance to do more musicals.

There were ten of us in the cast and we would go everywhere as a group, visiting many of the outlying islands. Lamma Island was unusual and the junk ride there was great fun but by far the best days were spent on Lantau Island. The island is in fact larger than HK Island but in total contrast is serene, quiet and very, very beautiful. The mountains look down powerfully upon the tiny villages, such as Tai-O, and the long stretches of uninhabited beaches reach out like silver threads around an aquamarine sea. There are many monasteries – we visited one in the mountains called Po-Lin – which are extremely colourful and have many Gods and Buddhas. There is little, if any, industry and the entire population is only 30,000.

On both occasions when we visited, the sun was hot, the sky a beautiful pale blue and the mountains a severe grey. I imagine Hong Kong Island was like this once, with tiny villages nestling in the hills. Soon a bridge is to be built from the New Territories to Lantau, involving two million people, so I'm glad I saw it as it is now.

The dream ended when I returned to England and came back to Earth. Washing-up, cooking, launderette, Tesco's. All a bit of a shock after a month's holiday. But I'm used to it now and Simon is well and happy.

That's half the excitement of our business; the constant ups and downs and the anticipation of what's happening next.

We're thinking of moving in July. This flat is miniscule and we need to spread a bit, so we're looking for a little house with a garden. Not easy.

I'm taking driving lessons again. I really must learn to drive. I keep putting it off as it's so damned expensive.

Oh well, must go now. When is your birthday Alex? Must be soon or have I missed it? (25 is nothing.)

Take care my friend. Always yours,

Love Fiona

Coming home to a tiny flat after the glamour of Hong Kong would be unsettling for most people. However, I was just thrilled to be home with Simon, playing my favourite role of housewife.

HM Prison Parkhurst
30. 3. 1978

Hello, My Friend – Welcome Back!

You paint a wonderfully vivid picture of Hong Kong (you'd make a wonderful PRO for their tourist bureau!) and of your experiences there. Tremendous indeed! But I am particularly pleased that the show went well for you.

Yes, it really was depression, lass, nowt else – or I'd have told you about it. It's okay, I'm out of the hospital now and back on 'normal' location. There is a doctor coming to see me shortly, he is from Grendon Prison, near Aylesbury, Bucks. Grendon is a medical prison that specialises in group therapy treatment. I was there in 1974 for two months – I got thrown out because I tried to escape over the wall. Anyway, I want to go back there and it's for this reason that Dr. Barrett is coming to interview me. I'll let you know what happens. Fiona – I made a promise to you that I'd keep out of trouble, since then I've stayed well away from it. That promise will always be good – so don't worry, I won't try escaping again, nor will I look for trouble. You say you like to think you do me some good. You'll never know. I owe you a great deal; you're the first person who has accepted me as a person also – and not just a convict. That is a valuable thing to me.

Oh yeah, I forgot – I've started oil-painting – having knocked out two pictures already. You ought to see them. Terrible. I'm going to become a <u>lousy</u> painter. I've had a vision.

Well, 'Angels' is back on television soon – next week, I hear – but it won't be the same with this new cast. Will you be watching it, Fiona? Me, I'm waiting to see 'Dick Barton – S A' (I grab up the TV Times every week to see if there's any news of it). Last week all the wings here were allocated one colour TV set each for the first time. Wow – what a difference! 'Top of the Pops' is <u>fantastic</u> in colour. Fletch is 'Going Straight' (very true-to-life, 'Going Straight', behind the humour).

My cell looks like a junkshop. You know how I feel about spiders (horribly superstitious, me, so it'd be bad luck for me to harm one), well I've had a spider in here for some time now. And it's spun this dirty great web under my locker so that every time I breathe out it gently billows. My mate, Chilly, reckons I should take a contract out on it and have someone hit it but I can't agree to that as I would be guilty by association … (if Paddy – that's its name – Paddy Longlegs – it's an *Irish* spider. If Paddy knew us humans were ganging up on it, I'd have a paranoid spider on my hands – and *they're* capable of anything!).

So, Dear Fiona – take good care of yourself and stay happy. Follow your heart.

Always Yours, Love Alex

Picture

Cubic box of concrete stone
With painted bricks in monotone,
A plain deal table and a chair
That someone put together in despair.
Sixty watts light up the space
Where flies and gnats and spiders race

From window sill to iron door
A distance of ten feet, no more.
Books and pamphlets line the shelf
(Possessions of a greater wealth)
That do not collect dust or grime
The year hands on my Clock of Time…
A friendly picture on the wall
Marks the spot where sunbeams fall;
A modern miracle to adore
Only gloom was ever there before.

Alex 1978

Alex was not suffering from depression at this point but had refused to take some experimental drugs that were often handed-out to Category-A prisoners, so he was sent to F2. All prisoners are forbidden to complain about their treatment or conditions in any written material, so all of his letters to me were censored. Some didn't make it through at all and others he was made to re-write completely.

London
28th April 1978

My Dear, Dear Alex,

Please excuse this brief note but things are rather hectic at the moment.

However, I couldn't leave it any longer to say how much I loved the recent poems. You really are very clever.

As for me, well, I miss Simon very much as he is away doing his sailing film, 'The Riddle of the Sands'. However, next week I start rehearsals for a comedy starring Arthur Lowe, called 'Caught Napping', so that should keep me out of mischief! I play the female lead, Jill, who is the rather dotty headmaster's daughter. We go on tour for 14 weeks starting in Billingham and I'm hoping it will be interesting.

I have already visited Simon in Holland for a week and enjoyed it very much. Amsterdam is such a clean, tidy city and Enkhuizen is like a model village. Cobbled streets, sweet little canals, neat rows of tiny terraced houses, thousands of tulips. Enchanting. Plenty of diamonds in Amsterdam too!

Talking of diamonds – I've been asked to wear £25,000 worth of Cartier jewels at a charity ball next Tuesday at the Dorchester Hotel. I can't believe it. I think I'll be a little upstaged.

I return your letter from the Home Office. What can I say? I'm very disappointed for you, dear Alex. I wish someone could explain. But please be patient.

Mum and Dad have been staying here this week. It's been great as we've been shopping and seeing plays together. My dog was here too, so it was rather cramped in my little flat.

Must go now, I'm afraid. You're my dearest friend Alex. Take care. Will write again soon.

Love, Fiona.

HM Prison Parkhurst
15. 5. 1978

My Dear Fiona,

Many thanks for your letter, as always I felt wonderful hearing from you, you're always like Spring and Summer to me – even in the gloomy and cold days of Winter. It's true! And I am filled with admiration and pride for you constantly – and much respect, you understand.

I think it is terrible that you must be separated from Simon so often; you must miss each other very much. Still, with so much to do to keep yourself occupied, the time should go by very quickly. Think how awful it would be if you were a commuter, or, worse still, a housewife!! (There's a bloody great motor-mower going full blast outside the window and it's doing my brain in. I don't know what's being cut out there – there's hardly any grass, only concrete and weeds).

Yes, Amsterdam <u>is</u> a dream of a place, isn't it? A friend of mine – doing six years in Long Lartin – owns a big nightclub over there; all the big bands appear there regularly. Kraftwork, Abba, Sasha Distel, etc. Very successful. The place only gets raided once a year. But you refer to the tidiness of the streets and the countryside. Yes. No-one loves natural scenery more than I. I'm very happy that you had such a nice time – and I'm so glad you're well and happy, too.

£25,000 of Cartier jewels … These people who requested that you should wear them … these people – these connoisseurs of beautiful art - they chose, out of all the beautiful girls in London, they chose only you, Fiona, to be worthy of setting off those fine jewels! If you did feel a little upstaged, well <u>that's</u> natural! Hey – guess how those jewels would have felt if <u>they</u> had emotions!

I am keeping out of trouble. Whenever I feel it in the air, I remember my promise to you and I think I have become much quieter over the past few months, too. I am also much more aware of what is going on about me – see what influence you have!

I gave up smoking again last Tuesday – and started again two days later. Ha! And here I am boasting of my strength of will …!

The rest of this letter could not be found. The next two crossed in the post.

Theatre Royal
Bath
22nd July 1978

My Dearest Alex,

Being on tour is all very well, great fun and all that, but it does tend to put a strain on relationships with friends and husbands, etc. I only see Simon on Sundays, which is very upsetting and you, my dear friend, haven't had a letter from me in ages. I apologise most profusely. However, here I am putting pen to paper at last.

Firstly, thank you a million times for the beautiful card you sent us on our anniversary. I was really moved Alex and it meant a lot to me. We had a lovely day on the 10th and are both very happy now. Not only are our careers going well but we've just moved into a beautiful little house and are absolutely thrilled with the way it is coming along. It's amazing how exciting it is to have stairs in one's house, and a garden to potter in, and a garage for the junk and one's own front door!! I wish you could see it Alex.

It is a little mock-Tudor cottage built in the 1930s, in North Ealing, and the area now has a conservation order on it. All the houses have the black and white timbered effect with cherry trees and roses in the front gardens. Ours needs a <u>lot</u> of interior redecorating, but Simon is a dab hand with wallpaper and paint and I love choosing colours and co-ordinating fabrics and carpets. We're trying to create a very warm, old-fashioned atmosphere inside and I have been raiding the local junk-shops and antique markets everywhere on tour, to see if I can pick up any bargains!

The play 'Caught Napping' is going very well and enjoying great success wherever we go. As you can see we are in Bath this week, which is such a lovely town that it makes our stay twice as enjoyable. We are a very happy company and Bill Pertwee (also in Dad's Army with Arthur) is our group leader, so we usually do all the local beauty spots and historical monuments during the day, which means that I'm seeing parts of our beautiful English countryside that I would never normally see. I went to Stratford-on-Avon for the first time the other day!

Is it warm on the Isle of Wight? We never know what weather to expect as one week we're North and then we're South again.

Well, my dear friend, take care and write soon as I love to receive your letters. The poem 'Picture' made me cry it was so beautiful.

Thank you for being so patient with me. I think of you often. Will write again very soon. Be good.

Much Love

Fiona

HM Prison Parkhurst

23. 7. 1978

Dear Fiona,

Something <u>is</u> wrong this time, isn't there. There are some bad people in prison, Fiona. I have to live with them, but I can't keep an eye on them all. Some put on such a good act, though, that it's only when they are released from prison do we find out whether they're bad or good.

I have always kept your letters out of the way of other people. <u>Please</u>, Fiona, write and tell me what is wrong! Believe me, lass, I would <u>never lie</u> to you! Believe me, then when I say I don't know what is wrong. You must write and tell me.

I can never ask you for things – you gave me your friendship and nothing could make me happier than that or be more valuable than that. Let me know what's wrong – if someone from here has been pestering you (all the time I have lived with this fear) <u>let me know</u>!! I'll put a stop to it.

Dear Fiona, whatever the future, I will always be your friend.

Write back if you feel like it. If not, thank you for getting me through two years imprisonment, I'll never forget. Take care, Princess.

Love and Respect to You

Alex

Getting Through the Night

Strains of martial music played
Through acoustic recesses of the brain
Whilst flashing strobes of consciousness
Blow apart the realms of tiredness
And leave in place of fairy lights
Consistent fireball of delights.
Then tossing brain cells of the mind
Refuse to let my eyes unwind
But fight it out in tedious duels;

Magnetic tape gone mad between the spools
Of nuclear piles of flickering blue
In Technicolour Powercolour view.
Subconscious dynamos hum and whine
Beneath this useless skull of mine
Spitting lightning voltage streaks
I pray to God and-lo! He speaks!
With bated breath my eardrums wait
In human stereo solid state …
God produced a scroll and read
That unofficially I was dead
And so I rose from where I'd lain
To commandeer the Astral Plane
Where I spoke to ghosts of the past
And caught a star and held it fast.
Upon a thread of silver glow
I travelled back to me below
And sat up screaming in my bed
With sweat-drops littering my head
And cold and darkness all about
Inside a box please let me out!
Within a dream I find a stream
And gone is noise where noise has been
And water, grass and air is sweet
And magic toadstools laugh and greet
My fumbling presence with delight
Providing me with glad respite.
Drifting now through woods and glades
Toward a morn with reddening shades
And silhouettes lighten as the sky
Announces that a day is nigh
And with relief I wake to find
Another night is left behind.

Alex 1978

Poor Alex. Having not heard from me for three months he was clearly concerned that something was amiss. But his anguish was to inspire one of his best poems and 'Getting Through the Night' displays a mature talent full of haunting images. However, no sooner had he posted this letter than he received mine.

Since I rediscovered Alex's letters I have read them over and over again and the following is one of my favourites. With the privilege of hindsight, the dream he describes never fails to move me.

HM Prison Parkhurst
26. 7. 1978

My Dear Fiona

Please forgive me for behaving like an old woman in my last letter to you. Last April I unpardonably left a letter from you lying on my cell table while I was out. When I got back one of the cons was waiting for me and I was sure the letter had been moved … I worried about this because the bloke was about to get released and, if he had read any of the contents of the letter he could've memorised the address and rung you up posing as a friend of mine. Anyway, he got out in early June and, not having heard from you I feared the worst – that he'd tried to see you. He was only an old man – and for that reason I could very easily visualise him looking for an easy touch for a grubstake; it happens all the time. I believed he'd tried it with you and that you were mad at me as a result. It would look as though I'd betrayed your trust.

So up to last week I was battling within my mind whether he <u>had</u> read that letter or whether he <u>hadn't</u> – so I <u>had</u> to write that letter to you to try to find out!! As it turned out he hadn't. But that's the last time I leave a friend's letter lying around! Fiona, I'm so sorry. (I'm not being rehabilitated in here – by the time I get through this lot I'll be a <u>paranoid schizophrenic</u>! Hah!).

When I got your letter today – well, I don't think it can be described properly on paper, but it was a fantastic feeling to know you're still there! You know how it is, Princess, you're my best friend. I'd self-destruct rather than do or say anything that might hurt you in any way – but, you know that.

I don't know what perfume it is that you use, but – pow! It ain't half got a punch! Lovely. It matches with you. Beautiful. They ought to call it 'Fiona'.

So now you have found a house, at last! Wonderful! But you'll miss the flat, you know, you both worked hard on that place, painting and papering and now you have to do it all over again – phew! Still, you do seem delighted at the prospect.

Funnily enough, I had a dream not long ago and it's always stayed with me. It was a strange dream. I think perhaps it is related to dreams, thoughts, and memories going back over the years to when I was small. There was a palace. Somewhere, I don't know where. On a star. And inside was constructed of gold floors and walls, with rich carpets and gossamer-silk drapes dotted with tiny jewels, light was coming from somewhere making the silk glow and the jewels sharply burst into a thousand coloured lights. I turned my face upwards and saw neither ceiling nor sky – it was a tower and stretched upwards into infinity. The occupant of the palace was a young woman wearing a rainbow, or so it seemed, but it was actually a long flowing gown the colours of which were constantly changing and moving. Her head was covered by a white cloudy veil, which hung to her shoulders.

She was the loveliest woman imaginable – I knew this although I made out no certain lines of body – nor could I see her face. Nor have I ever. But I saw and felt her presence … which, through some form of telepathy, told me words of communication, which I understood and listened to . All the wisdom of mankind radiated from the presence.

She grew bigger and filled my whole vision – concealing from view the room of gold and jewels and silk and the deep carpets …. at this point the whole scene changes … A city street … With hundreds of people walking to and fro on the pavements – but all are faceless. One day a young woman will turn around and I'll see her face. Or feel a presence.

If I told the psycho that he'd nut me off without a qualm …

'Alexandrovitch! – ve haff decided to Broadmoor you go! Pack your kit! By da left – Quvik monkey-hop! Left, left, left – right – left, left, left, right!'

So you finally hit Stratford-upon-Avon, then! Great – did you visit Shakespeare's birthplace? Or Anne Hathaway's cottage? Stratford … you know, I've got a lot of time for that place, I spent many happy days there and met a lot of very nice people.

I am glad you liked the poem 'Picture' and it is, of course, your picture I am referring to in it. The subject matter for my poems is very diverse – it all depends on how I feel and so out of 20 poems, say, someone will like five or six. It would really make my day (month and year) to see what <u>you</u> can do, Fiona. Promise me you'll try sometime, lass?

There was another great film on the TV recently, starring Ingrid Bergman –'Anastasia'. This delighted me because Princess Anastasia is to me what Lady Jane Grey is to you – furthermore I believe Anastasia <u>is</u> still alive and was not executed with the other members of the Russian Imperial Royal Family in 1918. Have you ever seen this film?

I've begun doing exercises in my cell and at present I feel like I've done five rounds with Rocky Marciano. I began last week doing 66 press-ups and 700 skips a day – now it's up to 100 press-ups and 2,000 skips and I'm feeling much fitter although there's aching pains in my chest, stomach and calves. They'll go away though if I keep at it. I got terribly out of condition through sitting around all day doing nothing! Anyway, my dear Friend, I must finish for now. The weather down here is lousy. Take good care of yourself, princess, and always be happy.

I Send All My Love

Alex

If it hadn't been for Alex's wonderful imagination carrying him to far-off places with 'gossamer silk drapes, dotted with tiny jewels' and his voracious appetite for literature, I think he would have succumbed to the system much sooner.

'I was becoming criminalised. Prison is another world, a darkened society. If environment does determine consciousness — and I believe that it does — the prison environment induces a darkened consciousness. If prisoners are subjected to an abnormal environment, they too, after a while, become abnormal.

Colin began swallowing razor blades and bed springs. He was taken to the local casualty hospital where his stomach was opened up and the metal removed. But no sooner was he brought back, than he started eating more bedsprings. It reached the stage where the doctors warned that they would not be able to keep opening him up every few weeks. Colin disappeared one day. The word had it that he'd been "nutted-off" (sectioned) to Broadmoor or Rampton.'

Cardiff
25th July 1978

Dear Alex,

Spent last weekend with my parents in Blandford, Dorset and Simon
came down too, as they all saw the show in Bath and thoroughly enjoyed
it. On Sunday, Arthur Lowe joined us for lunch in the Officer's Mess on
the camp, where my Dad is the Commander, and he charmed everyone. It
rained all day Sunday, unfortunately, and I <u>lost</u> at Scrabble!

I've just been offered the lead in Oscar Wilde's 'Lady Windermere's
Fan' to start in Guildford and then go to Rhodesia and Canada. How
about that? Nice part to play but I don't like the idea of South Africa
much. Don't want to leave Simon again either.

Ah well, my dear Alex, bet this was a surprise this morning!

Be Good

Love, Fiona

HM Prison Parkhurst
28. 7. 1978

My Dear Friend,

I'm very happy for you about the new invitation for the lead in 'Lady Windermere's Fan'.

But you're not happy, my friend. South Africa ... That's where I stop feeling glad,
because all the time I'll be thinking of you living in the midst of so much evil. No prison
in the world would hold me if anything happened to you, no prison. And I'm sure
Simon would be concerned for you – and of course you don't wish to leave him again.

There's too much hatred and violence in Rhodesia these days and the situation
isn't getting any better. Only worse. You'll be playing to white segregated audiences
and your very presence will indicate (rightly or wrongly) that you sympathise with
the regime. Whether you do or don't is neither here nor there to me, you can do

no wrong in <u>my</u> eyes – but I just don't want you going anywhere that isn't 100 per cent safe for you. Back home all the producers who are anti-apartheid will have to pass you over – purely as a matter of principle – that's standard procedure. Please, Fiona, weigh all this up before you make any final decision, hey? Take the advice of a friend; drop this one.

You'll never believe this … Last Sunday I <u>won</u> at Scrabble – and it must have been the first time I'd played it for some 8 years!! I ended with 301 points. Remarkable?

You take care of yourself, now, alright? And be wise!

Love and Peace, Your Friend

Alex

The creative skills that Alex possessed were becoming more accomplished with age. He was still only 25 but he could draw, paint, sew, write poetry and prose and his handwriting drew on a form of artistry as well. I have described how tiny and perfect it was, the lettering conjuring images of an elfin typewriter, and I suppose he developed it in order to cram as much as possible onto each page. But now he was excited to find that he could achieve something else. This was to have rewarding results.

HM Prison Parkhurst
30. 7. 1978

My Dear Fiona,

I've managed to write the Lord's Prayer two and a half times – on the back of a post-age stamp … how's <u>that</u>? Keep on smiling, Princess – 'Never Let The Storm Clouds Bother You'! Wishing you every success with the show.

Alex

He enclosed the stamp with his letter and it was the most astonishing thing I had seen. One-hundred-and-forty-eight words on the back of a four-and-a-half pence stamp, written with an ordinary blue bic pen, and without any special visual aid. I discovered later that he perfected this skill in order to help some of his mates smuggle information out, avoiding the censor. All that was required was a little judicious licking around the edges of the stamp.

Brighton
4th August 1978

Dear Alex,

I'm feeling a bit under par as I have a blood-shot eye, headache and hunger pangs. All I want to do is to go home to Simon.

Are there any fat men in prison? I would assume that they would lose weight in prison quite quickly, but maybe I'm wrong. They probably feed you very well! Hope you don't mind me asking.

I thought 'Getting Through the Night' was brilliant Alex. It summed up a million feelings and emotions. And the stamp is AMAZING!

You talk about Anastasia in your letter. Well I can't remember if I ever mentioned that I played Anastasia in the film 'Nicholas and Alexandra' when I was 14. Consequently I read many books about her and I too believe that she could have lived. I'm now reading a new book called 'The File on the Tsar', which claims that they all lived and has startling new evidence to prove it.

By the way, may I send you books and things or is that not allowed? Do let me know. Dear friend, thank you for your letters and warmth. I will write as soon as I can—but fret not!

Be v. Good.

Love—Fiona

HM Prison Parkhurst
6/7. 8. 1978

My Dear Friend,

I'm very pleased that you liked the poem – and, of course, the stamp – but you ain't seen nothin' yet. I am sending three more for you with this letter… let me tell you about them.

No 1 is the 'Lord's Prayer' written on a stamp, No 2 is the same – but written half as small and No 3 is half as small again – but in pencil. I had a letter a couple of weeks ago from Norris McWhirter who compiles the Guinness Book of Records. It seems that, to become the world's smallest handwriter – I have to write out the 'Lord's Prayer' onto a stamp – ten times! (Phew!) Anyway, I have managed to write it six times and I know that – given a few month's practice – I'll be able to write it out half as small again; twelve times. Howzat? And I don't even use a magnifying glass. Do I win a coconut?

Anyway, I was totally amazed when you wrote that you had played Anastasia!!! Even now it hasn't sunk in properly … This is Anastasia – the only member of royalty I have ever been interested in and know anything about – I mention her in a letter to you and it turns out that you have actually portrayed her! That is some coincidence! Wow. Strong medicine. (Hello, Princess.) Excuse me for a moment while I roll a cig. So my two favourite actresses – you and Ingrid Bergman – have played Anastasia? Crazy. I am astounded at all this!

And you believe that she may have lived? Fiona – I'm sure that she lived, more – convinced! The girl who was pulled out of the Berlin canal was, I'm certain, Anastasia. I have this feeling – very strong.

My own family – on my father's side – moved to the Ukraine not long after the Revolution. This area became Poland. The family name; Alexandrovitch became Alexandrowicz (which sounds exactly the same, only the spelling is slightly changed, the Russian 'vitch' being swapped with the Polish 'wicz'!). My father, as a young officer, returned to Russia to serve in the army through the War, then, in the early 1950s came to England and married my mother. Nowadays my father refuses to mention anything about his life previous to coming to England – I only know of my grandparents living in Odessa. So there is a mystery.

Now there are a few – not many – a few people in the Soviet Union who bear my family name, the Czar, Nicholas Alexandrovitch Romanov also bore it. It is highly unlikely that the royal family were any kind of relations to us – though, indeed, there were many far-flung branches of our family connected with the high bourgeoisie at that time. I have no way of knowing. But I have some kind of sixth sense about Anastasia that tells me she did not die with the others in 1918. Perhaps my conviction lies with something I may have overheard while very young. I don't know.

You ask if there are any <u>fat</u> men in prison? Well, I've come across them now and again but they're really few and far between. On our wing I can think of three guys you could call fat – it seems they have glandular trouble (as my mate Stewart would say: 'They've got technical difficulties'). When I came in prison I was fairly hefty – not fat! – but over the years, due to the hunger strikes and frequent losses of appetite I've lost some 2½ stones so that now I weigh in at around 11 stones. I seem to be losing weight all the time.

They probably feed us very well? What is this? I thought <u>I</u> was the comic around here! We get one orange a week – and that's our total weekly supply of fresh fruit. I think we'd all be down with scurvy if it weren't for that orange! The only milk we get to drink during the week is the ¼ pint we have on our Sunday cornflakes – and even that's watered-down.

Fiona – there are two things that I badly need and if you could get them for me I'd be eternally grateful. One is a wristwatch (not digital). It would prove really invaluable to time my essays, studies and physical exercises – but it would be impossible for me to buy one, as, except for my £1.39½p wage, I have no other income. The other thing is a 'soap parcel' – a bar of soap and a tube of toothpaste. Can do? If anything's addressed to me here I'll be able to have it.

I sympathise with you over the bloodshot eye – whatever have you been up to? Overwork? What do I always say? – take care of yourself! And headache with hunger pangs – you sound as though you've been in Holloway Prison for a night!!

Down here in the Solent area the rain is still coming down in showers, the air is very close and oppressive and it looks like a bit of thunder is on the way. But I can fix all that – listen, I have a magic pencil … when I wave it in the air … the rain stops. Watch this … God, Fiona; <u>nothing</u> works any more around this crummy joint!!

I do feel *alive* tonight. For some reason. It must be the bats. What do you think of the world, Princess – do you reckon we can change it for the better? You bet!!!

Regards to Simon and All My Love to You.

Alex

Alex describes a hostage situation that happened around this time:

'One day I heard a screw come upstairs and unlock one of the cell doors. Then I heard: "Just make one wrong move and you're dead".

I recognised the voice. It was George. He was built big and violent. He had the screw round the throat and had a Stanley knife held there. He stopped outside the next-door cell to me and yelled, "Get this fuckin' door opened."

A Welshman called Gary unlocked his door and let them in. So now George and the screw/hostage were in there with Gary.

Within half an hour everything was shut down and all cons were banged up. C-Wing began to fill up with screws—none of them had gone off duty—and because I was next door, I could hear what was going down. George told the screws that if any of them tried to jack the door off, the hostage would be killed.

He demanded a prison van and a driver to take them to a helicopter to fly them to an airport…etc.

A marksman with a rifle had arrived and was positioned across the yard.

The "situation" went on all day and into the evening, until eventually a police detective inspector turned up. Standing outside Gary's cell he tried to reason with them, negotiating to take the place of the screw. After an hour or so the copper managed to convince George to let the screw go.

He said, "Listen carefully George. I'm going to handcuff myself to the railings so that when you let the officer go, I'll be here and you can take me in his place, OK?"

I heard the screw go to unlock the door. Within a few seconds I heard Gary and George release the hostage and then the copper shouted "Move!"

The copper and the hostage sprinted down the landing leaving Gary and George standing outside Gary's cell. The whole wing reverberated to the sound of fifty pairs of screws' boots as they charged towards the two cons. The screws smashed into them and both cons were injured. There were animal screams. I was asked to mop up the blood afterwards. It quarter-filled a mop-bucket.

Both Gary and George were put down the block (into solitary) and after being sentenced to another five years each, they were both ghosted out. George went on hunger strike in Strangeways and died as he was being transferred to Gartree Prison. Both he and Gary had been made desperate by the system.'

HM Prison Parkhurst
21. 8. 1978

Hello Princess,

Oh, Fiona, we don't have a colour television set anymore – one of my mates picked it up and threw it up and down the TV room one afternoon. They won't (quite rightly) supply us with another colour set so we're back where we started, with black and white. Fiona, honestly, if they ever filmed us in here they'd end up with a longer running, more successful series than Coronation Street! It would take ten years for the public to get over the initial <u>shock</u>!

I was watching television the other night, half asleep, when one of the cons in the row behind me started hitting me over the back of my head … I thought, 'Hello', and turned around pretty quick. The guy concerned started patting me on the shoulder saying; 'Sorry, Alex, sorry, Alex'. What he'd done was he'd lit up a smoke and flicked the match away (it's dark in the TV room) and the match had landed in my hair setting it on fire. He'd hit me over the head to put the fire out. Luckily my hair is very thick and he'd acted fast so there was only superficial singeing. Without distractions like that I'd soon be bored stupid. (There was a terrible smell all over the TV room of burned hair afterwards).

Come on, cheer up, lass! Watch – I'll pull a funny face. Christ! That even scared <u>me</u>! To be serious, though, I must close for now. So, Fiona, take good care of yourself and keep the sun shining – okay? I'm still living up to my promise to keep out of trouble – my slate's been clean for two years now. Is that okay?

All My Love to You, Finest Regards to Simon.

Yours, Alex

As usual there was a lot more to the television set story than Alex could tell me. They were all watching a Rolf Harris programme when a con called Doug walked in, slowly picked up the TV and threw it across the room where it exploded like a bomb, showering the room with slivers of glass. He then went calmly to play table tennis.

Doug was sent down to F2 for 'treatment', which relieved everyone because they knew he had a short fuse and was mentally unsound. However, he was back on the wing a few days later.

Alex was on his way to give Doug a few roll-ups, when he was distracted by a friend enquiring as to whether Alex would sell his budgie. So he asked a guy called Bob to drop off the cigarettes.

'A few moments later, Bob walked back in. He looked an odd shade of grey and he was puffing nervously on his roll-up, his hands shaking all the while.

"Alex, Doug's door was locked so I couldn't give him the fags. I looked through the spyhole and there's somebody in Doug's cell with him..."

"What d'you mean? Who?"

"I don't know, but whoever it is I think he's dead."

Doug had a cell just a few doors down the landing. When I got there the door was banged up. I looked through the spyhole and saw Doug in front of his table with his head on his arms as if he'd fallen asleep. Then I saw, on the cot, one of the other lifers, a guy called Brian who was doing time for killing his lover, a male nurse I think. I knew it was Brian, although his face was going black with odd splotches of purple covering it. He looked as if he'd been stabbed and garrotted. Murdered.'

The warders yelled for 'bang-up', locking everyone in their cells and the prisoners were given doses of tranquillisers and sleeping pills. In the middle of the night, while heavily drugged, Alex was awoken by two police officers investigating the murder. They asked him about his movements the previous night.

"Well, I didn't go down the pub, I remember that."

"Very funny, ha ha. The quicker we get this over with the quicker you can get back to sleep."

Fortunately I had an alibi of the best kind. For most of the evening I'd been working in the pantry and a screw had been with me throughout.

Next morning we discovered that Doug had received a bad letter and had simply decided to kill the first person that came into his cell. I couldn't help wondering what might have happened if I'd gone to his cell earlier in the evening with the cigs I had for him … Doug was a big lad. Strong. I may well have taken Brian's place.'

London
4th September 1978

Dear Alex,

Home at last. Here is a little soap parcel for you. Hope it's O.K. I like sending you things, so every now and then I'll send you a surprise package. (As long as you're v. good and keep your toes crossed!!)

Thank you for the stamps. Your handwriting is truly incredible and, as you say, with a little perseverance you might well break that record (You deserve more than a coconut). Did you know that the one Lord's Prayer that you dedicated to me (with the pretty red and blue edges) is upsidedown?? The poor Queen is on her head! Is it accidental?

Mum, Dad and my dog Sunday are here with us this weekend, as they went to a wedding on Saturday (without the dog!!) and it's Mummy's birthday tomorrow. It's nice to see them as we all get on very well.

Funny you talking about singeing your hair, as Simon's just done the same thing, with his eyelashes, eyebrows and moustache getting crinkled edges too. I reckon he narrowly escaped a very nasty accident.

In haste. Sorry this is so short.

Regards from Simon

And much love and admiration from me.

Fiona

It is interesting that I enjoyed sending Alex certain items and having analysed these feelings, I can only assume that I was treating him very much as one would a friend. I cared about him. It is also true that the giver derives as much pleasure from the gesture as the recipient, so it was not entirely altruistic.

HM Prison Parkhurst
14. 9. 1978

My Dear Friend.

Innumerable thanks to you for the things you sent, Fiona, they are greatly appreciated, I assure you, an enormous help. I'll make you a Commissar one day! Or something. You're a fantastic girl – do you realise that? You mean a great deal to me, as though you were my sister, and this is how I shall always think of you – for life! I feel this.

If you and I, never having met one another, can become such friends, I wonder why everyone in the East cannot write to everyone in the West … then the whole world would learn how to be friendly – whole peoples would begin to love and respect one another and there would be no more wars and no more hatred.

My mother has been down here visiting me over the weekend, I was overjoyed to see her again and we had lots of things to discuss. I learn that my sister is getting married next month, October, and that everything is in a state due to this. My sister's name, incidentally, is Susan. They will be honeymooning in Barbados. I am a little sad about the wedding – I would have liked to be there, you understand. I haven't seen Susan since she was a little girl of 13 – and now she is a grown woman of 21 and about to be married! I think I shall ask the Governor if I might attend the service, sometimes these things are allowed on compassionate grounds.

Do not be depressed, you are too vital to the world for that. Whatever troubles you, when things seem too big to cope with, then let me know! Quite often it is better to talk about things than have them eat your heart out. Remember; 'we are lucky, are we not, just to be alive?' – your words; and so very true. I worry about something yesterday – today I think; what a silly thing to have worried about … I needn't have worried at all!

Well, Princess, here's autumn once more – isn't it amazing how time flies! I am having a Category-A review this month and, should they take me off the A-list, I could be out of here within two years! So will you cross your fingers for me? – then I can be <u>sure</u> they'll take me off Cat-A!

My Love to You, Your Friend and Brother

Alex

Memory Be Kind

Quietly, lazily,
My soul takes wing
To rest on bowers, clothed
                    verdantly for Spring.
Tranquil and serene
Thoughts blossom fair;
Love's as free as cumulus
Pure, high in the stratosphere!
And visions of my youth;
Those childhood dreams;
Once lost, are now regained
As the bumblebee and breathing grass,
Melodious as the rain,
Sing lullabies, soft and low,
That as a child so long ago
                    I knew,
And loved each word.
Now, within this woodland glade
Resting on Earth's bosom round,
I *can* recall my childhood days
With every sight and sound!
Then let me keep my dreams of love
Through the space of time;
Let not my youthful fancy die;
Memory, Be Kind.

Alex 1978

'If you and I, never having met one another, can become such friends, I wonder why everyone in the East cannot write to everyone in the West … then the whole world would learn how to be friendly – whole peoples would begin to love and respect one another and there would be no more wars and no more hatred.' Why indeed? These were powerful words to someone like me with a simplistic attitude to life based on a lack of political knowledge. And yet, through his melancholy about his sister's impending wedding, he takes the time to try to lift my mood out of the depressive state I kept finding myself in. These mood swings were to become increasingly difficult to control.

HM Prison Parkhurst
27. 9. 1978

My Dearest Fiona,

A theme has been running through my mind of late: 'I'm a failure, I'm a failure, I'm a failure'. It's now given way to 'What shall I try now? What am I best fitted for? Where is my place in this world?' In every book I read, I look for that pursuit which might give my life direction again.

I am a man of passions, capable of doing foolish things. I speak and act quickly when it would have been better to wait patiently. This being the case, must I consider myself a dangerous man, incapable of doing anything? I do not think so. But the question is to put these self-same passions to a good use. For instance, I have an irresistible passion for music and books, and I want continually to instruct myself, just as I want to breathe the air, you understand.

It is almost eight years now that I have been without a normal environment, languishing here and there. And during that time I have been going downhill, deteriorating.

If I don't study, if I don't go on seeking any longer, then I am lost. I want to become a great writer and poet. My only anxiety is; how can I be of some good in this world? Cannot I serve some purpose and be of some good? I think through the medium of writing.

Have you ever heard of Nadejda Philaretovna von Meck? She and Tchaikovsky were corresponding for years, they never met – and yet he produced his finest work for her. My finest work shall be for you.

I must sign off for now, Fiona, but I will write for you for centuries. Take the best care of yourself and be happy.

Much Love, Your Friend and Brother,

Alex

Unknown Destination

Upon a dark, cooling night
The footsteps of a child are heard
With echoing sadness, weary tread,
They falter, sometimes race ahead
Then stop, and turn to face about
As compass needles paused in doubt.

Along a country lane they ring;
Supplying sound that amplifies
Into a lonely magnitude
Defying human latitude.
Magnets pull — the feet are drawn
Incessantly, to the dawn.

Over bridges over stiles
The feet run on for miles
With purpose now they seem to say;
I know the way! I know the way!
In ferment intoxication …
What end? What Unknown Destination?

Alex 1978

Alex was fighting a losing battle with the authorities over the amount of medication being administered in prison and exactly what it was. He feared they were being experimented on and that the drugs probably contributed to Doug's state of mind when he randomly murdered Brian. He didn't recognise a new drug that he was taking on C-Wing, because of its side-effects of deep restlessness, and became convinced it was an experimental compound that was being used in the Soviet Union.

He decided to make an application to see someone from the Board of Visitors (now the Independent Monitoring Board). Members play an important role in dealing with problems inside prison. If a prisoner has an issue that he or she has been unable to resolve through the usual internal channels, he can put in a confidential request to see a member of the IMB.

When Alex met with a lady called Heather, two warders accompanied him. He showed her the sample, explained that he thought it was experimental and asked her to have it analysed. She said there was nothing she could do until she consulted some other members and asked him to hang onto it. Alex suggested that as soon as he left her office the two warders would probably take the sample away from him. He was told not to be so paranoid and to keep the phial safe.

'Dismissed, I left the office and headed back to my cell. A minute later the cell door burst open and half a dozen screws piled in. I was given a strip-search. The phial was taken off me. The screws searched every inch of my cell—even inside my correspondence and between the pages of my books. They took the cell furniture apart and pulled photographs from the wallboard, tearing them in the process. My radio was dismantled and "accidentally" dropped on the floor.'

Having tried to go through the proper channels and failed, Alex decided on further action. He set up a human rights group made up of prisoners themselves. The group was to become The League for Human Rights Observance (LHRO).

HM Prison Parkhurst
23. 10. 1978

My Very Dear Friend

Did you have a nice Birthday, Princess? Was it the best Birthday in the world? But of course it was – I told you it would be! Whatever my thought on October 10, it always included the image of my far-away-friend Fiona, whose happiness and friendship I prize more than the oxygen in the air that I breathe. How I wished on that day that I could have provided for you some intangible thing, which would have enabled you to experience something so intensely joyful, so purely delightful and glad – some essence of all these things. Alas, no such thing is available to man – but give me time …

I have your photograph before me – the one in which the white carnations appear with you – and you look so radiant … I feel so guilty that there is no likeness of me that I may give to you! I steadfastly persist in requesting permission from the Home Office that I be allowed to have my photo taken – without success. They seem unshakeable in their belief that – should it be allowed – the thing will be doctored in such a way that I appear in front of crossed Red Banners or something. Ridiculous. I do exist though.

My sister is to be married on Saturday to this guy called Kevin who I have never seen, and who has never bothered writing to me, even to say hi! What do you think, lass – shall I send the boys round? Seriously, though, all it takes is 'Dear Alex, I'm marrying your sister'. What am I getting for a brother-in-law? All I need now is to find out he's a secret member of the Conservative Party. I don't approve. And you're the only one I'll admit that to.

I heard part of Tchaikovsky's *Fourth Symphony* last night, and I found myself totally captivated – held and entranced by this wonderful music. The performance was of exceptionally high standard, so often these compositions are 'experimented' with and one is apt to hear so many variations of the same work – but this performance was excellent. As the station was a foreign one I missed the name of the orchestra but I think it must have been the Berlin Philharmonic. Are you familiar with the Fourth Symphony, Fiona?

Where would I be now, I often wonder, if it were not for you? You steer me away from trouble and give me additional strength to take what comes, and to deal with difficult situations in a new and more peaceable diplomatic way.

It's not been easy, so far – being an A-man carries a gigantic reputation and I often have other cons coming to me saying this and that and 'Alex – lend your assistance to this plot and that scheme'. Where I once would oblige I now remember you, my friend, and my promise to you that I'd keep out of trouble – when once my aspirations were to become an extremist; now they are to become a poet and to serve human- ity rather than become a destructive element in it. All of this is down to you, Fiona, down to your friendship, understanding and encouragement – and what do <u>you</u> get out of all this? You have got a <u>true</u> Friend, Comrade, and you have my unswerving dedication and loyalty, the greatest thing it is possible for me to give. Please – I beg you not to take what I say lightly. My one hope and wish is that, one day, I shall be granted the privilege of being of service to you.

Here is a poem that was inspired by one of your photographs.

Ode to a Pane of Glass

Peering through a pane of glass
Surrounded by a window-frame
You watch the snowflakes dance around
And flutter, expirating all too soon
        Upon a stony ground.

The glistening frost veils your face
To lend your beauty mystic air;
A snowflake sticks … It would appear
That melting, running down the mask,
        Your eye has shed a tear.

A toast, then, to that pane of glass
For presenting me with such a view!
That contrasted the cold of frost –
With the utter warmth of you …

Alex 1978

Simple yes, but manages to put over a message.

Well, I must now draw to a close, all is quiet – as usual when writing letters it is early morning, all is dark outside and Radio Victory has gone off the air. Tomorrow is today, suddenly, the 24th of October, 1978, and there are 68 days left until 1979 and another new year. With luck I'll be crashed out in half an hour's time. So, 'so long' for now, take care of yourself – okay?

Peace, Princess. All my love to you and finest regards to Simon.

Write soon.

Alex

Alex seemed to be having a prolific spurt of poetry running through his veins and in this letter enclosed yet another poem, dedicated to me. His love of Lancashire is clearly evident in this poem but I find the line 'images existing only in my mind' heartbreakingly sad. Once again, it is an example of how, all these years later, I am appreciating his poetry far more than I did at the time.

Visit

Chimneys on the rooftops wheeze, and cough out from their rheumy hearths
A sooty dust into the air—this, the blackened snow of Lancashire.
In pouring rain I stand alone and watch the spot that, as a child
I called my secret hiding-place … are these really raindrops on my face?
And there's the house where Nina lived (whom I loved but never told),
Where I spent so many hours building gold and diamond-ivory-towers
So lonely now, an empty place bereft of all but images existing
Only in my mind—I turn! I leave them all behind;
With no clear purpose in my head I wander through the dismal streets
Barely taking in this scene that what now is—is what has been.

Alex 1978

155

London

30th October — 8th November 1978

My Dearest Alex,

I feel dreadful about not writing to you for so long. Your letters bring me so much pleasure and your poetry never fails to move me. A million thank yous for my birthday card. Yes it was a lovely birthday – we had a meal by the river. Simon gave me an opal and ruby ring. Opals are my birthstone and they are very mysterious as they change colour with the light. My favourite gem is still the emerald. I'll never forget the little saying you put in my 21st birthday card ...

> 'Twenty-one years ago today
> According to tomorrow's legend
> Was the day the world discovered
> The Brightest Sparkling Emerald.'

I think that's quite exquisitely beautiful.

Since I finished the tour we have been working on the house. Simon does all the major jobs with me assisting (or hindering!) and when he's not here I potter around doing basic housekeeping stuff.

Then on October 15th for a week, our company put on Simon's one-man show, 'The Importance of being Oscar', at the local theatre. An eminent Irishman, Michael MacLiammoir, wrote it about the life of Oscar Wilde, and we bought the rights earlier this year just before Michael died (I can't remember if I've mentioned this show before, if I have, forgive me for boring you).

For three weeks prior to the opening I was dashing around putting up 150 posters in various shops and restaurants, on foot! The main problem was letting the public know about the show, as the theatre is a tiny members' theatre club, hidden behind a bush in the depths of darkest Ealing, so it isn't easy to find. Being a very new company we're still learning about administration and the various aspects of production.

It also meant writing dozens of notes to friends and acquaintances telling them about the show, answering phone calls, taking bookings, getting furniture for the set and setting up press interviews. This is why, my dearest Alex, you haven't heard from me for a while.

Anyway, it went quite well and Simon settled into it better during the last performances. Being on stage alone for two hours wasn't easy.

My job during the show was front-of-house manageress! In other words, taking ticket stubs, selling programmes and in the interval I ran a tea-bar selling tea, coffee and fresh sandwiches (made by me). I had some helpers and we made a profit due to our friendly smiles luring them away from the bar.

Goodness, it's only 3.30pm but it's so dark in here I can hardly see. Wait while I switch a light on ... Aha!!

As you know, Simon did a film called 'Death on the Nile', which had its Royal Premiere on October 23rd, two days after we finished 'Oscar'. A few of the stars were there and it was a lovely evening, except Simon's chauffeur-driven car didn't turn up, so in a panic we had to drive to Leicester Square in our tiny Fiat 500. My dress was bigger than the car! The next day our picture was on the front of the Daily Mail.

I think we may go for a short holiday soon. Poor Simon has been under great mental strain recently, trying to cope with everything and his new 'status'. The press have done some nasty articles too, so he still has a lot to learn, whereas I went through it all many years ago (Makes me sound very old and wise!!).

I'm so glad I finally received the 'lost' letter as it's a lovely one and the poems from 'What Day Is It Today?', are excellent, especially 'Ode to a Pane of Glass'. I am very honoured and flattered that the collection is dedicated to me. Thank you Alex – I don't deserve it. By the way, not all publishers want poems with 'complicated twists and turns' – I think your simplicity is what keeps them so meaningful, direct and sincere.

How did your category review go? I've had my toes crossed as well as everything else.

As for your 'I'm a failure' phase, everyone goes through that. I often get depressed thinking that I'm no good at anything. But as you said in your letter, you want to become a great writer and poet and you *will* be a great writer and poet one day, I know you will.

It's most important to have a goal, an ambition. You're not deteriorating – you're too wise and alert for that – because you use your brain, stretch it, when you are writing.

But you must convince yourself, promise yourself, that soon you will be able to start afresh. You can acknowledge and learn from what has gone before, but leave it far behind, looking ahead to a more determined, positive life. Use your experiences in your writing, which will set you apart from the rest. Freedom will bring new dimensions to your poetry, when you can smell the scented air again.

So Susan and Kevin are married now. Don't be sad. If you are so fond of her you must be happy for her. I'm sure Kevin is a reasonable guy and will write to you in due course.

Yesterday was the anniversary of the Russian Revolution in 1917 (Poor Anastasia – I wonder if she's still struggling)

Did you hear about the American tourist in St Petersburg who was looking at a family tree of the Romanovs? She said, 'My, my. How amazing. They all died in the same year!'

That reminds me, I went for an interview the other day to play the part of Romola, wife of Nijinsky in a huge film that is going to be made about the ballet dancer. Imagine! Another Russian! I don't think I've got the part though.

I am returning your Jimmy Boyle book, with many thanks for letting me read it. Also enclosed are a few things I thought you might like to look at. We went to Michelham Priory when I was on tour and I thought it was fascinatingly beautiful.

Well, Christmas will be upon us very soon. I shall be sending you something you requested in a little Xmas bumper bundle. OK?

Be good, my dear friend. Your welfare is of great concern to me. Warm regards from Simon and strength, admiration and love from me.

Fiona

HM Prison Parkhurst
Sunday 12. 11. 1978 to Monday 13. 11.1978

My Dearest Fiona,

How happy it made me to receive your wonderful letter! Such a long one too. Occasions like this are the most pleasant things in my life, so thank you Fiona, a great many times over.

I must make a confession; you see, I had never heard of Michael MacLiammoir!!! He must certainly have been a great and distinguished man. Let us hope then, that 'The Importance of Being Oscar' will prove highly successful for your company! You have certainly thrown much energy into this production, losing a fair amount of shoe-leather yourself on the promotional side, it seems.

I had to laugh at your description of the Questors Theatre; 'Behind a bush in darkest Ealing …'. I see. Indeed. Behind a bush … it sounds like something out of 'Lord of the Rings', doesn't it? One must be either a Boy Scout or a Hobbit to <u>find</u> the place! Never mind.

If there's one thing that makes me ill at ease it's the thought of being in a crowd attempting my best to be sociable, making 'small talk' with one person after another. I'd run a mile. I can't stand loud voices, stupid remarks and embarrassing silences; all the things that go with socialising with groups of people. I never raise my own voice, and I am always most relaxed when having a quiet conversation on a one-to-one basis. However, if it meant squeezing through a crowd to reach your sandwiches, I'd be in there without a second thought!

I've been carefully noting the progress of 'Death on the Nile' ever since you first mentioned it prior to your Egyptian visit. The Queen has always considered herself an Agatha Christie fan of long standing. Yet, at the royal premiere, she's supposed to have asked Peter Ustinov who the culprit was … well, hadn't she read the book? Some Agatha Christie fan …

You ask how my Cat A review went. Well, I know all the staff here sent reports that recommended I be taken off it (for the second year running) – but it appears the Home Office still consider me a top-security risk. It's so ludicrous! Anyway, application refused. Maybe I'll have better luck next year.

I'm very grateful for the sound advice you give me in your letter, it is very sensible, Princess, and I want you to know I'll do my utmost to follow it and to justify your confidence in me. I want so much to do good in this world, Fiona, there's no badness within me, I couldn't hurt anybody. God, I've seen more a in the past eight years than a soldier sees in a lifetime and I'm sick of it through and through. If nobody else believes me, I don't care – but <u>you</u> must! If there's one person in the world I can be honest with it is you. Let this be our bond; Truth and Trust, and may the friendship between us never die.

Here's another poem for you.

Nomadic Princess

Nomadic Princess of the Stage,
Your life's applause a radiance
Of gentle beauty stimulating
Warmth; to aesthetic principles.
Your Epithet is Nature's Kiss —
Fraught with ethereal garb
Of chameleon zephyrs, changing
Constantly, discarding stars
For galaxies and galaxies for less.
Stem not your Heart of Latitudes
That choose to keep your footsteps gay –
And all around you Happiness
That as a Cloak of Magic Air
May never melt, nor fade away.

Alex 1978

Guess what? A snowstorm has begun to rage outside.

Alas, I come towards the end of another letter to you. It seems very strange that you will have this in your hand, reading it, only hours after I ink in each word from this cold place. Strange.

All My Love to You

Alex

'I've seen more violence in the past eight years than a soldier sees in a lifetime', Alex wrote. It seems that the violence in prison is something played down by the Prison Service and hardly mentioned in the media. The truth is quite shocking. Alex witnessed many horrifically violent situations, which often led to recurring nightmares. On one occasion he was queuing for his lunch when another prisoner barged in front of him, stabbed the guy in front and calmly walked away. The victim collapsed in a pool of blood and died. By all accounts, bodies were always removed by the mortuary van in the middle of the night, when everyone was asleep.

HM Prison Parkhurst

4. 12. 1978

My Dear Friend,

I'm sitting writing this in the middle of the night. As always at this time the place is unnaturally calm and silent, save for the subdued rattling of water pipes in the recess across the landing. It seems they can't sleep, either!

It seems funny to know I'm getting more out of today than anyone else in here, Princess – writing to you is better than dreaming of freedom. Jesus – it's quiet, I feel like yelling out of the window at the top of my voice; 'I'm aliiiiiiive, you bastards!!!'

I've fallen in love with this girl – are you ready for that – who lives a billion miles away on the other side of the Wall and who certainly doesn't know I exist. People say I have this habit of creating problems for myself and I'm beginning to understand what they mean. But – to look for something, one has to know it exists. I'm sure It is Communism that is keeping me in prison. I will not betray my cause, so they can't take the risk of letting me out. They seem to hold this misconceived idea that the word 'revolutionist' is synonymous with 'anarchist' and 'terrorist'. Not so.

Vincent Van Gogh was a Revolutionary; he expressed himself with paints. Paul Robeson was a Revolutionary; he used the medium of song to express himself. Tchaikovsky used music. I will work and work to express myself in writing. But the authorities won't accept that. They prefer to see me throwing petrol bombs and organising sinister subversive commie groups … that way it's easier for them to justify keeping me locked up.

Some things they can't take away from me, our kid – I can look out of the window and see the stars, I can walk in the compound and breathe fresh air and I can return to my cell and see your picture – these things are my world, and while they exist so will I – no matter where they put me. That you contribute so much to my world is something I can't thank you enough for – just having you to write to, knowing that someone out there cares enough to read what I write – and I'll always be grateful to Simon, too, for putting up with me writing to you.

It won't be long now before they move me to Grendon Prison – probably soon after Christmas. At least it will be a step in the right direction, Grendon is Britain's only prison, which specialises in 'group therapy', there's only one other place in Europe like it – somewhere in Sweden. If I can convince them there that my purpose on being released wouldn't be to sling things about – then I have a fighting chance. If I <u>don't</u> convince them, I'll probably get nutted-off to Broadmoor or some other place like it. The thought scares the hell out of me. I don't really think they could get away with doing anything like that, though.

Anyway, Grendon should do me a lot of good; I really need the group therapy because I've been in prison so long I'm losing my ability to converse properly! (You don't believe that?). It's true. Keep smiling. Take care of yourself Fiona

Love Alex.

Alex was desperate for a transfer to Grendon but wasn't averse to disobeying orders. This led to another spell in solitary. I had not been in touch for a while because I was busy renovating our new home.

HM Prison Parkhurst
14/15. 12. 1978

Hello Fiona,

Currently I'm down the Block – nothing serious, I hasten to add. What happened was they wanted to move me onto another wing and I was against it, because I'm happy on B-Wing. I've only been on B-Wing three months and it's taken me that long to get settled down. A move now would mean starting all over again … So I barricaded myself in my cell. I've just been in front of the governor and he's given me three days down here – but I've won to the extent that I'm being allowed to return to B-Wing when my three days are up.

Well, lass, please take care of yourself, Princess.

All My Love, Your Friend and Brother

Alex.

The punishment 'down the block' was effectively solitary confinement for 24 hours a day with one half hour exception. Alex would have to remove his metal bedstead at seven o'clock in the morning, only to drag it back in at lights out. There were no privileges. However, he would be back on B-Wing in time for Christmas but received the shattering news that he would not be transferring to Grendon.

- 6 -
A New Transition

HM Prison Parkhurst

1. 1. 1980

My Very Dear Friend

Hello, Fiona! I hope you're okay and had a fantastic Christmas this year and didn't put on too much weight after the mince pies and festive spirits.

Listen, I've got to be admitted to the local mortuary soon for observation. Nothing serious … In fact it's too bloody silly for words – apparently my molecular structure needs recomposing and my embalming fluid's wearing off. No see-through turkey slices this time, only a bit of hen, things are getting hard these days. Outside, too. Soon you'll be paying £1.25 to keep Kermit in drinks and 20p for a Mars bar.

My mother is re-marrying this year (rather, 1980), but I don't know anything about the fellow concerned, what with being in here – but if he treats her alright it's OK with me. I still wish she would've gone back to my father, though, because I know he still loves her very much and is very unhappy without her – even after six years of separation. Still, I guess it's a reflection of the times we live in, sadness seems to be an ever-increasing norm to more and more people, and the dream of a happier existence for the future recedes further away. It's a great pity.

Have you heard Pink Floyd's No1? I think it's fantastic, we're all going round singing it and sitting in corners and humming it; all in all it's just another brick in the wall.

I've just been up at the window-grill looking at the night and I managed to get my nose past one of the bars – have you ever realised, Princess, that clean air smells funny? Well, I think it does, anyway. Sort of clean, you know, almost knocks you out.

I had a letter from the Probation Office in Oxford just before Christmas and it seems they're quite willing to help me get fixed up there when I get out. So that's part of the load off my mind. Also I've got in touch with an organization called 'Justice' to find out whether they will approach the Home Office on my behalf. They are a very professional group of people, who, if they take up a case, refuse to let go. And I've heard my case was discussed at a large National Council for Civil Liberties meeting in London last month – so maybe something will be finally picking up steam at last.

Take good care of yourself, Carrot, and stay happy always.

All My Love, Your Friend and Brother

Alex

Alex was depressed about his impending move to another prison. He wanted to get out of Parkhurst, but not to go to Gartree, which was another maximum-security prison, located in Leicestershire. He felt betrayed by the authorities and bewildered as to the reasons why.

'I was told I was not going to a Category B prison after all but making a sideways move to another dispersal gaol. When I asked why I was being moved to another top security prison, no-one could come up with an answer. Gartree had just had a riot, but I was assured it was a less restrictive nick with a relatively open programme of activities. I was told I'd probably be moving within a month or so but true to form they wouldn't tell me exactly when. I kept packing and unpacking my cardboard box and people were coming to say "Goodbye" to me every day.

They all brought gifts. Joe gave me a kettle (kettle on the hob, hob fob, fob watch, yeah?). Clive Duck and Dive came round with a Grundig radio and Crazy Horse gave me a flick knife. Shit, I thought, "What do I want this for?" I gave it to a mate and asked him to get rid. If the screws had searched me and found the knife, I'd have lost something like five years and been put back on Category-A.'

Trelawney Lodge
Isle of Wight
3rd January 1980

Dear Miss Fullerton,

When I visited Alex in Parkhurst last, which was just before Christmas, he asked me if I would send you a photograph of himself, which he had in his pocket. As this was forbidden and we both knew it, I refused after some thought, but told him the least I could do was to write to you.

I forgot to ask him if you were aware of my existence – my name is Gillian and I'm one of several Voluntary Associates, private individuals attached to Newport Probation Office here on the island, who visit and write to prisoners with the approval of the authorities.

I've visited Alex for over two years and we've got to know each other pretty well under the circumstances and we often speak of you and your career and that of your husband. Your letters and news and photos mean a lot to Alex and it's splendid of you to keep in touch with him in this way, he gets very low at times – who wouldn't – and is really unfortunate in having a life sentence for his particular crime. One hopes so much that he manages to keep on an even keel and reasonably cheerful while waiting seemingly endlessly for a review of his case or at least a similar hope of a sight to the end of his sentence.

As you've probably realised his politics and beliefs are bright red and this hasn't exactly endeared him to the powers that be; he regularly receives publications from Russia and wrote articles about the Soviet, which probably got no further than the prison censor!

Believe me he's very grateful indeed for your interest; I know it helps him and I hope you can find the time in your busy life to continue this contact.

With Best Wishes for the New Year.
Yours Sincerely

Gillian Crews (Mrs)

Mrs Crews was one of a special team of individuals who visited prisoners. Reading between the lines, she had formed a warm friendship with Alex and was concerned about his impending departure, and the disruption it would cause. Therefore the only constant thread she could see in his life, was me. I'm afraid the weight of that responsibility did not fully impact on me at the time, as I was pre-occupied with auditioning for a new musical.

HM Prison Parkhurst
21. 1. 1980

My Dearest Friend

Hi Fiona, I'm just writing to let you know that I'll probably be leaving Parkhurst on Wednesday 23rd en route to Gartree Prison somewhere in the Midlands. I'll be going to Wandsworth Prison first, maybe for two or three days, so I'll most likely be there on the Thursday and Friday 24th & 25th.

As Wandsworth is in London I thought perhaps you might like to come to see me there? I would be very happy for the chance of a proper talk with you and even just to see you would do me a world of good. I'm enclosing a gate pass, which is valid at Wandsworth and will get you in okay. If for any reason you're unable to make it, I'll understand, but will you try for me? I don't know anyone else in London that I particularly want to see; in fact you're the only real friend I have there. I just hope this letter gets to you in time and that you're able to follow it up. Please try.

Take care of yourself, Princess, and be happy. Give my regards to Simon, your Mum and Dad, and Sunday. All my love to you, and keep smiling!

Your Friend and Brother.

Alex

Unfortunately, I did not get the above letter until it was too late, as I was in Brussels at the time. However, it probably saved me from the awkward dilemma of whether or not I should visit Alex. He had not asked me directly before and I remember feeling that it might ruin our friendship. The next day he wrote again after discovering that he was to be sent to Wormwood Scrubs and not to Wandsworth.

HM Prison Parkhurst
22. 1. 1980

Dear Fiona

Another very brief letter for, at the moment, I'm afraid things are rather hectic, what with my leaving here tomorrow and everything. The main thing is that, since yesterday, another topsy-turvy move has been made in that I won't be staying at Wandsworth but The <u>Scrubs</u>. I think I'm in for yet another magical mystery tour some-how. So. That's where I'll be at – Wormwood Scrubs, anyway, so, again – if you can make it – it may be a good idea just to give them a ring to make certain I have arrived.

If I don't see you, I shall most likely be writing again from Gartree Prison soon after I get there, okay? Keep smiling, Carrot, I'm keeping out of trouble but it's one hell of a struggle at times to keep my temper, it's only my promise to you that really makes me think twice.

I hope everything's alright with you and that the rest of your family are well, and that you can make sense out of these often-jumbled letters of mine!

As Ever, All My Love

Alex

In his 'Prison Chronicles' Alex writes:

'I ought to have been feeling glad to leave Parkhurst behind but, strangely, I felt a sadness. I guess it was because I'd spent so long there that it had become a kind of second home and I was going to miss a lot of sound people.

For the first time I was being transferred as a normal prisoner, and not as an A-man. The prison bus left the island with half a dozen convicts aboard, plus five screws and a driver. I was cuffed-up to a guy from Watford doing a ten stretch for a series of burglaries, or so he said.

As the bus pulled in to Leatherhead Police Station for a refreshment break, the bloke I was cuffed to gave me a nudge with his elbow; when I looked down, I saw that his hand was free — he'd slipped the handcuffs. I spat on my wrist and tried to slip them but couldn't get past the wrist bone. The principal officer was checking handcuffs before letting anyone off so my travelling companion pushed his hand back into the handcuffs. If he hadn't, we would have been well and truly nicked and I would have been put back on the A list.

When I got to Wormwood Scrubs, I was told I'd be "lodging" there for a week. It was virtually a 23-hour bang up every day.'

London
30th January 1980 (Sent to Gartree Prison)

Dear Alex,

I've just returned from an eight-day trip to a film festival in Brussels with Simon and found your two short notes. As a result I was unable to do anything about contacting you here in London, and couldn't see you in the Scrubs; I'm so sorry, but hope this finds you okay in Gartree. Two nights in the Scrubs and then off to a place you don't know? I'll have to find out where it is. What is the move for? Did you request it? I'm worried about you.

Well Alex, I've been offered a leading role in a new English musical called 'Barnardo'. I'm so excited! I play Syrie, who in 1870(ish) met Dr. Barnardo and started helping out as governess and nanny in his orphan-age. Eventually they marry and have children. It's an enchanting story with catchy music, lovable kids and gorgeous costumes. I'm very excited about it because, as you know, I've always wanted to sing more. However, this is basically an actress's role as it's very dramatic but I do have two very good songs. One is a ballad and the other is zippy and huge! Today I had my first costume fitting and we start rehearsals in March. It will be at the Royalty Theatre, London and everyone is hoping for a long run, but that depends on how successful we are. So there is a lot of dashing about doing photos, meetings and PR. It's the way I like to be.

Mum and Dad are busy in their new home in Winchester. Did I tell you my father is now a Brigadier? I'm so proud of him – he's so clever. I'm always slightly intimidated by his cleverness, in case he thinks I'm silly. But he's proud of me too.

It's a lovely day today but my garden looks awfully bare and boring. Keep that temper in check, darling Alex, and I'll write soon.

Fondest Love,

Carrot

HM Prison Gartree
Leicestershire
31. 1. 1980

My Dearest Fiona

Well, I'm in my new prison. I don't know what it's going to be like. I guess I've got too old to start again in a top security place, everyone in Parkhurst said I would be going to a semi-open prison where I could work towards getting released, but I should have known better than believe that. Now I end up here. What I can't understand is that I really did keep out of trouble, so I don't know where I went wrong. I've only been here 2 hours and I can sense something strange – as though I'd like to chop down a tree but can't do it because I'm certain it will fall on my head. I don't know anybody here and I would rather do without getting in with the mainline cons again – so I'm going to try to keep myself to myself, which may be disastrous – a loner is classed as unsociable by both sides.

I really don't know what to do. But one sure thing is that I'm not going to get depressed over this, it's one of those things in life you have to accept, and to survive it may make me a better person when it's over.

My time at The Scrubs was pure hell, it's a terrible place and I was praying each day for a visit from you – although I do accept your decision not to come as the correct one. Perhaps, in fact I'm sure, my asking you to visit was in many ways unfair – considering your career – it could have had an adverse effect if you were recognised visiting a penal institution. People might have got the wrong idea, connecting you with the underground. So, as I said in my letter from Parkhurst, I do understand perfectly your reticence. On top of that you have many commitments, which probably you had to deal with. I fully understand.

I would have loved an opportunity for us to learn new things about each other and the chance to have a serious chat, without the spectre of censorship determining what we must say in correspondence, which, in effect, leaves the most important things left unsaid. For it is still a fact that you are the only person I have grown to respect and trust without hesitation.

Please write again soon, Princess, for I value your friendship more than anything else.

I will write again when I hear from you – could you forward an alternative address where I can reach you more effectively? I will treat it in strictest confidence. Please take care of yourself, Carrot, and give my regards to Simon and your family.

As always, all my love to you.

Your Friend, Alex Xx

Receiving this made me feel terrible as I realised our letters, once again, had crossed in the post, but luckily he *had* received my letter on February 1st.

HM Prison Gartree
8. 2. 1980

Dearest Fiona

The relief of hearing from you is enormous – better than anything! I received your letter on the day after arriving here and it was like having a friend with me. Very difficult to express what I mean. You always did turn up at times of crises to calm things down for me, and it's something I shall forever wonder at. How on earth did you find out where I was so quickly!!?

Even I didn't know the address of this place until I actually got here. Are my letters getting to you alright through [your agent's office in the] Kings Road? And thank you too, for the birthday card; it was great of you to remember (I, myself, had forgotten, therefore your card came as an added surprise). You're the only person I got a card from this year, Princess, though I expect my parents sent a couple to Parkhurst, so they would have to be re-routed.

I'm extremely glad for you over 'Barnardo', it sounds as though it was specifically written for you – it must surely be a tremendous success because I know you will enjoy playing the part and making it radiate with feeling.

Also, it was fantastic to hear of Simon winning the award for being the most promising newcomer! And, from what I hear, it was Carrot who stole the night completely. Naturally, naturally. All the critics seem to agree over <u>one</u> thing, at least – that you both will be in great demand for the 1980s, I'm very proud indeed. I've always known you've got what it takes. Always follow your heart.

I've started to do my press-ups again and my daily task is to do a hundred, when I find it comfortable to do that, I'll move the task to 150 and so on. One of the troubles, though, is that I'm back on a sedative again. I take it at 7.30 pm and by 8.30 I'm crashed out until the next morning, so exercise in the evenings is out. Also here we're locked in our cells at 8 pm – except for three days a week when the time is 8.30 pm, which is in contrast to 9 pm at Parkhurst. I'm finding it very difficult to settle down here, there's one or two guys I know from Parkhurst but they aren't the kind of people I should have too much to do with at this stage in my sentence.

I do feel very badly let down by Parkhurst who told me I'd leave there to go <u>out</u> of the top-security system, to somewhere like Maidstone, Kingston or Lewes, and instead I get moved to this place. Fiona, there is absolutely nothing wrong with me that might pose a threat to society; God knows what the Tories see in me. I think they are frightened of what I might write. Not without good cause.

My best pal in Parkhurst, Steve B, went on a week's home leave last month. It would be the first time he'd be with his wife and child for more than two years. He came back and we all made fun of him because he was covered in love bites all over his neck, he tried to say he'd had a bit of trouble shaving.

He brought me back a stick of rock (honest!), two cigars and this awful pen – which also has one of those stamped motifs on the side which reads; '4th Gosport (Sextons Own) Cub Scout Pack'. Weird.

Another guy who went on home leave, one of the 'gangsters', came back and we found out he'd been mugged by two girl guides in Putney. I don't know what the world's coming to. I think he put a contract out on Brown Owl.

One of the first things I must do is write to my friend Gillian on the Isle of Wight to thank her for visiting me over the past couple of years. We had some fascinating discussions, and I don't want her to think I've forgotten her already! She, together with the Welfare Dept. at the prison, did a hell of a lot to bring my case to the attention of the powers-that-be, and I know they share my disillusionment at this move to Gartree.

The cells here are much smaller than at Parkhurst, too. Two and a half paces across and three paces lengthwise. As though to compensate, the windows are larger, and one can see through them. All I can see is the security fence and the 25ft wall and a load of barbed wire. In between there's a bit of grass with a sapling in the centre, at present devoid of foliage, and the grass is a bit green, like your eyes, where sparrows, starlings and pigeons pick up breadcrumbs we have thrown down. The food's a bit better here, also, and my pay is 20p over what I was getting on the island. The water tastes like antiseptic mouthwash; I hope they aren't producing bromide in varying flavours.

I've just finished reading Orwell's 'Animal Farm' and was a little disappointed, as it didn't make much of an impression on me; I guess it's really a book to read for the children. Have you read anything good recently, Fiona? Something you can recommend? As it stands I'm just about to begin Tolkien's 'Lord of the Rings' again – I think I went through it much too quickly the last time, so I'm going to go slowly. I keep glancing up at your picture. All the submarines have been launched. I think you're fantastic.

Dearest Carrot — Thanks a million times. Your letter was great for me and I'm very happy things are going well for you, kid; and the birthday card was lovely. 'Sunday' looks a tremendous bundle of fun, doesn't he? Keep yourself happy, Princess, and always be as you are. You'll always mean the world to me.

Take care of yourself. Give my best regards to your Mum and Dad, and to Simon – and all of my love to you.

As Always,

Your Friend and Brother.

Alex

On the 2nd March Simon and I flew to Los Angeles so that he could attend meetings and auditions for new television projects. This is always a busy time in LA as they cast all the up and coming series in March. It is known as 'Pilot Season'. Meanwhile, I sat around getting extremely bored, so I started writing little stories and even some poetry. I didn't feel confident enough to show any of it to Alex.

HM Prison Gartree

3. 3. 1980

My Dearest Fiona

Hi! Guess what's happened. Remember a couple of years ago when I was doing that writing on the backs of postage-stamps? I think I sent you an example? Well, the most extraordinary thing has happened —

I've just been reading Tolkien's 'Lord of the Rings' and I was so impressed with the songs and poems that I thought I'd write them out on stamps. It crossed my mind that if the elves and hobbits actually existed, then the size of their handwriting and writing-paper would be approximately equal to what I've been doing on stamps. I wrote to the Burnbake Trust, enclosing an example, and said I was thinking of writing out Tolkien's songs and poems – what would be the feasibility of having the work exhibited? Back came a reply that they would mount the exhibition for me, etc…! I'll enclose their letter so you can see. I just wanted you to be the first to know.

Keep smiling! Stay happy! I'll write properly soon, it looks like I'm going to be busy for a change. Write when you can. Best regards to Simon and your parents!

All my love to you, Carrot – take care of yourself,

As Ever, Your Friend and Brother

Alex.

PS This will be my first exhibition!
PPS I'm dedicating it to you.
PPPS Things are beginning to work out now. Apologies for the handwriting.

'Gartree is a modern gaol, in the sense that its buildings are redbrick and of a 1960s design. The cells are all single ones but have no integral sanitation facilities. The old Victorian system of "slopping out" applies.

I went to work in the light textiles shop using different types of sewing machines. On the wings there were cooking facilities where we could fry up a pan of hash or a few eggs. These items had to be bought out of our wages, which were around three quid a week.

One evening, I was in the TV room when one of the cons, Heavy Metal, came in with a chip pan full of boiling fat. He poured it over the head of the guy sitting in front of me, who let out a high-pitched, almost silent, scream as he clawed at his face and hair. He went to hospital. Heavy Metal was given an extra five years.'

London
12th March 1980

Dear Alex,

I'm thrilled about the news on your stamps. I agree that your handwriting should be exhibited for all to wonder at.

Thank you for your letters and poems, my friend. I understand how disappointed you are at being sent to Gartree, but maybe it is only for a short while. How are you settling down now? Have you made a few friends? New places always take time to get used to – we all find that.

I've just returned from ten days in Los Angeles with Simon, only I've left him there because he's doing a play for two weeks and I'm about to start rehearsals. The trip was awful because we were staying in a friend's flat, which is always difficult, and I didn't have a car so couldn't get around (LA doesn't have public transport) and was stuck in the flat. I hardly saw Simon and felt very neglected. He never gives me his full attention any-more because he's preoccupied all the time.

I'm very depressed now as I miss him so much and there's no reason why he has to do these showcase plays in Los Angeles, he's just as success-ful here. I can't sleep – maybe I should try your sedatives.

My daffodils and tulips are leaping up in the garden and should be opening very soon. It'll be nice to have some colour at last. The blossom is nearly out too. England is so pretty in the spring.

I hated 'Animal Farm' too. One of my favourite light authors is Gerald Durrell. I read this book ('My Family and Other Animals') on the way out to LA and it made the journey go very fast. I hope you like it.

As for Lady Jane I think that may be a dream that will probably never materialise.

Please take care of yourself. (Hope I get the heating fixed in here—it's freezing!!)

Fondest Love,

Fiona

PS Hope you like the enclosed. Same old face!

HM Prison Gartree
17. 3. 1980

Dearest Fiona

Just received your letter this morning. The book I'll get into tonight. The photograph is fantastic – I have it in front of me now, and you're as lovely as ever. Same old face, hey? I'll tell you something, friends may come and go but I wouldn't swap you for a million of them. I'm your friend, and <u>proud</u> to be so.

Why are you depressed, Nomad? Simon loves you, and he naturally wants your future to be secure – and more often than not a secure future can only be brought about by hard work. Does this figure out to you?

I once used to drink a hot cup of tea before going to sleep at night and I <u>had</u> to have a book to read. Often I became so absorbed in what I was reading that, when I turned to the cup, the tea inside was stone cold. Surely, he must know you're unhappy about him being out there? So he'll probably get home at the earliest opportunity. I would if I were in his place.

Fiona – don't worry, everything will work out for you, you'll see. Don't touch sedatives whatever you do! Sure they'll get you to sleep – but you'll get hooked if you use them for more than 3 days and they won't do your body any good.

I got a letter from Rose at the Burnbake Trust the other day re. the stamps. I sent the first batch off last week and we're trying to come up with the most practical way of exhibiting them. The best idea, a butterfly case, has come from Rose, so far. She's going to see Lady Casson on Thursday – who is one of the Koëstler's organizers and might be able to suggest something constructive.

Alex mentions the Burnbake Trust, which, like the Koestler Trust, helps prisoners and ex-prisoners keep out of the penal system by introducing them to the arts. The support he received from them was tremendous and also meant that his extraordinary handwriting would reach a wider audience. His poetry, and later his paintings, were all exhibited to the public.

I've already had my work described by BBC Radio Leicester as 'unbelievable'! Rose is a mass of helpful advice for other schemes, such as paintings on ivory, fine jewellery, etc. At least now I'm confident that if I get out I'll be able to do some form of specialised work, over and above writing, for a living. It's nice to know. I've gone off politics completely, now; but I'm gonna revolutionise <u>something</u> if it kills me! I'm freezing, too. Wish you were here. Could do with a little help getting the windows fixed.

I'm not in the right frame of mind these days to look at the better side of life. I've got used to the routine here, but I can't say I've settled down. This is just another People Container; just another brick in the wall, there's no incentive to do anything. The breaks come with hearing from you and, to a lesser degree, the Burnbake Trust. Other than that I'm still dead, don't know how long this will last.

I have my first big case review coming up in August by the Parole Board, if they recommend to the Home Secretary that I be released, and if the HS endorses their recommendation, I could be out within 18 months. Conversely, if the Parole Board <u>doesn't</u> give me a favourable review, I'll have to wait another 2 years for my <u>next</u> case review ...

Look at the situation at Parkhurst. For six years I got to know everybody there. Last year, <u>all</u> departments; governor, welfare and Church, told the Home Office I should be moved from the Dispersal system to a prison where I could work towards release. Then an almost unknown thing happened! The Home Office refused to accept Parkhurst's recommendation! The HO dismissed six years careful evaluation out of hand. I was sent to another dispersal prison – Gartree. The reason is obvious.

Don't get me wrong, Fiona – I'm not complaining. I've been hurt so much I just don't hurt any more. I'm not bitter or anything. But my purpose is to stop other people being hurt, and to this I'll give all that I have.

Fiona, my dear Friend, forgive me, if you can, for bringing such things into my letter. All I know is the world is a really terrible place – and all I want is to make it less terrible. There has to be some answer, some idea, to grasp – is that really <u>politics</u>…? Do you ever look from your window and, upon sighting a rainbow, feel a wish to race to where it begins or ends?

Do you not search for something indefinable? Maybe I'm a fool. Then again, 'all that glistens is not gold, all who wander are not lost.' Ah, well, what will be, will be.

My thoughts are always with you, Princess, and I want you always to be happy. Look after yourself, okay? Sure I'll be good. For you, the world.

As Ever, Your Friend and Brother

All My Love

Alex

Alex's frustration with the stagnant nature of his sentence and the refusal of the Home Office to listen to the various recommendations from Parkhurst, was leading to an uncertainty about whether to continue our correspondence, as he wrote in his 'Prison Chronicles':

'I was still writing to F, although my letters were becoming increasingly emotional and I was beginning to feel a hopelessness about the lack of movement around my case. My letters couldn't have made easy reading and I began to think of a way to stop the correspondence with her. She deserved better from me. Letters were not supposed to put the reader on a downer, but I knew that's what mine were doing. At that time I believed I'd never get out of prison, ever.'

London
16th April 1980

Darling Alex,

A million thank-yous for the lovely Easter card. I was thinking of you and wondering if you were sharing this glorious sunshine. I was in Cambridge for Easter with my in-laws, who treat me a bit like a daughter.

Simon is still away in LA for another three weeks – and I miss him desperately. I'm in rehearsals now and prone to a little innocent flirtation, but sometimes men misconstrue the situation. Some (arrogant) men seem to think I want something else (Ho-ho … they should be so lucky!). But, I'm just lonely.

D'you know my friend, I open my heart and innermost thoughts more to you than to any other person I know. One day I will tell you everything.

Maybe when I'm gone, you will write a book about me. I have had a very full and complex life but I'm a very moody person and I loathe my moods sometimes. I want to sparkle all the time, but can't. I'd love to be enigmatic. Mysterious. But I'm too open and honest for that. I tend to say what I'm thinking and in this business that often isn't a good thing. Ah well. Being an only child is complicated! I wish I had a brother.

Oh Alex, Alex, I do adore you.

Will write more soon. Be good and take care.

Fondest love – FF xxxxx

HM Prison Gartree
21. 4. 1980

My Very Dearest Friend

Countless thanks for your beautiful letter. I've been reading it over and over, and this is how it'll be for days before I put it away.

I don't like arrogant people, either. Christ, did I sound arrogant in my last letter? If I did, I'm <u>appalled</u>!!. I really am sorry, Fiona. <u>Really</u> – I guess I've been reading too many books … anyway, I <u>told</u> you I was stupid. Damn.

The most important thing to me, the <u>most</u> important thing, is for me to know that you're happy. When I know that you're not, it's as though the stars have gone out and I want to do something to light them up again. But how to do this? All I have is a pen and some paper. I can't telephone through or come down for a chat … it's really very frustrating, to say the least. So all I can do is create things with words – and there are certain things about the written word that can be easily misinterpreted. Often, after signing my letters I'll read through them and there may be a paragraph that does not 'sound' as I intended it to; but rather than delete the offending words (which I hate to do – it makes the whole thing look so untidy) I let it go and hope for the best. <u>Not</u> the proper thing to do. You see, I can't just reach for another sheet of paper and begin again because we can only use the stationery we're issued with – and this is strictly regulated.

I know all too well what it is to be lonely, Carrot – look at <u>me</u>, hey? – every minute, every hour, day, week, month, every year for almost a decade now (a long, long, time) I've been lonely. My life and everything I care for are way beyond my reach, outside the prison walls; I can't see them and they can't see me. For a decade … wow, that is <u>some</u> loneliness! But, you see, whilst most people have forgotten my existence, there's one person who hasn't. To me you're a sister – and this is how I'll always regard you; as a sister, Princess, never doubt me in this. I don't deal in dishonour. So you <u>do</u> have a brother, and a very devoted one at that, I can tell you. For I'll stand by you and fight for you, <u>exactly</u> as a brother would.

Whenever I get word from you, look what happens; all of a sudden I'm not lonely at all, you're still there, and as I read your letter time ceases to be so oppressive and, instead, becomes irrelevant.

If you can make <u>me</u> happy in such a way, then I have this vague hope that it might work the other way around too; that my letters can give you some kind of strength in return. I dearly hope so. For, being in here, I've nothing else to give, and this is terrible.

Do you know when it was I last actually spoke to a girl? I'll tell you – 1971. 1971! Can you imagine that? Damn prison! I often wish I'd been shot or hung on a lamp-post; Infinitely preferable to this slow mindless death.

Sometimes – correction, most of the time – I think I will never get out of here, and this leads to a certain anxiety, which I try to fight so that it won't develop into depression. Every so often, though, depression wins and at such moments I feel really hopeless and panic-stricken. I want to get out of my cell, go for a walk – anything – but I cannot. I can't even sleep. My one question is; 'Why are they keeping me in prison for so long??' Lifers who are in for murder are usually in a pre-release prison by nine years and here am I, in for GBH (a fit-up, at that), and <u>still</u> in a top-security prison. It doesn't make any sense.

The moods you speak of, it makes my heart ache to hear of them, but nonetheless they're a part of that process our parents describe as 'growing-up' (I get them, too), the trick is to overcome them.

When you start feeling blue, say to yourself 'OK you creeps, you wanna make me feel down? Well, here's a surprise – I'm not going to let you. Not this time.' Fiona, they're just a bunch of cowards, good for nothing. But you have to keep a sense of humour.

Gerald Durrell <u>was</u> a laugh, I really enjoyed the book. I'd <u>love</u> to write an auto-biography of you. How about beginning it yourself, in case I don't make it? All you need is a portable tape-recorder and a supply of blank cassettes.

This is your journal in which you record everything of personal significance – then have a secretary type the tapes onto foolscap and – there's your manuscript!

Rose has just managed to put someone's exhibition on at the Haymarket Theatre in Leicester; paintings, I think, hung in the foyer. I've asked her to try to have mine exhibited at the Theatre Royal for 'Barnardo' – it's the first book of Tolkien's songs and poems and consists of about 50 postage stamps. Of course, it will be up to the Royal's manager whether the exhibition goes ahead or not; Rose says she wrote to him a fortnight ago, so we're waiting to hear the decision. If he does agree would <u>you</u> want it to go ahead? – I ask because it's dedicated to you.

No, I'm afraid I didn't catch much of the sunshine – we only get ½ hour's open-air exercise here each day. Anyway, now I got to go. I adore you too – one hell of a lot! The tree outside my window has its new coat of green – Spring's here, Carrot! Winter's over at last.

Your Friend and Brother, as ever

Alex, Xx

For me to complain of loneliness to a man in a prison cell was probably a bit rich but Alex responded with his usual grace. I was being selfish and not a little panicky about 'Barnardo', a show that was beginning to resemble *The Titanic* — very cumbersome, too many people and sinking fast. But my costumes were nice.

HM Prison Gartree

7. 5. 1980

My Very Dear Friend

Just a few lines. Of course, true to form, I got the name of the theatre totally wrong in my last letter (!) It's the Royalty Theatre, isn't it, not the Theatre Royal. Luckily, I realised my mistake the day after I wrote the letter and managed to let Rose know in time, so she has now written to the Royalty manager. Yet she also wrote to the Theatre Royal manager and he said if they ever gave a Barnardo-type performance he'd be happy to show the stamps!!

I'm sorry,— I've been feeling like a crushed Weetabix recently, all over the place. I wish I could do something about my memory. I'm beginning to get a complex about it.

Is there any possibility of you coming up for a visit sometime, Fiona? When 'Barnardo' is finished? I don't know. I'd like to see you some time, you know, when it's convenient and when you're not so busy. That would be great. Make a change from being psychoanalysed by this crummy environment.

Just had my hair cut. It looks very horrible; the guy who did it must have something against me because I know plenty of people who could have done a better job with a Flymow.

Listen, Fiona – are you serious about my writing a book on you? I mean, <u>really</u>? I'd <u>love</u> to do that, you know.

As Always, Your Friend and Brother,

Alex

Rehearsals for the new musical, 'Barnardo', had not been going smoothly so I was unable to write to Alex for a while and completely overlooked his suggestion of a visit. (Quite unwittingly, which must have hurt him). The show was a rather crass attempt to emulate the success of 'Oliver' and 'Annie' so we had dirty Victorian streets and lots of cute singing orphans, which understandably upset Barnardo's the charity. The Royalty Theatre was a rather ugly building, on a side street just off Kingsway, so it wasn't strictly 'West End' as far as the purists were concerned and my dressing-room was a horrible little hole. Really tiny. The Palladium it most definitely was not. This was my first major London musical so I desperately wanted it to work. We opened on May 22nd to the most resoundingly awful reviews.

Alex's exhibition of Tolkien poems, written in miniature handwriting on the back of standard size postage stamps, was hanging in the Circle Bar of the theatre. I should have told him how wonderful they looked, but didn't have time to put pen to paper.

HM Prison Gartree
30. 5.1980

To My Very Dearest Friend

Hello, Princess – hope you don't mind – just a few lines, tracks of time. How are you? I sincerely hope things are much better for you now that 'Barnardo' is under way and that you're finding great satisfaction working with the cast.

I think I have some of my stamps displayed in the building somewhere – have you seen them? Please let me know what you think of them, my friend, for they were done only for the purpose of showing you that I am capable of something. What you think is very important. The exhibition itself is so tiny that I doubt if many will even notice it; ideally, I'd like it to be a component part of some larger exhibition, perhaps in a library somewhere, but I'll have to wait and see.

I am getting a visit from my mother on Saturday. This will be the first time I'll have seen her since my visit to Manchester in 1978 – over two years ago – so I guess there will be a lot to talk about. She is bringing with her a man who looks like becoming my stepfather in the near future. His name is Arthur. She has mentioned him quite a lot in her last few letters   now I'll be able to put a face to the name. As long as he makes her happy, that's the most important thing, isn't it?

Best wishes to Simon and your family, not forgetting little Sunday.
Always Your Devoted Friend, All my love

Alex

London
12th June 1980

Dearest Alex,

Many, many apologies for the long gap in letters, but the show has been consuming all of my time. Your last three letters are all treasures and give me no end of joy. Thank you for all your wonderful words of wisdom, and your patience too.

Yes, your stamps with the Tolkien poems are proudly displayed in the Circle Bar at the Royalty Theatre!! They have been beautifully mounted, along with a letter from the Burnbake Trust and a typed dedication, all in one frame. You should be very proud. I was really moved when I saw it Alex. It is exquisite, the work you have done.

They have fixed up a magnifying glass too, so that people can have a closer look and Mr Mossellson has received many compliments on the display (He's the owner of the theatre). Simon has taken a colour photo of it, which we will send to you as soon as poss.

How was your mother when you saw her? Two years is a long time. I'll bet she was overcome at seeing you again – it must be very difficult. I have thought a great deal about visiting you Alex, but can't decide whether it's a good idea or not. Forgive me. Obviously it is out of the question while the show is running, but I'll have to think about it.

The show, by the way, has been a disaster. 'Barnardo' was roasted, panned, slated and killed by the critics. They hated it because it is blatant commercial entertainment. But what's wrong with that? We wanted to make a few people smile and the show has all the right ingredients. But as a result of the bad press our audiences are only 50% full and the management have gone bankrupt! We are now in the hands of the official receiver who is trying to run the show in order to pay off creditors. We think we have another three weeks to start making money or we come off. It's very sad because actually the audiences love the show. It is very spectacular and has a company of over 50 but morale is quite low now because suddenly we're all going to be out of a job.

I love doing the show, although it's hard work, and luckily the press were very kind to me but I suppose one has to experience a real flop in order to enjoy a real success.

Simon is very well and busy rehearsing Macbeth for the Ludlow Festival. He is playing Big M with Gayle Hunnicutt as Lady M. The role of course is mammoth and poor Simon is still trying to learn all the words but I'm sure he'll be very good in it. I do admire anyone who can get to grips with Shakespeare.

I'd like to spend some time in the country this summer. Maybe Cornwall or Dorset for two weeks. What do you think?

You misunderstood me when I was talking about arrogance in my last letter. I didn't mean to insinuate that you were arrogant. Christ, no. And you're not stupid either. You're one of the cleverest, wisest, wittiest (how do you spell that?) loveliest people I know. Honestly.

Mum and Dad popped into the theatre last night to see your exhibition and asked about you. They always do, as they know how fond of you I am. They send their regards.

I'll tell you a secret. There is a very handsome actor in the show. He is terribly in love with me. Isn't that sweet? He keeps buying me presents. I kinda like him too but he isn't a patch on Simon.

Got to go now. Will write soon.
Bye, bye Alex. Be good.
All My Fondest Love,

Fiona xxxxx

Experiencing a theatrical flop of that magnitude was a sobering experience. Audiences were flocking to the theatre just to see if it really was as bad as the critics said! I think they, the critics, had it in for Ernest Maxin who wrote, directed and scored the show, but with hindsight I realise the show was probably just too cheesy and cute to satisfy most critics. A lot of people lost a great deal of money on it and two weeks later we were all sent packing.

HM Prison Gartree
16. 6. 1980

My Very Dear Friend

Hello, Princess – just got your letter. Great to hear from you.

What's happened? Really – I thought everything was going really well with the show – certainly, as you say, the press has gone a bundle on you; I saw one or two articles with nothing but praise for you. Yet the management's gone bust? Well, one thing we know – it certainly isn't through any fault of yours.

Your handsome actor is in love with you? Oh, aye? Well, he isn't alone, by any means, sister … ! That's what you get for being so beautiful, you see. The poor sod. Oh, Fiona. Be nice to him, but don't let him fall too deep because he'll only make a fool of himself and in the long run it's not worth all the hassle – and you're right, perfectly, when you say he isn't a patch on Simon – and remember, only two people in love with each other can ever afford it to be known … and can ever be happy. Isn't that right? Oh, well, something like that.

That's great news about the stamps! First I've heard about them since the show hit the road. I'm very glad you liked them, you know, being the motivating force, so to speak, behind them (But I can't do anything more like that, because my eyes aren't so good anymore. As it stands I can't even go in the sunshine as my eyes can't take the glare – after five minutes there's one hell of a migraine).

I've just been throwing some bread down to the sparrows – they fly to within six inches from my hand, having got used to me by now. They're going to have a rough time of it tonight because it's been blowing a storm all day and that makes it harder for them to find food. There are quite a few pigeons about but no sea-gulls like at Parkhurst. I feel sorry for the sparrows because the crows, pigeons and starlings goose-step all over them and sometimes nick the grub that I've thrown. Aye, well, that's life.

Yes, my mam was very upset when I saw her and, sure, I forgot most of the things I'd intended to say. She brought 20 of my cigarettes and by the end of the 2 hours I'd smoked the lot (it's no use trying to give it up) – which perhaps sums up better than anything else how I was feeling. She said she would write to the Home Secretary to press for my release and also see our MP. She also brought along the chap who looks like being my stepfather – I found him a very quiet, unassuming bloke and I must admit I took a liking to him. We got on all right – his name's Arthur.

Don't worry about not being able to visit me here, Princess – I weighed up the pros and cons of it a long time ago and there are far too many cons. So why do I ask? You know, things happen and situations change, often I just want somebody not connected with this place to talk to. More often than not these are just moods and pass by fairly quickly, you understand.

At last I've got a probation officer <u>properly</u> assigned to me from Oxford – so I can now find out a bit more about where I'll be going to live.

That's a good idea of yours about getting into the countryside. A very good idea. Get out of the city, it'll do you a world of good! It's not very expensive, you know, and the food is always the best, the cider's cheap and there's thousands of things to see. When you get home you'll be a different person.

You're a Treasure, you know. I'm sorry about the state of my handwriting, I hope when I get my new specs I'll be back to normal, meanwhile you'll have to forgive me. I <u>hate</u> writing untidy letters! Well, Princess – give my finest regards to your Mum and Dad, Simon and, of course, Sunday. Write when you <u>can</u> – I know you're busy. And keep all the 'late runners' at arms length! Be happy!

<u>All My Love to You, Carrot.</u>

Your Friend and Brother, as Ever,

Alex

XXXXX

London
3rd July 1980

Dearest Alex,

How time flies. No sooner had I finished my last letter to you, than we were given notice that the show was to close in two weeks. We were all very sad but there was nothing we could do. In a way it was a relief as tension was spreading throughout the theatre. So we went out with a bang and had a big party on the last night. The sad thing is losing all those close friends one makes on a show. We became a very close unit and then suddenly it's all gone. However, I enjoyed most of it and learnt a lot from the experience.

Now, after only three weeks I start rehearsals for another musical! I'm playing Polly Peachum in 'The Beggar's Opera' at the Lyric Theatre, Hammersmith for a short four-week season. It's a sort of 17th century bawdy comedy about an opera being performed and I'm thrilled because I have loads of singing to do and it's a very classy production.

Thank you for your beautiful cards with the exquisite paintings inside. They are really gorgeous. Also thank you for our anniversary card. Four years! How kind of you to remember.

Isn't this rain appalling? Very boring. Everyone's moaning like mad. Simon has been working like a slave in the garden since his return from Ludlow. I let it get a bit jungly, I'm afraid! Lazy you see.

His stint as Macbeth was a great success and I enjoyed it immensely. It was performed in the castle, against the ramparts and was spectacular to look at. The surrounding Shropshire countryside is breathtakingly beautiful and was a welcome change after three disappointing months in London.

I nearly bought a spaniel puppy on the spur of the moment, but luckily saw the huge responsibility it would bring and decided to let it go to a home with a more regular lifestyle. He was beautiful though!

Must go now. Keep busy and keep writing.

Fondest love as ever and regards from Simon.

Lots of Love Fiona x

HM Prison Gartree
28. 7. 1980

My Very Dearest Friend and Sister!

Warmest Greetings! I hope you don't mind me writing while I'm stoned out of my mind? Explanation: just had my sleeping draught. Got your last fantastic letter in front of me and I shall now make an extra dynamic effort to answer it. Excuse, if you will, my terrible handwriting, but I can't help it – my pen's moving of it's own quite independent volition. Are you okay, Princess? Happy? Let me know if you come up against any pebbles on the beach.

I am really sorry that 'Barnardo' finished so soon, but I <u>know</u> you can easily take this in your stride and your new show at the Lyric just goes to show how highly you're held in the regard of the Theatre administration.

Listen, my parole review is next month and I'm a bit on edge about it. I'm hoping it will be favourable and as a result I'll be sent to a less restrictive prison where I can work out what I'm gonna do with the Future. Keep your fingers crossed for me, will you, and throw some salt over your shoulder? That's what it needs. A lot of luck.

Well, I'm enjoying the Olympics immensely – are you watching them on TV? Steve Ovett beat Sebastian Coe today in the 800 metres qualifier, but I am hoping that Coe will win the actual Final. The one thing that's certain, though, is that Britain will pull off a 1-2. Great.

I have this idea about reversing the crime rate: legalise cannabis and severely restrict the sale of alcohol. Ready for that? Can you imagine all the potential villains walking around Happy instead of being dead Drunk and in a foul mood? You know, the way it seems to me, something comes along that makes people happy and – wham! – there's a law against it!

That should keep me in another 10 years. What the hell. Listen – about writing your autobiography, were you on the level? If you still want something like that done, Princess, let me know – it would be <u>fantastic</u> to do; wouldn't it be fantastic?

Last night was great. Thunder, lightning – the works! I was at the window watching it happen, humming the '1812' – for four HOURS! The lightning never struck me once – so the Fates haven't anything against me (maybe I <u>will</u> get a favourable review …!) I'd love to stand on a hill on Dartmoor or the Dales during a storm like that. Oh boy!

It's getting really late now and the Chloral says crash out but I'm determined to keep writing for as long as I can. I feel as though I'm floating on air and if I stand up I wobble about, like a football-shaped brick, all over the place. The radio's blasting out the Rolling Stones, even though it's really turned down low. I hope I'm keeping to the lines on the paper because I'm getting double vision and things look a bit blurred.

Fiona – sorry about the state of my writing in this letter, at present I'm on a down-hill slope on the graph – hope I'll start going up again. I'll write again when I hit that upwards movement. Take best care of yourself, Princess, and stay as happy as possible! Best wishes to your Mum, Dad and Simon.

All My Love,

Your Friend and Brother.

Alex, X

Alex was finding it almost impossible to settle at Gartree and the tone of this letter is indicative of his darkening mood. The poems had stopped coming and he was now on heavy doses of medication to keep him calm. If he had known at this point that he would still have another 13 years to serve, he would surely have taken his own life. His strong sense of betrayal by the Prison Service at being sent to another top security gaol was compounded by his constant protestations of innocence. The trouble was, the longer he maintained his innocence, the longer the authorities would keep him inside. It is a well-known Catch-22 situation for an innocent life-sentenced prisoner, that if he does not acknowledge his guilt, he jeopardises his position in relation to eventual release. This is because he is unable to do the necessary courses, express remorse or 'address his offending' to use the official jargon.

Meanwhile, I was busy rehearsing 'The Beggar's Opera' and finding the vocal score a satisfying challenge. The director however, thought it was far more important to take us to the Hogarth Museum to study pictures of the period than to stage the musical numbers. Rehearsals were utterly shambolic.

Simon was becoming restless at home.

HM Prison Gartree
23. 8. 1980

Very Dear Friend

I hope you're okay and that all is well with you. I meant to write earlier but have been down the Block here since the 14th – 14 days solitary for smoking cannabis. First time I've been nicked since that rooftop thing at Parkhurst in March, last year.

Fiona – something important I'd like you to do. Those two Photostats I sent you early last year – the ones detailing my arrest and conviction – will you please send them to the following address:

CITIZENS COMMISSION ON HUMAN RIGHTS
SAINT HILL MANOR
EAST GRINSTEAD
SUSSEX.

It's very important. Thanks very much.

Things pretty dim at present, but when they change I'll write and let you know. Take good care, Princess! Stay happy and stay beautiful.

As Ever, Your Friend and Brother.

Alex XX

London
9th September 1980

My Dear Alex,

Why did you do that? I'm very disappointed. Fourteen days solitary when your parole review was due. What happened? Does this affect your record? Anyway, my dear friend, I'm sorry for the delay in replying but suffice to say that I was very worried for you.

'The Beggar's Opera' opened on August 27th and I got very tired during rehearsals, as I hadn't really recovered from 'Barnardo'. Simon was here for my opening night but the show had rather lukewarm reviews. Some of the critics were nice about me, others not so nice. The production is not as good as it could be.

Funnily enough I don't enjoy doing this show nearly as much as I enjoyed 'Barnardo'. I think it's the company atmosphere. There are bigger egos and older actors in this and as a result, more backstabbing and bitchiness. This is the side of showbiz I really hate. Is it really worth it? All I want is a quiet life with someone who loves me.

I retook some shots of your Tolkien stamp display as Simon botched up the last lot (They came out black). Will send them soon as poss.

Yes, I would love you to write a book about me, but not for a while. Over the next few years we can amass the necessary research material and I can record memories onto cassette and then Wham! One interesting point: both my father's parents came from an orphanage so I have no traceable family tree.

I have sent your Photostats to CCHR as requested. OK?

Fondest Love as Ever.

Now behave

Fiona x

During the run of 'The Beggar's Opera' I had become unwell with a virus and the antibiotics brought on another spate of depression. Simon and I started arguing about trivial things and I hated doing the show. It was the first time, I suppose, I realised that a thick skin and impenetrable self-belief was an absolute necessity in show business. My line to Alex, 'All I want is a quiet life with someone who loves me,' is very revealing.

HM Prison Gartree
15. 9. 1980

My Dear Friend

I'm writing this having just put down your letter. I wish I was getting out of here tomorrow; to begin with I could sort out that lot backstage … I hope you don't have much longer to do there, Carrot, really.

God I've been ill over the last couple of weeks, I still am – I don't know whether it's an ulcer (apparently they are characteristic of folk who worry a lot, so I should have a stomach full of them) but I'm having rather severe abdominal pains. Consequently I have to suck these enormous tablets the size of old pennies! They taste of Horlicks.

I'm sorry I haven't been able to write much of late, things haven't been too good and I hate writing letters to you when I know they'll only serve to make you worry. That's no good. I'm not the same as I used to be, years take their toll, you understand, but having you as a sister has slowed up that process very much. You know that.

Why did I get into trouble? Well, at the time I wasn't conscious of doing anything diabolical, all I did was smoke a bit of cannabis to get me out of the mood I was in. It made me forget and I had a good night's sleep. I know it leaves no harmful after-effects (unlike some of the 'acceptable' muck I've been prescribed over the years).

Fourteen days. No, it does not affect my record – from all I've heard it wouldn't surprise me if the magistrate lit up a joint in the car on the way home. Some countries have legalised cannabis, including parts of the USA, and it's only because Britain is so far behind the times that it isn't legal here – all it is is a superior type of tobacco, minus the nasty and harmful nicotine drug, with properties that stimulate rather than destroy the senses.

But okay. I promise I won't use it again in prison if you feel strongly about it. Perhaps, anyway, it's too stigmatised. Sorry. For worrying you. I didn't mean to.

You ask is it all worth it? It's only worth doing anything if it brings you pride in yourself. If, by what you do you were able to make people happy – even for a couple of hours – then I'd say that was worthwhile. And that is what you do. But if you're unhappy with the way of things, then give yourself a break. It's the little things that are important, simple things. I would relax and keep in step with my own drummer and sod the brass band that everyone else is galloping to.

In my case I think a quiet life would be essential if I get out … and that's a big contributing factor in my desire to get off the ground as a writer. So I can regulate my own pace and avoid the mesh of routine. Take things a little easier, Fiona – when you're finished with 'Beggar's Opera', give yourself a breather, you're not a machine.

Thanks for sending the Photostats off for me, the CCHR will hold them and make certain investigations … all I need now is an investigator to see the person I'm alleged to have hurt for the GBH charge, and one question will be enough to prove that I wasn't the person involved. One question on my physical description – ID. But first I need the investigator and I'm going to request that from the CCHR.

Rose Murray went to the Royalty Theatre because she needed the stamps for an exhibition at St. Paul's Cathedral(!) but couldn't get in, so that was an exhib. I missed – though, as consolation, some of my poems were there and quite a few people asked for them. Did I tell you I'm working with the Trust to get a volume of prison poems and verse together?

Well, Carrot, now I have to wind up to meet the postal deadline. Another weekend almost over, another day survived. Stay well and keep in high spirits, don't let other people's attitudes get at you!

All of My Love to You, as for Always

Alex XX

Alex continued to sabotage his review by aggravating the Home Office.

'One day at lunchtime, I was told to pick up a letter from the censor's office. I knew something was up. I was given a large brown paper envelope and inside was a brief letter saying that a booklet was enclosed, but there was no sign of it. I asked the censor where it was and he said I would have to make an application to the governor, as it had been stopped.

He held it up for me to see. It was "The Liquid Cosh". At last the Parkhurst League for Human Rights Observance reports had been published! The censor explained that it was "inflammatory literature" so I made a request to see the governor.

The next day the governor denied me possession of the booklet but gave me ten minutes to check it through. Not much of a concession but at least I'd be able to view the pages.

It was published by the Church of Scientology for the Citizens Commission on Human Rights (who investigate forms of abuse in prisons) and was very hard-hitting. It had been contributed to by a doctor and comprised a grave indictment against the system, describing how prisoners were often given experimental drugs and their effects analysed.

Much of the text was written by me and credited to me. There was my photograph also, so this was the first time that I had become "visible" to the Home Office. All previous LHRO reports, when sent to the media, asked for anonymity thus ensuring that whoever wrote the report would be protected from any possible repercussions. Now, the cat was well and truly out of the bag — as far as I was concerned.

Sure enough, a couple of weeks later, I was paid a visit by a Home Office official who warned me to wind up the LHRO or all of us would have our sentences extended. After lengthy discussions, I gave up my position as secretary and circulated a letter stating that, because of Home Office pressure, the LHRO was to be wound up.'

It closed down on 2nd February 1981. If the Home Office were worried about Alex before, they were REALLY worried about him now.

London
23rd Sept 1980

Dearest Alex,

I'm very sorry to hear you haven't been well. Hope it's not an ulcer 'cos they are really painful. Do they give you sufficient treatment when ill? I do hope so. Keep sucking the tablets and stop worrying. Hypertension won't help at all.

Also very, very sorry you missed the exhibition at St Paul's Cathedral. I feel awful. I will ring Rose and let her know how to get hold of the stamps.

This will be just a quickie 'cos I can't sleep and have been up for the last two hours reading some of your old letters. They really do cheer me up enormously. I just found your 'Carrot' poem – it's so funny and very clever indeed.

The milkman's just been, so excuse me a mo … Nothing like a good cup of tea. Mind you, this is a ghastly cup of tea, but never mind!

Simon was tossing and turning in bed last night and I had things racing around my brain so I decided to get up. That was 4 am. It's now 8 am. It's so quiet here … just the birds coughing!

Some cousins and other family came to the show last night so we had a bit of a celebration. 'Don't you sound like your mother' they said of my singing. I was flattered because my Mum (being Welsh) has a lovely soprano voice and would have turned professional if she hadn't married my father so young.

Unfortunately, one of the older actors in the show upset the lady with whom I'm sharing a dressing-room. She's a very grand, middle-aged actress who's been in the business 40 years and claims to know everybody. They're always annoying each other and I had to put up with all the bitchiness throughout the entire performance. I find listening to her more exhausting than doing the show. Non-stop gossip too.

We're into the last week now. Phew! I think I will take a breather, as you suggest, and recharge my batteries.

Wednesday 24th September

I've been pottering around the house all day doing all those house-wifey things, the radio is blaring out and I can get on with the hoovering. I'm a very tidy person – always have been – I suppose being brought up in the army and then boarding school drills it into you. I'm now sitting at the dining table in my blue tracksuit, with a freshly scrubbed face (all that stage greasepaint isn't doing it a lot of good) and Simon has just returned from the hairdresser. We go to the same guy in London and basically have the same cut(!) as mine is so short now.

It's funny how quickly things happen in the business. I said I was looking forward to a break, well, I've just been offered the lead role in a musical called 'The Biograph Girl' which starts rehearsing on Monday! It's about the early days of the movies with Mary Pickford and Lillian Gish carrying the story. However, having just read the script, I think I'm going to turn it down. I may regret it but something tells me this is not the right thing for me now.

Well, the afternoon is wearing on and I have to leave for the theatre at six, so I think I may take a nap now.

Be good for heaven's sake. Get well soon.

All My Fondest Love, Fiona x.

PS Did I tell you I have a rose-bush in my garden that is labelled 'Alex Red'? Appropriate, eh?

HM Prison Gartree
9. 10. 1980

My Dearest Fiona

Thanks for the letter and things, the photos were great – Simon looks fantastic and you, as ever, like a million roubles … I'll see if I can change it into a portrait on canvas, that's going to be one of my foremost ambitions, it's a job for a perfectionist, which I am in my work. And the book you sent was a classic touch, if I may say so [a biography of the Marx Brothers] – now I can tell you I'm reading Marx with an easy conscience, right?

The leaves are beginning to die on the little tree outside my window, another year will soon be over and then it'll be 1981. I hope it comes quickly and doesn't drag itself out like 1979. I'm very conscious about the seasons, you know, every time the weather changes I catch 'flu. Ha. I'm glad you're taking a breather when you close at the Lyric, Carrot, you'll feel all the better for it. Utilize the fresh air and green open spaces, if there are any in London, and watch the grass grow and the clouds move across the sky.

I've just come off the psychotropic tranquilliser Largactil, so it's possible the cold turkey process is inducing a reactionary effect to my system. But I'll get over it eventually.

I see Tony Benn's been spouting on about reincarnation on the National Health – or its equivalent in nationalistic terms, he does tend to get a little carried away. It's a pity Callaghan wasn't christened William – can you imagine Bill and Benn leading the Labour Party … !

What's this rose bush you mention? Is that <u>really</u> the name of it? You look after it then, and don't let the weeds get near; it won't like weeds, being a symbol of Freedom! Viva! Alex-Red … well, I never.

I'm trying to conjure up a picture of you in a blue tracksuit … I can just about manage it and the vision is very beautiful indeed – you're a wonderful person, Carrot, and the world that I know is a better place for it.

Now I must close, but will write more fully soon. I am okay at present, still pushing for a place at Grendon. Keep in good spirit and enjoy all the wonderful things around you. Above all, be happy! Until I write again.

All My Love, Your Friend and Brother

Alex, Xx

My career was going exactly as I wanted it to, with interest in me growing as a musical theatre performer. Having starred in three big West End shows, and having turned down 'The Biograph Girl' (which closed after 57 performances), I knew that my career lay here in London. Having chopped off all my hair, I was featuring in magazines a great deal and the press couldn't get enough of Simon and I, as the new golden couple of showbiz. However, the atmosphere at home was strained to bursting, with Simon behaving like a caged lion when the movie roles eluded him.

- 7 -
Rule 43

HM Prison Gartree
21. 10. 1980

My Dearest Fiona

Hello, Carrot. Hope you had a decent rave-up on your Birthday and that you're black-listing French apples in the national interest. Personally, I'm blacklisting green peppers because I can't stand the taste; it's bad because the cook keeps putting them in the soup, so I'm blacklisting that, too. It could get worse.

Do you wish, sometimes, that you had a crystal ball to look into, you know, to find out what the future's all about? Well, maybe I'd better stay in the present. *A dreamer lives for eternity.*

By the way, there's a very illuminating new documentary series beginning on BBC on Wednesday about – it should tell you more than I can in my letters about life inside. It's on every Wednesday (I think) though, of course, we won't get to see it in here.

I want to write, Fiona – and in here I just can't. It's impossible. I mean, like the bloke in the 'Elephant Man' – you know, 'I'm not an animal … I'm a man!' Well, sod it all. This is crazy. Spiritual genocide.

Thanks a million for the package you sent the other week, Carrot, that was very thoughtful of you, but in future I won't be able to receive things like soap and tooth-paste, etc., or glucose tablets because a recent ruling says that prisoners are not allowed such things to be sent in. Another brick in the wall. Books are okay though. Speaking of which I'm finding Groucho's letters immensely enjoyable, I'm reading the book a little at a time whenever I feel a bit low and it usually works okay. Viva!

Dear Fiona

I've come out of the Mainstream here and now I'm down the Block again on voluntary segregation (Rule 43). One of the guys was getting me wound-up. He knew he could get away with anything with me and I wouldn't retaliate because I'm under Review and can't afford trouble. Anyway this cardboard gangster was taking digs at me in front of other cons and, to be honest, I was about ready to go for him – but if I had it would have set me back maybe four years until my next Review. So the only other alternative was to disappear, something I intensely disliked doing as it'd mean going on 43 (that part of the prison which is segregated from the rest, to accommodate those prisoners who would be in danger from the main bulk of prisoners on the wings, such as child-killers, rapists, grasses, etc.).

Really, there was no choice at all – I couldn't go to the screws and tell them about this guy because that would be grassing – so now I'm down on 43. Can you imagine … so as far as I'm concerned, I've resigned. I'm staying down here until they give me a transfer to a non-dispersal nick where, incidentally, I should already be at this stage in my sentence. Also I'm going to get a lawyer to help with the ID problem, I've had enough. These places are sick and the people who send others here to be *contained,* like *turnips in a field,* must be sick, too. '1984', George Orwell – not as daft as people make out. So what's 43 like?

Oh … Fiona, not very good. It means 23 out of 24 hours each day spent locked in the cell, no TV, no hobbies and nothing much else. But as I'm not on punishment I can have my mattress and blankets during the day, radio and tobacco, pens and paper.

Also I get to see a newspaper every day. The weekly pay is only £1.60p and I can see that disappearing for the tobacco, somehow I can't give up smoking – though if I get out I certainly shall. All in all, I can only stick this situation out for a short while, but, whatever happens, I'm not going back onto any dispersal mainstream.

I must close for now but will write again when the clouds pass. Carrot – take good care of yourself. My finest regards to your Mum and Dad and to Simon, hello to Sunday.

All My Love, as Ever, Your Friend and Brother

Alex Xx

PS Keep the rose bush strong.

My poor Alex. He must have been experiencing very threatening behaviour for him to seek protection under Prison Rule 43. Being segregated from the rest of the prison is usually only sought by sex offenders, who are at the bottom of the prison hierarchy, police officers and so on, so he must have been in grave difficulty and feeling vulnerable to take this course of action. He had been inside for nine years by now but already he was displaying the charactcristics of a lifer who had been in for 15, such as increased introversion, less interest in social activities and a greater dependence on routine. David Wilson says in *The Longest Injustice*, 'Surely we can all sympathise with the cumulative impact of an indeterminate sentence, which must increase feelings of helplessness and powerlessness'. Alex had no idea when, if ever, he was coming out. Having chosen segregation, the boredom was intense and his mind started to play nasty tricks.

Simon and I were in Ireland. He was thrilled to have been cast in a lead role in a major American mini-series called 'The Manions of America'. I was tagging along for a restful break, after 'The Beggar's Opera' and my mystery virus had left me exhausted and under weight. The series starred an unknown Irish actor called Pierce Brosnan and Linda Purl, a sweet girl from the hit TV series 'Happy Days'.

HM Prison Gartree
31. 10. 1980

Dearest Fiona

Hello sister. I've never been drunk in my life but I would love to get drunk now, into a stupor to beat everything and go on for a thousand years. I'd drink vinegar if there was alcohol in it. The truth is I've never been so bored in my life, oh, wow, it's crazy just lying around trying to think of something but nothing ever comes … I can't even write a poem, not two lines. I'm beginning to wonder what the hell's happening – whether I'm mad or everybody's mad and I'm normal. Well, I got all the solitude I ever wanted – and now I've got it I'm just beginning to realize how dangerous it can become. It's self-alienation, I think and I can remember reading somebody's thesis on that subject a long time ago – maybe it was Marx or Faust – and it's supposed to lead to a kind of split personality, which doesn't do anybody any good, when you think about it. I've always told myself I have the spirit in me to survive anything, but I feel as though something is draining it slowly away and I'm trying to fight it and Christ, it's sure one hell of a struggle.

OK it's taken ten years to get me to this state and I'm proud of that. I think I've lasted longer than most and don't get me wrong, I'm not beaten yet, all the heavy artillery's held in reserve. The trouble with being a lifer, Fiona, is that everybody, every step of the way, is trying to psychoanalyse you, probe into you, find out what makes you tick and they're not interested in your good points – they dig out your bad points and weaknesses and catalogue all these to make you into some kind of Martian. And more often than not, you have more good points than any of them. Psychology is the intellectual's insurance policy.

Because I am a revolutionist the authorities take a very dim view of me, I'm afraid. That's why they're holding me in prison for so long, you can bet a million. But unfortunately the Home Office stereotype the word revolutionist along with 'extremist' or 'agitator' or 'subversive', 'anarchist', 'commie'… they see me as something I'm not, or they see me as they want to see me. But I want to stress again, for <u>your</u> benefit, my dear friend, that I am <u>not</u> a danger to anybody, that all I want to do when I get out is <u>write</u> and that I certainly won't be drawn into any kind of extremism. I will be concerned only with Truth and Freedom – and that, really, cannot be such a bad thing. Except to those who fear such things.

Did you ever get a gnome for the bottom of your garden, Carrot? They say that on one special day of the year – nobody knows exactly when – all the garden gnomes come to life and go for a general meeting in Bradford with the parliamentary under-secretary of state for the Gnome Office. He lives at a place called: 'Piggot's Bottom' near Dingley Dell in Westminster, according to the radio.

After the meeting they have a clog dance, get a baked potato each and some beans and four bottles of Celtic dew, known among mortals as Guinness, upon which they really become Chopin and Liszt. But, when they all get home to their respective gardens – an hour before dawn – they sit themselves down an inch away from where they sat hitherto. They crumple the beans into a fine dust and throw it around themselves into the garden. Then, for another year they turn to stone. But the bean-dust doesn't die, and every plant touched by it will grow happy and strong. And the people who live in the houses will eventually notice the gnome and say to themselves – golly, I'm <u>sure</u> it's moved …! But, as they always do, they'll dismiss the thought as stupid and absurd and go about their ways… perhaps to admire how well the flowers and shrubbery are growing …

Fiona, it would be really marvellous if Poland was to achieve national independence, but that would be most unlikely due to both geographical and political circumstances. A pity. One day, maybe.

Well, now to get some sleep, Carrot. I feel better so I'll close for now. My finest regards to Simon and your parents and to Sunday. And to the garden – if the grass was as green as your eyes it would be sweet all year through and snowflakes would melt on it. Peace.

All My Love, Your Friend and Brother

Alex Xx

When I received this letter it moved me to tears and I was riddled with guilt that I hadn't written to Alex for two months. 'I'm not beaten yet,' he says and in the midst of all his pain he could write with such sweetness and charm about the gnomes. I felt a desperate sadness at my inability to help him. In Ireland, I was unaware that I was hurtling towards a devastating chapter in my life.

Kilkea Castle Hotel
Castledermot
Co Kildare
Ireland
3rd November 1980

My Dearest Alex,

I am very sorry to hear of your latest situation. Rule 43 doesn't sound bearable but if it is the preferable alternative, then you must do it. How can one guy do so much to make your life a misery and get away with it?

Can't anything be done? Anyway, I am thinking of you and praying for you and hoping that you get a quick transfer.

Yes, that really <u>is</u> the name of one of my rose bushes. Alex Red. It is the official name that it has been given by the Rose Breeders Association. My mother-in-law brought a whole load of rose bushes for us to put in some empty beds. When I saw the label on this one, I couldn't believe it! So it went in pride of place at the front of the end bed and gave us beautiful rich red blooms all summer. Alex Red.

As you can see we are in County Kildare staying in a very impressive Norman Castle, which was built in 1180. Simon is filming an American TV series called 'The Manions of America', about an Irish family who settle in America in 1847. He plays one of the leading characters, an English Hussar who falls in love with an Irish peasant. David Soul from 'Starsky and Hutch' is in the cast and a young Irish actor called Pierce Brosnan is the lead. We have been in Dublin and Galway and I'm having a wonderful holiday really, just relaxing and recharging the batteries. I feel happier and fitter than I have done for ages.

The countryside is really beautiful here. I've just been for a long walk and the sun was shining on all the golden leaves and the river was twinkling and the air smelt rich and pure. It has been raining a lot recently (which probably accounts for this being such a lush, green isle) but today it is bright and warm with hardly a cloud in the sky (Can't believe it is Nov. 3rd?).

I am sitting at this desk in our room in the castle turret, looking out over newly harvested fields, huge assorted golden, reddish trees, cows grazing lazily and a little ruin of a stone cottage that may, perhaps, have been the keeper's home once.

Sometimes I go on location with Simon and hang around all day but I can't do that all the time, so on other days I pass the time here with the other actors, who are all very friendly and pleasant company.

Yesterday we went for a long cycle ride and then had a picnic. We also play billiards, which is great fun because I beat them all!!

I probably won't stay here all the time, as there are things to be done at home, so I may go back to London for a short while.

How are your mother and Arthur?

I've tried ringing Rose on the home number and left a message with a gentleman there (her husband?) as to how to get hold of your stamps. Hopefully they will be at the House of Commons on November 10th.

Well, I guess I'd better go now. Keep well and take great care. I'm glad the book is making you smile.

Regards from Simon

Fondest, Warmest Love, Fiona

Unusually, I didn't hear back from Alex, who was struggling to keep his head above water. Between these two letters, however, my life had begun to unravel at an alarming pace. Having enjoyed my time in Ireland with Simon, we came back home for a few days, as he had some time off. He said he had some meetings in London. What I didn't know was that he had arranged to meet a divorce lawyer.

London
5th December 1980

Darling Alex,

So, Christmas is nearly here. I can't believe this year has flown by so fast. Thank you for your lovely letters. They are of immense comfort and I count you as one of my closest, most special friends.

No gnomes as yet. I've always fancied a gnome in the garden but haven't ever found the right one! I'm convinced they come alive more than <u>one</u> day a year though. In fact, they have a lot to do with the quality of one's garden. Be nice to your gnome and your garden will prosper etc!

Simon had a week off filming so we're back in England now, as he wants to do some business here.

Please excuse my writing. I'm in a slight state of shock at the moment and the booze is helping to ease the pain. I'm calmer than I have been for four days however, but the fact is, Simon has suddenly announced that he is 'not happy with our marriage, has felt dissatisfied for about a year and that if things don't change we ought to separate'.

Well, you can imagine how I feel. As far as I was concerned, everything was fine and dandy. I was happy being with him in Ireland. Very supportive, loving and willing to forfeit everything to be with him. I can't go into details or this letter would take ages to write, but basically he is saying that his ambition, work and energy are his whole life and that I am putting him under pressure by being around and needing love and attention. His whole argument seems totally selfish in that he wants to throw away his responsibilities and commitment in order to pursue his longing for fame and fortune. This shook me up greatly. I had no idea that he felt having a wife was 'a great burden'. When he mentioned phrases like 'splitting up' and 'not needing you any more' it was all news to me. We haven't been having rows or screaming matches or anything, he's just decided that he'd be better off if I was out of the way.

However, as yet we are <u>not</u> separating and Christmas will be a family affair but after the extremely hurtful things he has said, I can't imagine that anything I do will make a difference. He wants me to throw myself back into my career (I haven't long finished the show) and lead a more independent life but there still has to be love and togetherness. The change in him is incredible.

Obviously I want to work at it. I'm willing to persevere because you can't just chuck it aside if something seems to be wrong. But now I've stopped crying and can be rational about it all, I've realised that perhaps I <u>can</u> live on my own and start again. Why not? I'm sorry to burden you with this but somehow it helps to write it down. I hope you understand.

How is 43 now? Do you have plenty to read or can I send you some books? Please be good. You shouldn't really be on 43 should you, so the sooner you're away the better. Anyway, I think about you a lot. Take care and write soon.

All My Love,

Fiona

'The show, by the way, has been a disaster. It was roasted, panned, slated and killed by the critics'.
In 'Barnardo' 1980 with James Smillie.

**'All the screws are in love
with one or the other of you!'**
With (l to r) Clare Clifford, Julie Dawn Cole, Karen David, Lesley Dunlop, and Erin Geraghty—original cast members of 'Angels', 1975. (Courtesy BBC)

'How's this for coincidence; soon you'll be on stage in London and I'll be on stage in Parkhurst'.
In 'Cinderella' with Richard O'Sullivan as Buttons, 1976.

'I was a proper tourist. Even went to
Hemingway's hideaway on the island of
Torcello'.
Travelling alone for the first time.
Venice 1981.

'Hong Kong is the most fascinating,
beautiful, mysterious city I have ever visited'.
In the musical 'Something's Afoot' with
Virginia McKenna (far left).

23 AUG 1978

C- Wing,
H.M. PRISON,
PARKHURST,
NEWPORT,
ISLE-OF-WIGHT. PO30 5NX

Dear Fiona;

Hello, lass. Got your letter today along with the wedding photograph
of Simon and yourself, you look extremely beautiful. If people can say beauty cannot
be carried to extremes you have made history by proving them wrong, and how happy
you look! Let me just say how glad I am for you and that the same kind of happiness
will remain with you forever! Now I am decorating...! I have to find somewhere
in the cell to stand this photograph! No, this photo. does not belong in any prison
cell, I think instead I will leave it with your letter in the cupboard :- then, when I
get a bit rough I'll bring it back out and things will change for the better. Zap!

You find me interesting. Wow! Mutual. I find myself interesting, too.
I can't make it out, honestly. A lot of people from every walk of life have said they
find me interesting and I am baffled. Well and truly. This copper once found
me asleep, around two o,clock in the morning (I was about thirteen years old), in
a telephone box at Kettering 'bus station. He marched me up to the local cop-shop
and reported to the inspector what he had found. The inspector looked at me
and said; "interesting". Oh, wow, I thought. And he took my snake-belt off me.
Happens all the time....

Fiona, I know how busy you are, and of course you cannot go writing
me long letters! Let me tell you I consider myself most fortunate indeed to actually
know you, and that is enough. My hope is that, one day, you will be able to count
on me as a friend — a very valuable thing, friendship, never to be taken lightly,
a commodity to be regarded with the utmost trust and respect. May we one day
become friends, then.

No. 243 30563 7-10-68

P.T.O.

Yes, all is well with me and this sunshine is appreciated. Or, rather, it was. It's been here too long, this heat, I think I would prefer Lancashire right now and a few of its thunderstorms. The grass up there is greener than in any other part of the country and the flowers are not dehydrated like down South here. May we get rain soon!

Do you still have sugar-cubes wrapped with paper and printed 'BBC' at the Corp? I've heard some interesting tales of the mechanisms of the 'BBC' from a mate of mine. He used to have to suffer make-up - something about Number 7 (F) brushes, 'Matte Plastic Sealer' (!) and 'C.T.V'. Is this true or is he pulling my leg? Something else about translucent powder. The mind boggles!

Well I will be looking forward to the next series of Angels, I'm only sorry it will be the last, Fiona. Is the work very hard? Anyway, you will be in some of the programmes and that makes such occasions special to me, you project a wonderful personality, you know. It's kind of contagious, it's catching. You'll have a brilliant future ahead of you, no mistake about that. Hold on while I roll a smoke. I smoke too much. In ten years' time I'll be coffin me lungs up. I hope they legalise pot .... could do with a trip somewhere. And it's not half as dangerous as this lousy tobacco. Think I'll write to the Queen.

On second thoughts, better not... It's not far from Christmas now, is it? How's this for coincidence; you will be on stage in London and I think I might be on stage in Parkhurst! This year we're thinking of doing a concert. On C-Wing we have two guys playing mouth-organ, an accordianist, two drummers and a couple of guitars. I think the governor would like us to sing carols, perish the thought! I have three or four guys who could make the San Quentin concert look like 'Jim'll Fix It by comparison. All I need is a mike' and a Copy Cat and Buddy Holly lives again!

Well I sound okay in a bathroom ..... rather like the Titanic coming up. You still haven't said when your birthday is. Fiona, what's your favourite disc in the Charts? I like Wings a bit, hey; here's a short poem for you —

'GRASS'

I am simple like breathing

nothing more, alas,

I am not a rock, a mountain peak,

I am only grass.

Winter winds blow over me —

an uproarious riot.

I lie under a blanket of snow.

I am quiet.

Spring will come — a silent thunder,

and then I'll appear

Passionately, like a dream, like the sky

blue and clear.

Men and women in love

will walk upon me.

For them quiet, green and blue

the world will be.

And if they decide to mow me

to make hay,

Believe me, I shall grow again.

I shall stay! I shall stay!

——— * ———

I think poetry is beautiful, though I'm only into modern poetry. I suppose one day I

have to get around to Tennyson & Co. Fiona, there's so much to do! And one has only a little time to do it. Ever get that feeling? I don't know what it is. I always need to get things done quickly, though, at the same time, I can find endless patience.

I got all the newspapers that you were in and kept the cuttings. I don't think my last letter got to you, Fiona. You know, I wish I could send you a photo' of myself but none exist. I did apply two years ago to have my picture taken by the Authorities - my family wanted a copy - but the application was refused on political grounds. Such is life. In here one learns to accept such things. I'm sorry that I have to remain such a mystery to you.

I have written to a Moscow arts and culture magazine, if I have a favourable reply I may consider having them publish my own literary contributions after my release. They set an extraordinary high standard, of course, and so I would be very honoured if my contributions should be accepted — I still wish to live in the Soviet Union, there I would receive tutorage from a Master. No word has yet come from the Soviet Ambassador as regards my citizenship application, I will let you know of the result when it comes through.

I've just finished reading Erich von Daniken's latest book; 'In Search Of Ancient Gods' and am now a staunch Danikenite - have you ever read any of his books? They are truly remarkable. I mean, fancy producing a two-thousand year old electric dry battery! These books, that are becoming more and more widely recognised, throw the Bible and Darwen's theories upside down! I've no doubt at all that the world was once the home of a civilization, advanced technologically enough for space travel, and that we are descendants of that civilization. The other theory, that of Darwen's and the evolution from apes, I find unacceptable. Your views?

Well, I am running short of writing-space and so I shall have to finish for now. Enjoy yourself at work, and don't write back until you can find the right moment. Meanwhile, I'll be thinking of you; take good care of yourself, and Simon, too.

So long, Fiona — Yours, with affection;

Alex.

'**Soon you'll be more Russian than I am'.**
As Lisanka in 'The Death of Ivan Ilyich'.
(Courtesy BBC)

'**My hope is that one day you will be able to count me as a friend — a very valuable thing friendship, never to be taken lightly, a commodity to be regarded with the utmost trust and respect. May we one day become friends, then'.**
Alex and Fiona in 2012.
(Photo by Alasdair Kirk)

Alex Alexandrowicz, 2012.

(Photo by Alasdair Kirk)

HM Prison Gartree
8. 12. 1980

Dearest Fiona

I received your letter this morning and it's left me shattered, so we both know what that feels like. I'm still shattered. Simon has dropped to rock bottom in my estimation – a bloody fool – <u>and</u> one day, believe me, he'll reach the same conclusion for himself. If he doesn't 'need you any more' okay, pack up your things and go to stay with your parents for a while – if he really loves you (and this is what you <u>must</u> know for certain) if he really loves you he'll come looking for you and tell you so.

   If you do not love him any more, still pack up your bags and go to your parents until I can get you somewhere more central – I know my friend Vivien would be happy with a little company (she's in your profession, has the Celt in her, very warm and friendly and does not speak behind people's backs). And she'd treat you as a sister. <u>Do not remain on your own</u>. I want a phone number where I can reach you at any time; will you put that in your next letter? – don't forget. I'll need it to give Vivien so she can call you, also I'll have Rose and Teresa 'phone through occasionally to check you're ok and find if there's anything you need. Watch the booze, ok? And if you feel you need something to balance the gyro have your family doctor prescribe a mild anti-depressant.

   Right. There goes the cool, here comes the emotion. Why the hell? What's this guy thinking of? Do you want me to write to him? Do you want me to do anything? Jesus Christ. I love you, right? Remember you got a brother, a hand, an arm, you understand this? Whatever you want of me is always yours, Princess, forever, for keeps. You saved my life and I don't forget. What's fame and fortune when compared to you, my friend? I'm not concerned about Simon, I'm concerned only that you be happy. If you're married to Simon, that's fantastic by me – providing <u>you're</u> happy. I still hope your marriage patches up, but it's good for you to remember the things he has said.

   You're young, intelligent and quite apart from being just a bonny lass you have a hell of a lot more going for you, and you're right, you <u>do</u> have friends – sometimes they pop up from the most unlikely of places – but they're there. Yes, and some of them aren't hypocrites, some of them will stand up and fight by your side!

   Let's have a look at this objectively, working from the premise that you are going to split up for a time. In the first place, if you separated, you would not be 'starting again', Princess. Christ I remember the 18-year-old kid and I look at her now and I see a mature young woman there with a heart of gold. Look at that most <u>priceless</u> commodity you have acquired! It's called 'experience', it's what you've picked up along the way, experience.

There is much more to life than living, sometimes, you know, we got to die a little, too. You're suffering now, and my heart is aching for you, my darling, but remember it is not those who inflict, but those who suffer who shall conquer! You have a heart … Do what it tells you and you will be happy, no one can and no one ever will OWN YOU … Come on, our kid, how about a smile?

Ah … your face, it is sad. That is not good, it was made for smiling, your eyes were made to sparkle and there have been tears there … we have no need to be sad, sister, look at what we have beyond the windows, forests, meadows, streams, flowers, snowflakes, a robin and, yes, even raindrops – and beyond the horizon? Who can tell? A whole world and it is yours to walk in, to laugh, to whistle, to run in! And you may meet someone, who, like you, has been searching, for a thousand years, and …

Yes, I got your letter from Ireland, I didn't know how long you would be over there so I thought I'd delay writing 'til nearer Christmas. It doesn't matter now. I'm not going to be able to stay awake much longer, the drugs, you understand. I was going to ask someone to marry me but, sure, that's off now. Never mind 43 or books, they're not important – you are important, I love you more than I love myself, you understand this?

It means I love you more than life itself, so be good.

Did you get that album 'A BELT OF THE CELTS' by the Wolfe Tones? I had a copy of it in Parkhurst and it gave me strength when I was lonely. I hope it does the same for you. Please, Fiona, take care of yourself and don't let things get you down and please write back as soon as you can. Give my very finest regards to your Mum and Dad and to little Sunday. You're no burden, sweetheart, you're as light as a feather, you're my sister and I love you. This is all I can write for now but I always think of you too and pray for you every night. Das Vidaniya for now, then.

All of My Love to You, Happy Christmas.
Your Friend and Brother

Alex, Xxx — PS The photograph was beautiful, thank you.

The week in London had been a masterclass in camouflage, but incredibly painful at the same time. I had a feeling someone else, someone in Ireland, was involved with Simon but he vehemently denied it. We did a big photo shoot for a glossy magazine and he managed to convince everyone that all was well and that we were madly in love.

On the 8th December 1980 Simon and I were back in Ireland and woke to the news that John Lennon had been shot and killed. Everyone seemed to be in a state of shock, but no-one more so than me, having just discovered that Simon was in love with his co-star, the American actress Linda Purl.

HM Prison Gartree

9. 12. 1980

My Dearest Fiona

I hope that you got my last letter alright. I guess it must be terrible to share one's life with someone for five years and then hit a situation where everything shatters, kind of, like dropping a pane of glass onto the ground, it can only be repaired with much patience and the glue must be extra special if there's to be no evidence of the cracks in the future.

What Simon has said to you is inexcusable, though you may find it in you to forgive and forget, and keep your marriage together. This is what many people would do if only for appearances sake, but also, usually, for more basic reasons.

Possibly by now Simon has come to his senses and made it up to you. Whatever happens, I'm concerned only with you and your future.

We're survivors, sister, you and I, and if there's a nuclear war tomorrow make sure there's a mailbox on your nuclear fallout shelter! – Nothing has the power to put us down, nothing. We have a fighting spirit, you from the Celt, I from the Slav (what an awesome combination), and that fighting spirit will never die!

Ah, my princess, sometimes how I wish that things were different!

I guess I'll be out within the next 3 years, I have already been told I can expect a better move early in the New Year. This will mean my security status will go down and I'll be in a prison where hobbies and other things are allowed and there is a process of rehabilitation at work. It will be strange, coming back to Freedom after (what will then be) 13 years in clink.

It's funny how things work out. I remember when I first went to Parkhurst as an A-man – you know who told me to keep <u>out of</u> trouble, to go straight when I get out? Reg Kray. 'Alex, you shouldn't be in here. One day you'll get out and when you do, don't ever do anything to come back'. Well that was nearly six years ago now, but listening to another con wasn't enough. I needed someone out there to have faith in me, to <u>accept</u> me as an equal, a <u>person</u>.

God, times were bad then, Fiona; all I saw was this life sentence stretching way out in front of me. I'd arrived at Parkhurst with a reputation from Wakefield Prison. I was sent to Wakefield at the age of 20, I was into my second year of imprisonment and I was green, I didn't know the ropes all that well. This old guy invited me up to his cell for a game of chess, but when I got up there he tried to have it off with me, he was homosexual, you see. I ended up tapping him over the head with an iron bar and put him in hospital for a while with a fractured skull. I got 56 days bread and water. But the other cons spread the word – don't mess around with Alex. And so I arrived at Parkhurst with a rep. I wasn't proud of, but the reputation had started.

Then, one evening in the TV room I was watching a new series called 'Angels'. I saw a girl in the series and I thought, Jesus, and I said to myself 'try writing to her'. I never expected a response. I went back to my cell and wrote a letter, the rest is history. It changed the whole course of my life. It was this girl, this beautiful, wonderful girl who provided a balance between outside values and the savage values of the prison system.

I found myself writing to someone and gradually respect and love began to grow. I never again got into trouble (except for the minor rooftop demo), no more violence, and I knew it was a promise I'd made to this girl, which I could not break.

When things got bad, instead of breaking up my cell, I sat down and wrote – and always the reply gave me new hope, new courage and strength. She became a stabilising force – an anchor. Whereas hitherto I had been an active and recognised Communist, this girl's non-political stance had a profound effect on me, I wrote to my 'comrades' and withdrew my oath of allegiance – no other person could have given me the initiative to make this almost unprecedented move. It was a move, almost certainly, which motivated the Home Office to remove my high-security Category-A status … a big step towards my eventual release, which, as I say, could now be within the next 3 years.

If it wasn't for the fact that you were married to Simon, and obviously dearly in love with him, I would have asked you to marry me. I knew, of course, this could never be. But my love for you was (and is) so intense that I wanted to be second closest to you, and the role and very real (for me) responsibility of calling you sister, and all that entails, seemed to me to be the best and most honourable solution. At first glance, it would seem to the outside observer that this was a most strange state of affairs, that such emotional power could be generated through the restrictive circumstances that exist. Maybe, I don't know, maybe you yourself would call it strange also. But it is by no means unprecedented, my darling, and perhaps what you have read, Alex speaking from his heart, may show you the road that has been followed and that a junction up ahead may be in sight. I realise, through opening my heart to you, that I run the risk of losing you, but it is nonetheless time I made my true feelings known. I could never be dishonest or lie to you, never.

I still hope that Simon comes to his senses. Yes, for if that would make you happy, I would be happy also. Because when you love someone, really love someone, it is enough to be content that the one you love is happy. And I will continue to call you 'sister'; nothing will have changed. Except you and I, we will know at least, the true depth of feeling on my part, and you will know how I feel deep inside.

Perhaps, I shall never hear from you again, God knows, you have enough emotional problems on your plate without an idiot like me adding to them. If you do stop writing, obviously I'd be fairly cut up about it – but at the same time, I would understand and respect your feelings and would make no attempt to try re-establishing contact.

You are beautiful from the heart outwards – a rare thing in this day and age. Take very good care of yourself, Princess. I think of you and pray for you always. May your life become one of joy and real happiness, an example to the ideal of creation, and may you find what you seek.

I am, and always will remain, Your Friend and Brother.
All my Love to You, Princess, Das Vidaniya!

Alex

XXXX

I wish I could remember my reaction to this astonishingly emotive letter because he took an enormous gamble by declaring his feelings for me so readily. He knew it was a risk, but cleverly decided it was a risk worth taking. But how did a man, imprisoned from the age of 18, develop such a protective, caring nature? To be able to write with such emotional power about wanting to take care of me, gave me unbelievable strength at a time when my self-esteem was at rock bottom.

[This sanitised version of the awful attack at Wakefield Prison is, of course, far from the brutal truth as described earlier.]

HM Prison Gartree

15. 12. 1980

My Dearest Sister

Hi again, kid, the world is STILL HERE!!!

I'm thinking of you all the time now and my thoughts are that Simon has apologised and you're back to first base, but I guess I'm worried that this has not come about and that you need help but I'm locked in this bloody box and I'm so frustrated it hurts bad. But I have a feeling everything will be alright eventually, but no matter where you go or what you do always remember you got a Brother! Please excuse my lousy handwriting. Please write soon. Did I make an idiot of myself in my last two letters? If so, I'll do it again; I love you.

When I get out I have to get myself fit again, I think this will take a year of proper food and walks up and down Scafell Pike with a pack of bricks on my back. That's how to do it. Christ. I know those mountains like the back of my hand. I'll take a tent and a camera and from the top of Scafell (you can see for miles, right out to sea!) I'll take a picture of the tent and send it to you and there'll be the tent in the foreground and, behind it, this awesome panorama, and on the back I'll write: 'This is a picture of my home and my garden.' Please write soon, <u>will</u> you?

Das Vidaniya! Your Friend and Brother

Alex, XXX

For ever 'til the dark paths of time are
well-trod and lighter
I will always remember you're my darling
and the stars will shine
On the clifftops I'll wander and the seas will break
far down below me
No melody will sound so beautiful
no sound so sweet and clear
And it will be you, my sweetheart
that song I shall hear ...

Alex 1980

London
18th December 1980

My Darling Alex,

Thank you for your two beautiful letters. I wept buckets because I could
feel your love and warmth and that is what I need so very much.

The week when I first wrote of our trouble was horrendous because
we had to go through a farce of facing friends and having photos taken
together, etc. He then said, strangely, he would like me to come back to
Ireland with him and I thought I may be able to smooth things over. We
drove over to Dublin and for three days I put up with the most unbearable rejection and feeling of loneliness. He would ignore me and only talk
to the other people in the house. I was made to feel like a naughty child.

I finally broke down and went to a doctor who prescribed Valium. I
now take three a day and they calm me down. I finally decided to leave
Dublin (only there four days) and he seemed genuinely sad to see me go
but 'thought it was for the best'.

He will come home for Christmas where both families will congregate
at my parent's home in Winchester. I think it will be strained.

It just seems that his ambition is his whole life now. He even said on the phone last night that he would probably go to America straight after this. I <u>insisted</u> he come home first so we have some time together because if he doesn't want to come home, we might as well call it quits now. But he is very confusing, he says it's not irretrievable and then says he doesn't love me anymore, which is the most painful thing.

I know a lot of it is my fault but I can't face the future without him. I just need to be loved and cherished but Simon can't give me those things.

Oh Alex, it's so good to know you are there and your beautiful letters moved me so much. Of course I would never stop writing to you. Don't be silly. I value your friendship and love too much. Thank you a million times for your support. I love you dearly and will be thinking of you over Christmas.

All My Very Fondest Love, Fiona x

Quite why I returned to Ireland with Simon I will never know because it turned out to be deeply humiliating. Linda Purl was living in the house with Simon and would rise at five every morning to study her Bible. When I confronted her about the affair she said simply, 'It is God's way'. She even wrote me a letter detailing these sentiments. Presumably she wrote her husband, Desi Arnaz Jnr, the same kind of letter.

HM Prison — Gartree
Monday 22. 12. 1980 or thereabouts (Censored version)

My Dearest Darling Fiona

First of all, though you say don't be silly, I'm still goddamn relieved that I haven't lost you, all this week I've been chain-smoking like an expectant father, wondering how you are, how you're coping, what you're doing, whether you got my letters, okay, etc., etc. I'm thinking of you all the time now. If we could be together on a spiritual level then this has got to be it – I knew I'd get a letter from you today, I knew hours before it actually arrived. I was actually <u>waiting</u> for it … !

You're really going through the wringer at the moment, aren't you, lass? I don't like the thought of you being alone, you know. Watch the Valium – what colour are the tablets, yellow or blue? – if they're blue, three a day (30mg) is about right – but don't take more than three. In actual fact, down on the Island I was on 20 mg a day but only took the stuff when I felt I needed it, like, when I was under strain or had an attack of nerves (I'm very sensitive – almost hypersensitive).

Do not blame yourself, you're beginning to, you know – and that is not just. A more loving, devoted and loyal wife Simon will never hope to find ever again, that's the truth, and that fact makes his conduct all the more reprehensible; he ought to have enough savvy to realise how extraordinarily lucky he is in being married to you. But all he seems capable of doing is hurting you, this is terrible, terrible and wrong.

The tragic thing is you may still love him and if this is the case, then you're torturing yourself and, believe me you'll go through a lot of (unnecessary) suffering. I say unnecessary because you are young and strong enough to get the hell out and begin living again for today and tomorrow.

What is the future, anyway? – hell, kitten, we could all be wiped off the face of the earth tomorrow. Security? You <u>can</u> face the future, you know, because you're still searching – and there are so many beautiful things you have yet to discover … Really. I know you need to be loved and cherished, my darling, I totally understand this … what can I say?

All I know is that I need someone <u>to</u> love and cherish, Christ I have ten years of love bottled up inside me, Fiona, if you want it, it's yours. Of course, I never will love anybody else in the same way I love you – no matter what the future may bring or how Fate plays her hand, you will always come first with me; if I can use my life to help yours I'd consider it an honour, and consider myself lucky. I don't give a damn for myself, if I can only <u>give</u> to you, make you happy, then – you know what … I would be really happy – just by doing that! Believe me.

How do you feel about a trip up here so we can have a talk? I know I've mentioned this before and we've both dismissed it as impracticable – mainly my concern is that someone will recognise you and wonder what you're doing at a top security nick. But if you wear a pair of shades and don't dress too stylishly, no-one is likely to notice. Will you let me know what you think? I'd dearly like a chance to talk to you – and, it would give you something to <u>do</u> for a day … I'll even get a haircut! Christ they've been trying to make me have a haircut for months, I'll do it if you'll come up for a visit – bargain? Let me know. Okay?

You know what I would like? I'd like to sit opposite you with a fire in-between us and watch you smile, talk a bit, fly paper aeroplanes – pilot them, too – watch you reading a book or playing with Sunday, that's a couple of the things I'd like, and I'd like to hold you for a million years or so, give or take a thousand – see how crazy I am?

It's okay, it's only my dreams somehow appearing in front of me as the words come out of the end of my Bic; they're hard to stop at times, it's as though my pen is doing all the thinking and presenting the results before my eyes. Don't be offended, I'm bound to say stupid things on occasion.

They are stupid things because I'm a realist and I know they can't be real, it's just the revolutionist in me which says to hell with realism – is there such a thing as a brotherly embrace? That lasts forever? Because I <u>love</u> you, Sister, that's how it is.

Please Write Again soon, 'cos your letters mean so much to me, you know. I'll write again soon, too. Keep your chin up, Sweetheart! Don't cry – save your tears, girl, for when you're happy!!

All My Love and Deepest Affection. Your Friend and Brother Always

Alex Xxx

As well as channelling his energy into trying to save my marriage, Alex was also involved in another far more serious project. On November 17th, the Yorkshire Ripper had murdered his 13th known victim and everyone in the prison was sickened by the attacks. They all decided that the police didn't have a clue how to catch him and that they probably needed some help.

They decided to appeal to the underworld, on the basis that *someone* knew *something*, and would send information to a national newspaper.

'The appeal wasn't difficult to write and I'd finished it in half an hour. It had to be written in a certain way, using the language and terminology spoken by prisoners. The difficulty was in getting the document to the newspapers, because it had to go to certain prisoners scattered around the country for their signatures. Within days it had been to Long Lartin, then on to the Scrubs and down to the Island before arriving back at Gartree. Legitimate channels were avoided.

We had a meeting to decide which of the national newspapers to send it to and settled on the *Daily Mirror*, because most prisoners regard it as being genuinely concerned with social injustices. The appeal was duly sent to the paper and they gave it front-page coverage with a banner headline reading "GRASS ON THE RIPPER". We held our breath.'

Just three days later the Ripper was caught. Although the police might never admit it, their version of the arrest of Peter Sutcliffe may not reveal everything.

HM Prison Gartree
Boxing Day 1980

My Dearest Darling Fiona

Thinking of you. And I'm hoping you had a wonderful Christmas, regardless … has Simon postponed his foray to the States? Are you certain that his excuse is the reason he says – that it is career and not some other woman? Ouch. But you must be certain, kid. I should imagine that some other woman may find it easy to fall for the qualities which you yourself fell for in 1976. I could understand that, and I'm fairly damn sure that girls, if they've made up their minds, can usually get what they want from a guy, men being what we are. That's okay. Only it stops being okay when the guy in question happens to be married, and married to my best friend!

What are your ideas on this, Fiona? One thing – if there is another woman, get the hell out of it. The sea's big, plenty of fish in it, but you must make sure of your fish – watch out for the sharks, and squids and stingrays. Maybe you were making a mistake in 1976, most sharks are quite good-looking – but inside … not so good. Now we're into 1981 almost: you've grown up, and you're learning to distinguish what is bad and what is good; it's a bastard, I know, and you're being hurt in the process. It's hurting me, too.

This next sentence you must read carefully. If there is any *practical* help I can give you; if, perhaps, you need something checked, and you're out of your depth; if you want something done and you are not sure how to do it – for God's sake come to me. You do have a brother, and I care – you understand this? Some things I can do. For you – anytime.

Fiona – please write soon, I need you. I'll write again soon. Please, take good care of yourself, Princess – chin up and keep smiling, okay?

My Warmest Regards to your Mum and Dad. Hi to Sunday.

As Ever, Your Devoted Friend and Brother.

Alex, Xxx

Christmas 1980 was an experience I wouldn't wish on my greatest enemy. Both families—Simon's and mine—were together in my parents' house near Winchester. It was what we always did, but perhaps, with hindsight, it might have been better if we had altered the arrangements. The atmosphere was heavy with resentment. I knew Simon didn't want to be near me. He wanted to be with Linda. Who was also married.

- 8 -

A Sudden Departure

HM Prison Gartree

11. 1. 1981

My Dearest Darling

Listen – How are you, my friend? Are you still taking the Valium? Try not to stay on it for too long, it really doesn't help in the long run. In particular when you sign up for your next production, if the role calls for snap and vitality you must come off the Valium – it has a tendency to slow down mental and physical procession (as, no doubt, you have already noticed). I want to see the old Fiona back. Today is the first day of the rest of your life, as the guy said – do you feel able to see it that way? You must do, sugar, because you have so much to give, so much happiness to so many people. Hell, I remember when I was your age! I'd written my first letter to you – do you remember that? The submarines? Well, it has not changed a bit – well, maybe – now you're older and wiser, more beautiful than ever.

I've learnt a lot since I was 23. I've learned that life is for living, I've learned how to reach out to people, to relate with them. I've learned that all one has to be is oneself; I've learned that I can only be hurt if I wish it upon myself. Now, you have loved a person – but remember that love, like everything else, is a relative thing – you have yet to love life itself, in all its beautiful and wonderful splendour, its many and varied forms. Ah – one day you will understand what I am saying to you. To live! Not one of us knows what fate has in store ... the road is long, the mountain steep, but there are times when we reach a crossroads and have to make a decision, times when we

221

reach a mountain peak and can SEE with a startling clarity … what we could not see before. Then you will have truly found love. Turn again – to face the Sun!

I guess this Christmas has been for you very emotional and significant. I can almost picture the scene. Fiona – have you come to any decision about your future? It must be really horrific for you, my darling. It was never your fault, kid. Just as it isn't your fault if you turn over a stone and see what's underneath. You put back the stone and turn away. I remember something once said by Naomi Bliven: 'Behind every woman you ever heard of, stands a man who let her down'.

Please write soon, Fiona, I need to hear from you. In the meantime look after yourself and keep smiling, hey?

As ever, your devoted Friend and Brother.

Alex,

XXX

London
14th January 1981

Darling Alex,

Thank you for your many recent letters. They have been of great comfort to me. I hope you have not been over-reacting during this situation, by making these <u>enormous</u> declarations. You don't have to say you love me, just so that I feel loved. I love you too, but in a very special, platonic, spiritual way. I need you and value your friendship very, very highly but I'm afraid to come and see you because I think it may jeopardise the whole thing. Do you understand? I hope so.

What is so special about our relationship is the written word, not verbal communication, but pen on paper. It is the written word as opposed to the spoken one, which I feel I can express more clearly.

Simon says the whole problem in our marriage is 'communication'. He likes to have the upper hand and he always makes me feel stupid. In a discussion I 'clam up' because everything I say is either wrong or argued with.

Christmas was only just bearable. I was on Valium and wine and managed to stay calm, except on one occasion when we were all going for a walk and Simon didn't want to come. I knew why. You were right Alex. This is all about a woman.

His parents and brother arrived at my parent's house on Christmas Eve but S was very distant so the atmosphere was quite strained. We all behaved very respectfully but I couldn't be normal, so I kept myself busy in the kitchen with mummy. He gave me two ornaments, which I thought were rather impersonal gifts. Then as if to confirm my suspicions I received a phone message to say that a florist had been unable to deliver his large bouquet of roses to an address in JAPAN! To HER I assume.

He returned to Ireland on the Sunday and it was an unemotional goodbye. I felt numb. The next day Mum, Dad and I went to Dartmoor for a New Year's break. We stayed in Moretonhampstead and went for long, healthy walks along the moors, climbed Tors, waded through streams and got blown over by the wind. It was wonderful! Mum and Dad are still so 'together' and, being the only child, we are all very close.

New Year's Eve was very sedate. I don't like large parties and kissing people I don't know, so at midnight, after the fireworks, I felt sad. I was glad to be saying farewell to a bad year but anxious as to what this one may bring.

I have mixed emotions now, you see. I seem to cope with things much better when he is away. Maybe it's the actual 'DIVORCE' I'm afraid of – not losing Simon.

I'm home now and keeping busy with this and that. Mostly singing lessons. Mum, Dad and little Sunday send their love and I will write again soon. Thank you for being so wonderful.

All My Fondest Love,

Fiona

xx

The trip to Dartmoor was miserable as the hotel was rather formal and I just wanted to crawl into bed due to the Valium, which was keeping me calm and making me sleepy.

Alex's letters were incredibly comforting but I think I was slightly overwhelmed by his romantic declarations. They were from a man whom I had never met and I had no idea what he looked like, so the whole relationship was becoming slightly surreal. With hindsight I can see the attraction of receiving attention from someone who can't touch you. Who can't harm you emotionally. On receiving his letter of January 11th I wrote again.

London
16th January 1981

Darling Alex,

Thank you for your note. Yes, I'm smiling – I'm a bit stronger. I have my music – I sing for two hours every morning and that cheers me up. I love music and lyrics I can identify with. They're nearly all sad, I've noticed. Ah well. Practice, practice.

I hope my last letter made sense. I DO need you and love you. Like a brother. How are things at Gartree now?

Spoke to Simon last night, briefly. Very strange. Like talking to one's chiropodist. Very bland.

Here are some snaps, including some of your stamp collection (at last), which was so beautifully mounted by the Burnbake Trust at the Royalty Theatre.

Be good and write lots. I think of you always.

All My Love,

Fiona x

The Burnbake Trust
Burnbake
Wilton
Salisbury
Wiltshire
18th January 1981

Dear Fiona,

Have been meaning to thank you for phoning (from Ireland I gather?) about Alex's stamps. They were collected eventually and are on display at the House of Commons.

I saw Alex before Christmas – he looked thin, cold and miserable – so did his friend, also on the Rule 43 wing – something had gone wrong with the heating. They were wrapped in these awful grey overcoats – like something out of a Russian novel! But no doubt things will improve.

I gather A hopes to go to Grendon – good if he does – conditions are more 'natural', or so I understand.

Best wishes and thanks again,

Rose (Murray)

Art Director.

How poetic! The rebel was hanging around in the corridors of power. I'm sure the irony of having his stamps on display at the House of Commons was not lost on Alex.

Meanwhile, I was still numb with my change of circumstances and sought refuge in song. I'm convinced people underestimate the power of music and the natural high that one can experience from singing, particularly in a group. But even alone, singing along to my teacher's tape, belting out arpeggios as if my life depended on it, became hugely therapeutic.

HM Prison Gartree

22. 1. 1981

My Very Dearest Friend

A million thanks for your letters and the beautiful photographs, again you've made me very happy like nobody else can. What enormous declaration? Listen to me, I would not say I love you just to make you feel loved – I say I love you because I <u>do</u> … there is not anything wrong with that, sister, I'm a realist (though, okay, I'm also unconventional at times). I won't want anything from you except your friendship, there aren't any strings or angles, and as long as you're a friend of mine there is not anything I wouldn't do for you.

And because I am a friend of yours I am naturally extremely concerned for your happiness, otherwise I would not be fit to call myself your Friend. Our love <u>is</u> Platonic and it is also very special. For my part I will always respect your wishes no matter what. How can I put it? I want to see you find some guy with whom you can be HAPPY, for this would make me happy in turn. I want to be as near to you as a brother would be – not a husband – just some bloke called Alex who you can trust, who'll help you out whenever you call, someone you can turn to knowing my loyalty to you is 100 per cent tight. I'm not complicated, Fiona, I'm just somebody who will go along with whatever you say. If you say go jump in the canal that's what I'll do. You need not be afraid of some big complicated situation arising out of our friendship. I merely believe in letting things run their natural course, what will be will be.

The purpose behind my asking you to visit me is solely to have a chat and for you to learn more about me. I believe we understand one another sufficiently to hold a conversation and not get hung up about it. My reasoning was that we'd have to meet each other one day – so why not bring it forward a little? Still, I do understand your point of view and I <u>do</u> recognise that it's selfish of me to expect you to meet me in a <u>place like this</u>. As the guy said 'There's a time and a place for everything, and this could very well <u>not</u> be the time <u>or</u> place.' I guess that, between the two of us, you are the one who is being realistic over this matter and that you're probably right to let things ride, so I won't bring up this subject again, OK, kitten? Right.

I'm sorry for not replying to your letter sooner but this past week has been a bad one. I had the reply to that Review I had in August and all they've done is pass me over for another Review to begin in October 1982 – which is almost two years away.

No mention of a transfer. And this Rule 43 thing is getting me down, though I had to come off my daily Fentozine as it was beginning to affect my coordination – in the mornings I was weaving about all over the place. So I'm back with all this nervous energy, which I can't get rid of. The only thing that's keeping me going are the books I'm reading. I read one after the other like chain-smoking cigarettes. On average I get through ten a week and at the moment I have a Daphne du Maurier, 'Jamaica Inn', ready for when I've finished this letter.

I saw my probation officer the other week and we had a good talk, at that time we were both optimistic that the reply to the Review would be a good one, at the very least a move to a less high security prison. She also gave me a ticking off for writing that letter to the underworld, which the 'Daily Mirror' spread all over its front page but I'm not sorry for writing it and I haven't been disciplined for it – yet, I guess it wasn't actually approved of and may go against me. Everything just seems to be an enormous Catch-22 in as much as it's very difficult to do what is 'right'. What's needed is a crystal ball so we can spot the mistakes long before they happen. Ha! Then life wouldn't be worth living.

I can understand you having mixed emotions, Fiona; you're going through enough! From what you say (Simon's attitude toward you) I'd say to hell with it and get your divorce, especially if there is a woman involved. Mind you, that's Alex the non-conformist who's giving you that advice. But … forgive me, if two people vow to love each other and live with each other for life, then a bond is forged and for it to remain whole and strong both parties must stay true and loyal. In this case Simon has broken that bond and cannot expect you to go on as though nothing has happened. Do not be <u>afraid</u> of divorce, millions of people end their marriages, you won't be the first and you won't be the last, either.

You have Alex behind you, one hundred per cent. This is something Simon does not have. I do not know what resources you have available to you, but mine are fairly considerable when I choose to activate them. To help you, I will go all the way, my friend. If you give me the go-ahead I will endeavour to find you a competent investigator …

In the meantime, either destroy all my letters to you or put them in a safe place – this is MOST important. Do this as soon as you can.

I envy you your trek into Dartmoor, though I prefer the Lake District, the photo of Becky Falls, though, reminded me of better times and a wave of nostalgia swept over me. These are the beautiful things in life. I was <u>extremely</u> pleased too with the picture of my stamp display, it was the first I'd seen of it … and I'd have gladly given a penny for your thoughts there on Plymouth Hoe. Such 'photos' of you I like the best!

Take good care of yourself, my darling, stay warm and to hell with yesterday! I think of you constantly and pray each night that you stay well and safe. Goodnight, then, Princess. Things will work out right in the end. Please give my warmest regards to your Mum and Dad and a ruffle for little Sunday.

To you

All My Love, as Ever

Your Devoted Friend and Brother,

Alex, X

Sitting alone in his cell, the idea of being my eternal protector and my brother appeals to Alex's romantic nature, but why did he ask me to destroy all his letters? Did he think they would compromise me in some way?

London
2nd February 1981

My Dearest Alex,

Firstly, I keep forgetting to thank you for the wonderful LP you sent me, 'Belt of the Celts'. The music is very soothing, unusual and pleasant. I play it often. Thank you.

Secondly, I am absolutely devastated that you will not get another review until October 1982. I am so worried for you on Rule 43 and feel so helpless that there is nothing I can do. My thoughts and love are always with you though.

Simon was due to return home from Ireland today but he said his 'schedule' had been extended and will be home on Friday. Obviously we have a lot of talking to do, but now, in a way, I wish he didn't have to come back at all. I am keeping busy reorganizing my life, doing lots of singing and dancing lessons and catching up with friends. If he says he no longer needs me, we shall see what happens.

Every weekend I go to Winchester to see Mum and Dad and I gave Sunday a special 'ruffle' from Alex. We've just had a marvellous long walk across the fields.

Guess what? On February 15th I'm flying to Singapore for a week to film a commercial for Dutch TV. I'm so excited 'cos I used to live there as a kid. I've never done a commercial before but it won't be seen in this country. Imagine flying to Singapore to film a 30 second commercial for Holland!! Crazy. I'm very flattered to be chosen.

Here's an early birthday card. I will be thinking of you on the 8th [which was Alex's 28th birthday] and drinking your health.

Take care my dearest Alex. All My Love

Fiona x

This letter is hiding a lot of pain, because I remember sobbing throughout the entire walk with my dog. The countryside around where we lived is very pretty and Sunday never left my side, which was unusual.

HM Prison Gartree
5. 2. 1981

My Very Dearest Friend

Hello, Carrot. Peace. Thanks a million times for the card – it raised a smile – and your letter. You seem to be in much better spirits and I'm <u>glad</u> for that – and your trip to Singapore – Capital! Very good news indeed, I'm delighted for you.

Do not be worried for me on this Rule 43 thing, lass, I've gone through other situations much, much worse than this. I know how to take care of myself and how to get the best from a bad thing. Of course, I am <u>also</u> devastated by being passed over by the Home Office. I am a subversive, Fiona, in so far as the subject of human rights participation within British gaols is frowned upon, anyone actively engaged in this field is therefore classified as 'subversive'! Very ironic. I wish I could explain to you more fully my position, somehow I know that you would not disapprove of my involvement – although it is quite obvious that this is what is keeping me in prison. I have had that confirmed from various sources.

I am leaving the secretaryship of the League for Human Rights Observance to accept a new post, which will give me legal status as an accredited member of the human rights movement. This will be a precedent. It will be interesting to see what reaction comes from the Home Office(!). Most likely it will come in the form of a <u>further</u> postponement following my October 1982 Review. But I will not, under any circumstances, be blackmailed into renouncing my principles in return for being given a release date. Eventually my people will begin to question the HO as to WHY I am being kept in prison and when that time comes, believe me, they will find themselves in a <u>most</u> embarrassing position – for there is no justification whatever for them to have kept me under maximum security conditions for such a lengthy period of time.

I have had two interviews recently with a psychiatrist, at my own request, and I asked him: do you think there is anything wrong with my state of mind? He replied that I was as mentally fit as the next man. Anyway, I'll go down fighting, be sure of that!

I am enclosing a document consisting of three pages. I want you to <u>have</u> these. <u>Please</u> let me know <u>you have received them</u>, will you? In your next letter. They only explain <u>part</u> of it, but I desperately want you, of <u>all</u> people, to grasp part of what is keeping me in prison. And to understand.

But, my darling, you <u>are</u> helping me – never doubt that for a second. You're my anchor and my lifeline. My Sister! You have given me your friendship and an inspiration that I have received from no-one else; you've changed me, my friend, and whatever good I do in this world will be directly due to your influence and moral support. I owe you one hell of a lot, you know that? Well, for the moment I will close. Thank you for standing by me, it means more than anything.

Be happy and follow your heart. Keep Safe.

Your Devoted Friend and Brother, All My Love

Alex X

'But I will not, under any circumstances, be blackmailed into renouncing my principles in return for being given a release date.' This, of course, was madness but as many people who knew Alex understood, he was full of youthful ideology. The more he railed against the system, no matter how well justified this may have been, the more he put his release from prison in jeopardy. Yet it seemed that he was prepared to sabotage his chances of freedom with such statements. The papers that he sent me contained information pertaining to his arrest and the state of Parkhurst at that time. I have no idea how he managed to smuggle them out.

London
11th February 1981

Darling Alex,

I received your letter and the enclosed papers and will keep them in a safe place OK?

Simon returned from Ireland and I saw him for only <u>one hour</u> in which he said he wanted a divorce. I agreed to his wishes and we are now initiating the proceedings. The only grounds we have are irretrievable breakdown as <u>he</u> is filing for it, not me. He doesn't even live here anymore. He is going to the USA.

Will contact you when I return from Singapore. (Isn't it sad?)

As Ever, Your friend.

Fiona

The media had by now got a whiff that our marriage was in trouble when someone rang a magazine and told them not to run the photos they had just taken of us. This was the point I had been dreading but I realise now that it was more to do with my dented pride, than anything else.

However, my own loneliness was nothing compared to Alex's in solitary confinement on Rule 43. This was his choice because of the danger posed by another prisoner but after a while, isolated from the world, the mind can start to play tricks. The sensory deprivation and lack of contact with other humans can have a severe negative impact on a prisoner's mental state and may lead to depression, paranoia and even suicidal tendencies. Segregated prisoners may become withdrawn and can lose their interpersonal skills. Alex was 'swimming underwater' but his correspondence had come to represent a much needed lifeline. I was concerned that I hadn't heard from him since the 5th February.

London
4th March 1981

My Darling Alex,

Well, there we are. It's all out in the open now. Enclosed are a couple of articles relating to the divorce. Since I've had time to think about it clearly and objectively, and to talk it over with some wonderful friends, I realise now that I would have had to leave that marriage sooner or later. It was becoming unbearable. But my loyalty and beliefs were making me hang on, because I thought that marriage was for life and that I'd never find anyone as good to me as Simon.

Well, I was lying to myself and just didn't have the initial guts to do anything, but since he's made the move, I have felt a great sense of relief.

I don't have to answer to anybody and for the first time in my life I will be totally independent.

I know there will be lonely times – but I was lonely when I was married. Now I can go out and grab life for what it's worth, just like you said. I've discovered I have lots of great friends – people who care and want to help, so I should never be alone.

Singapore was lovely. A welcome break. It's a beautifully clean city now – so different to what I remember – and the Chinese are charming. Our hotel was so new that the swimming pool hadn't opened, so we had to use the pool in a hotel up the road! The filming went OK but I forgot to tell you that the commercial is for Dutch cigarettes and will be shown only in the cinemas.

We filmed for four days in the steaming, humid heat, with smoke machines filling our lungs, me puffing away on a hundred cigs and the Chinese people crowding around to watch! The director said he'd never seen anyone sit so still for so long. Must have been the drugs. I'm off to Milan on March 24th to do another commercial. This time it's for an Italian shampoo. Mamma mia!

6th March

Sorry for the gap. It's been a bit hectic all of a sudden. I didn't realise I had so many friends and they have been wonderful – the phone never stops ringing.

I'm trying to keep busy, so in the mornings I do singing or dancing lessons (I've gone into rigorous self-discipline), which is followed by lunch with either a friend or a work colleague, then maybe a photo-session or interview. Divorce has made me popular with the magazines! Then in the evenings I may go to the theatre with a friend or out to eat with a neighbour.

I'm suddenly enjoying myself in a way that I haven't done for ages. No use in moping around forever, is there? Life's too short. I've done all my crying now. My confidence is slowly coming back and I've lost a lot of weight but I feel fit and look better now. At 24 I'm young enough to start all over again. I'm just beginning!!

Having not heard from you for a few weeks, I hope everything is OK. I am worrying about you. Are you sleeping enough? Are you still on Rule 43? (I'm off the Valium now, by the way).

Take care of yourself and be good. Thinking of you as always.

Love,

Fiona

x

HM Prison Gartree

15. 3. 1981

My Very Dear Friend

I don't know how to put this, so I'll trust to luck and write things down as I go along.

I received your letter of March 4 ok – I'm delighted that you're back on your feet again, that's a girl! Now you have a whole new life ahead of you, Princess, and I know, whatever you do, you'll do it well and be happy. This is good. I'll always remember you, Fiona, more than <u>anybody</u> else.

Now you will have to forget me, my friend. Your new start will be just that, no more writing to an old lag in prison. I doubt now whether my book will be written, this hurts me because it was to have been dedicated to you, but the hurt is lessened because I know that many, many, others will dedicate things to you. I love you but I have one other whom I love, as Tolstoy once said: 'The hero of my story, who I love with all my heart, whom I have tried to recreate in all his beauty, and who was, is and will forever be beautiful is – Truth'. And Freedom. And, I guess, Principles. One day, you will understand. For these things, I fight!

May God go with you, Green Eyes, I shall always be with you!

If you'd like something to read on the flight out to Milan, I recommend a booklet, fresh from the printers, which will tell you a little more about me. It is called 'The Liquid Cosh' and available from my branch office.

Fiona, I love you. I hope you have got as much out of our relationship as I have, I am deeply in your debt. Goodbye, my darling, look after yourself. May life be kind to you. Never say die!

Yours Forever, Alex XX
Citizens Commission on Human Rights, Gartree

> The Road goes ever on and on
> Out from the door where it began.
> Now far ahead the Road has gone,
> Let others follow it who can!

> *J R R Tolkien, 'Lord of the Rings'*

I was devastated when I received this and felt full of remorse that I could have been so insensitive in my last letter. Had I prompted this rather poignant 'goodbye' note because I seemed to be getting 'back on my feet'? I didn't realise his darkening mood was leading to real despair — as he explains in the following letter.

HM Prison Gartree
27. 3. 1981

My Dear Fiona

I'm going to ask a selfish thing. I'd like to ask you to disregard the last letter I wrote to you, if you can. I've made a bloody fool of myself again. Owing to the situation when I wrote it, a number of things were happening, the accumulative effect of these things led me to believe it would be better for you to disassociate yourself from me.

You've had enough heartache over the last few months, I didn't wish to add to it now you're getting back on your feet. But a part of me died when I'd posted that letter, and it's more painful than the difficulties I was faced with at the time! Those difficulties seemed then to justify a letter to you to cut you off from my problems. But I was <u>wrong</u> and should have known. I underestimated by own capabilities of coping. I've always made it before and thought I was indestructible, that I could climb out from behind the devil's teeth and spit in his face afterwards. Well, that's what I have done again. It's all over now but at the time I really thought I was going down and I just had to get something to you before I drowned. It was probably the worst period of real despair I've been through. But I've made it.

It could have hurt you, Princess: I swear that wasn't the intention, and if it did I am dreadfully sorry. I guess your letter asking if anything was wrong, when everything <u>was</u> wrong, made me reply in the way I did … there was, you see, <u>no way</u> I could tell you <u>what</u> was wrong. So how could I reply? Write to you as though nothing was wrong and try to disguise the reality? No, you'd have seen through it. And, anyway, lying to you has never been on.

Someday, I <u>will</u> let you know what's been happening, and you'll see how that letter came to be written, the reasoning behind it, everything. We still pals?

I've just recently been told that I am to be transferred in the next few weeks to MAIDSTONE prison, which is out of the top-security system, and from where I'll have a real chance of being released. So, at long last – the light at the end of the tunnel. Things are much more optimistic now, and I know that if I continue to stay out of trouble I can be out within the next three years – and that's definite. Now I know where I'm going there is suddenly the incentive to work towards social re-adjustment, or whatever they call it. Now the programme is to regain my physical fitness, come off the drugs, push myself to regain all I've lost in the past 10 years, and I can do it. No problem.

In many ways I'm my own worst enemy, challenging the system, pursuing and rooting out the inhumanity that exists in the Black side of our democracy. I can never turn a blind eye to such things, and that's my only failing. The outspokenness. I'll have to learn to keep my trap shut.

Have you received 'The Liquid Cosh'? I think it's vital that you get a copy, for it will show you what I have used my life for. It would certainly give you a clearer understanding of this guy you write to, you know. You have more knowledge of me than any other person but to complete that knowledge this booklet is a must.

Today is the 27th, so you are probably still in Milan as I write this.

At present I am just keeping my fingers crossed that you will still want to continue with me (wouldn't really blame you for giving up). At the moment we are living in completely different worlds, most of your world, which I have not visited recently, is beyond my comprehension, and I am sure the obverse is true; that you know very little about prison, its stresses, pressures, Catch-22s; its psychology and utter frustration; its impracticality. Fiona – stay with me! Burn my last letter. It never happened.

However things work out, take good care of yourself, Sister. I think of you always. Write if you forgive me. Yes?

All My Love to You, Your Friend and Brother.

Alex Xx

After making the shampoo commercial in Milan, Venice beckoned. Having not visited before, I decided to jump on a train and do the tourist thing, alone. It was strangely empowering to be travelling solo, having just been dumped by my husband, and it was the beginning of a new found independence.

London
8th April 1981

Dearest Alex,

Thank you for your letter. I was very, very relieved to hear from you and to know that you are alright. I can't imagine what happened to you Alex – it must have been awful. But you climbed out of it. You are strong. Please, please take care of yourself. You are very special to me.

Briefly, I am OK and bearing up through it all. Sort of. I stay as busy as possible, though I would love to work properly. Filming in Milan was hectic, which I followed with a brief holiday in Venice. I went all on my own but had a great time and thought Venice fantastic. I was a proper tourist! Saw a lot in four days. Even went to Hemingway's hideaway on the island of Torcello.

One weird thing happened. Just outside the palace in St Marks Square I bumped into some friends of my in-laws. They asked how Simon was. That was, um, embarrassing. For them!

Enclosed are some pics of me in St Marks Square. Will write soon.

All Love, Fiona

HM Prison Gartree
11. 4. 1981

My Very Dear Friend

Thanks!!! I got your letter this morning and it was still in front of me an hour after I'd read it ... what can I say? Princess, you can't imagine how happy I feel. Or, maybe you can, because, my dear friend, you are also very special to me ...

Yes, what happened was awful, but what made things even more so was my reasoning that my friends must be kept out of this line of fire – when I fight battles I have always done so alone. If I think I am going to be hurt then I'll be damned if my friends are going to be affected in the process, and so I cut my friends off. I go it alone. The letter I wrote on the 15th March was the most painful letter I have ever had to write in my life, I just <u>prayed</u> you would read between the lines and understand what I was trying to say. Such things are so difficult to express on paper. And my reasoning was wrong. You have proven to me that your friendship is steadfast, I know now that I have one friend. And, in me, you have also one solid friend, may this always be so!! One important thing about having a good friend is that one has someone to <u>confide</u> in … but, because of prison rules and regulations it is often made impossible for a prisoner to describe what is happening to him. Complaining about prison treatment is forbidden – but I hope that one day I will be free to explain such occurrences to you.

You say you are staying as busy as possible, though you'd love to work properly. Suppose that I write a script for a play … would you be willing, if a venue can be found, to take a part in it? A kind of charity do, for maybe one or two performances? What do you think? At this stage it's just an idea. You could help enormously!

Well, inside the next two weeks I should be arriving at Maidstone Prison, it's down in Kent someplace. I'll have to spend maybe two years (maybe less) there before moving on to an open prison then another year and that should be <u>it</u>. Finish. I'll write to you as soon as I get there, let you know what the atmosphere is like. There will be quite a few people from Parkhurst there that I know, so I should get on alright. I'm off Rule 43 now, by the way, and am back on B-Wing, so at least I can watch a bit of television and do some more constructive work in the workshop.

By the way, I'm on packing … stacking finished garments into <u>bundles of 10</u>, wrapping them in plastic bags and sewing 10 bags into a sack, ready for shipment out. Very intelligent work I'll have you know.

Take good care of yourself, Sister, I'm thinking of you every day.

All My Love to You Princess.

Alex

Xx

While Alex was awaiting his move to Maidstone, I was undergoing a transformation at home. Simon had moved to Los Angeles to be with Linda Purl and sent his brother round to pack up all his furniture, paintings and books to be loaded onto a container bound for the USA. I remember sitting on the floor, while the house was stripped of all his stuff, and thinking that divorce was definitely not for cowards. Possessions cease to mean anything and the detritus of everyday life looks shabby. A girlfriend gave me a pep talk and told me to take charge of my life.

HM Prison Gartree

16. 4. 1981

My Dearest Fiona

'The Secretary of State has fully considered your petition. Arrangements will be made for your transfer from Gartree to Maidstone in due course'. I'm relieved that the Home Office has confirmed my move and I'm hoping 'in due course' will mean within the next fortnight. Hell's teeth, it's taken them long enough! Much of the rest of the day I have been thinking of you. I am hoping beyond hope that our bond will ever strengthen and never falter, whatever it was that brought us together I pray will keep us together. I know more than ever before that I need you so much. Ha! Whatever will you think of that, I wonder?

Yesterday a theatre group called 'Stirabout' came to the prison and gave us an hour and half's entertainment; they were very good indeed. The programme consisted of a multiple of sketches and a few songs. Two girls and two blokes made up the group, one of the blokes put on this pair of digital dark glasses, which blinked on and off – it was hilarious! And they were all very talented musicians (one of the girls suddenly appeared with a tenor sax, of all things, and played it fairly well). At first I wasn't going to go, but a mate of mine said why not, it'll make a change, so I said okay, and I'm glad that I went. I guess I thought they'd be amateurs.

I'll be glad when I get to Maidstone. I'll be able to start painting once again. The first two weeks may be rough, though, as they do not dispense sleeping draughts there, but it'll be okay in the long run. Touch wood. The thing is, you see, during the day we aren't in our cells very long, there's the workshops and association, etc. But from 8 pm in the evenings to 7 a.m. next morning we're locked in our cells continuously, so if one can't sleep there's little else to do but pace backwards and forwards or lay staring at the ceiling and walls. You can imagine how this can get at you.

Hopefully after the first fortnight things will become less tense, especially if I get some paints; painting is good for me because it relaxes me and I get a lot of enjoyment from it.

I've been doing another programme of press ups and Jesus it's killing me, I have to do at least 120 a day which is also approximately the number of roll ups I smoke; it's a real comedy. What is the best way to stop smoking, Fiona? I've tried everything, got any suggestions? Willpower's out – I need cigarettes to fuel willpower, and chewing gum is banned in prisons. The thing is – I want to stop (!) Caramba, I wish … oh, I wish a million things, a billion things. I could perhaps try counting my wishes at nights and maybe it would cure my insomnia, like counting sheep. But, no. One wish, just one, to come true … ! And there, I have made it, with fingers crossed in the orthodox tradition and also, with not a little discomfiture, two toes. Big Medicine! Do not be curious. Do not ask me about the wish – it is a secret, you see. Should it come true then I shall tell you of the wish, and you will laugh, yes? Viva!

So for now, please take care, Fiona … I am proud that you are my friend, may this always be so. Let me know how things are with you. My finest regards to your Mother and Father, not forgetting little Sunday!

Your Friend and Brother

Alex X

Winchester
17th April 1981

Darling Alex,

Thank you for your letter. Our friendship will never falter. I am here for you Alex. Come rain or shine.

I'm in Winchester with Mum and Dad for Easter and we all send you our warmest love and special thoughts over this period. Sunday sends an extra 'woof' to you too! The sun is shining and we've been working in the garden all day and are thoroughly exhausted.

I expect you are looking forward to your move to Maidstone Prison. It sounds good. V positive. Hope it comes soon. I'm sure it will be good for you. Take care my special friend.

Warmest Love, FF

HM Prison Gartree
27. 4. 1981

My Dearest Fiona

Good to hear from you – extremely good. And even from Sunday – Caramba! I think working in the garden is as good a way as any to spend a short holiday – the flowers will thank you come the summer! The main thing is that you enjoyed yourself, yes? I was thinking of you over Easter and about the past five years and every other day that floats by, this is a marvellous way of spending the time; I think so anyway. As long as you stay safe and happy then my mental energy is not being wasted.

There's a rumour going around that this year we are going to have a May Queen(!) and that the guy won't know about it until the actual day, ha! But I'll be at Maidstone for May Day; symbolic, I'd like to imagine. 200 press-ups a day, now, and increasing!! I'm beginning to really feel better – gets rid of the frustration and tension better than anything.

Today I woke up to a white world outside. Snow is still thick on the ground and it's quite cold; of course this is my element really. But it is strange that only three days ago men were stripped down to their T-shirts because of the heat! It's a shame because outside my window there is a patch of Spring daffodils, which were in full bloom yesterday, alas during the night the strong winds bent them over and the snow has buried their heads. Perhaps they will recover but much sunshine is needed … will you come and smile for them, it is their only hope!!

My probation officer, Teresa, arrived last Tuesday – half an hour early – so we managed two hours together and had a few laughs. She asked about you and I said you were fine, that you had just got back from Milan. We get on very well … I suppose because we're almost direct opposites.

The radio went dead again last night, I took off the back with a screwdriver and had a poke about but it seems one of the transistors has bust so I'm in trouble. Damn thing.

Stick with me, Princess. Today, I am nothing. Tomorrow, we shall see! You've known me through good times and bad and still you are there; you may never realise how much this means to me. My best friend. I will probably write my next letter from Maidstone! Until then, you take good care of yourself,

Alex, XX

The Strength of the Earth

The strength of the earth
though you may not see
holds you
and surely protects you just so
in mighty arms
never let them go
The trees are sighing
their laden bowers
softly sway
for you alone far down below
never let them go.
The flowers break into bloom
their joy a sweet profusion
Heavenly scent
and it is to you they wish it to blow
never let them go
My heart watches you
and is held entranced
caught in a moment of never-ending flow
never let it go

Alex, 1981

HM Prison Maidstone
Medway Wing
30. 4. 1981

My Darling Fiona

Well I have just arrived here at Maidstone. This morning was wholly taken up by the travelling, I came down in a Jag XJ6 and it took four hours to reach here. We had to come through London, New Cross, Lewisham and actually drove past the wall of Buckingham Palace. I was amazed at the amount of traffic and the number of people on the streets, it seemed like a world gone crazy, maybe it's because there are so many people out of work. We went past Victoria Railway Station and that, at least, hasn't changed much since the days I spent around there – also I noted that some of the London taxi cabs had gone two-tone! I guess that reflects more than anything the changing scene out there.

While all this was around me I couldn't help searching every street for a sight of Kermit . We did go past a green mini but there was some bloke at the wheel. Damn. What a disappointment!

This prison is not at all like Gartree, the atmosphere is different and is going to take some getting used to, but no doubt I'll adapt as always. Guess what? As I came into reception another prisoner arrived at the same time from Wandsworth – it was Chilly! We shook hands and humorously remarked how fate keeps us together – he has just got 2½ years; alas, he has gone onto a different wing while I am located on Medway Wing (the long-term wing).

In my prayers also I ask that the bond between us shall never be weakened: only strengthened and that we will truly become as close as brother and sister. It is you alone who has given me strength while I have been in prison, the strength to restore lost and dying hope into burning resolution. If I am released from prison – will you still be there to offer me counsel? – for I will need it then perhaps far more than whilst I remain here …

And so I am at Maidstone. And so begins another chapter.

I Remain as Ever, With Love, Your Friend and Brother

Alex XX

It is interesting that here Alex says, '*If* I am released' as opposed to his usual more optimistic '*When* I am released, in three or four years'.

London
Wednesday 6th May 1981
11.30 pm

Hello My Darling Alex,

Well. How's Maidstone? I hope the journey was OK (XJ6 huh? That's posh!!) and that you are well and now ensconced in your temporary dwelling (Oooh that sounds funny. I daren't say 'home' because it's not is it?).

Thanks for your last letter. The poem is absolutely beautiful. Very clever. I'd love to be able to perform it somewhere. Talking of which, you mentioned a play that you'd like to write for charity. Well, I think it's a splendid idea and of course I would like to take part. I'd be delighted.

Anyway, how are you? I do hope you are safe and well and all those ghastly problems have been left behind in G.

I seem to be alright-ish. Up and down you know. My social life is a bit of a whirl, which is nice occasionally but often I just want to stay at home and watch TV! Sounds very mundane, but the fellas always expect something from me after they've taken me out a couple of times. I find them all <u>very</u> boring. Why can't a girl just go to the theatre and have a pleasant evening, without the knowledge that she's going to get pounced on later? I mean really!!

It's very flattering in a way that I'm having so much attention from men at the moment, but I'm not crazy about a single one of them and, as I'm still in a vulnerable state, all I want is a good laugh, not silly games.

Anyway, I keep as busy as possible. If it's a quiet day I rush about the house like a tornado doing all the housework—my wretched Hoover has just conked out. Nothing exciting on the work horizon. I think I've got a lousy agent. He's not a hustler and neither am I.

Then there are the children that keep me busy. Have I told you about them? Three gorgeous little girls from three different families in my street. Shirin, 10, Sarah, 8, and Claire, 6.

They all come round here after school for tea and play in my garden and chat and generally have a good time. Yesterday, we all washed Kermit, my car. They are very polite and terrifically good company. Of course, they love it when I'm in the papers 'cos then they can show their friends and show off! We play games and have great fun. Last week I took them to Madame Tussauds (the waxworks) near Baker Steet but it was terribly crowded and the poor things could hardly see.

I hope you're not analysing this handwriting 'cos I'm rather tired now. You may of course; I'm dying to know what you make of my hand. Being a naturally inquisitive person I'm fascinated by things like that.

Ah well. Night-night. Sleep well my friend. I'll continue tomorrow. Zzzzzzzzzzzzzzz.

Thursday 7th May 1981

Hi Alex,

Just returned from a boozy lunch with a lawyer friend of mine (he's not actually representing me in my divorce, but being a good friend he gives me lots of practical advice) and what should be on my doormat? A gas bill and a letter from ALEX!! I was going to make some enquiries about the Maidstone address but now I don't have to. It's already here. How lovely of you to write so soon. I thought it would be a while before I heard from you, as I know it takes time to get settled. So Chilly is there too! How amazing. Even though you are on different wings, will you see much of him?

Keep up the exercises. They work for mind as well as body. I'm still doing my dance classes but find I need to be pushed before I work out properly. I tend to be rather lazy at home and not do them.

Yes, the bond between us _will_ get stronger, Alex. It will never die now. I'll always be here when you need me. I need you too, don't forget, so together we'll muddle through.

I haven't received a copy of 'The Liquid Cosh' but, if you can get hold of it, I'd love to read it.

Oh dear, I'm smoking far too much. Like you I'm trying to give it up but I haven't found the solution. No secret to it—just willpower.

Can I send you things at Maidstone, like books, soap, toothpaste etc?? If it is permitted, let me know what you require and I'll see what I can do.

What on earth did you wish for in your letter of 16th April? And why would it make me laugh? I know you told me not to ask but please don't wish for the impossible. Wish for something that is within reach and then the possibility is always there that one's wish will be granted.

I often wish and pray that you will be safe and well. You have far too great a mind and talent to be wasted. Do not search for ideals or lost causes. I don't really understand your politics and beliefs (as you know) but I do believe that you must live for NOW and use every minute to the best of your ability. Write, paint, think, compose, discuss. But stay away from danger. From trouble. The signals are always there, my friend. And when they appear, steer clear.

I've been near danger many times. I've nearly lost my life on three occasions but always the signal was there and I was able to avoid the danger (I think I have a guardian angel). Life is the most precious gift we have and what we do with it is entirely up to us. I can't fully comprehend why an intelligent, witty, talented, loveable person like you has got involved in a situation that has landed you where you are. And why you keep adding fuel to the fire I will never know probably. All I care about is you. So please, please be good and keep safe.

Must go now. You mean a lot to me Alex, so I look forward to your next letter.

Fondest Love and Affection,

Fiona

x

Sadly, this is the last of my letters to Alex that were brought back to me. All my letters from mid-1981 to 1988, when I received Alex's final letter, are missing.

By this time Alex had served ten years and was still only 28-years-old. He thought his situation was improving but the harsh reality was that he was to serve another 12 years. This seems incredible to me but in his letters, which became increasingly sporadic, I could sense that his resolve was wavering and that his fighting spirit was being radically reduced by the amount of medication he was being given.

HM Prison Maidstone
Medway Wing
23/25. 5. 1981

My Dearest Fiona

Hello again, Princess, I hope you received my last letter okay. I have just re-read your own letter, which I got on the 11th.

You sound very well in your letter and I hope things have not changed since – your only problem seems to be concerning men; ah, I have no answer to that, my friend, nor advice to offer … one can easily understand the situation for you are so indescribably beautiful! Of course you are going to have men attempting to get you into bed if only to satisfy their egos, very selfish I know; but there's nothing wrong with finding yourself a young man that you <u>like</u> … if he truly respects you and isn't on an ego trip, he won't pull any Funnies.

I will do an analysis of your handwriting next and it will arrive with my next letter to you. From what I see you are still a little depressed – this comes over in the slant of your lines. A useful tip is always to write each line dead horizontal – as though you were using lined notepaper. In particular use this method if writing to someone with regard to a job of work.

Having said that, you are certainly happier than over Christmas – given another few months and you will be right back on form again. My dear Carrot, you don't have to understand my politics or beliefs, I am not involved with politics any more. But my beliefs are strong, and yet they are simple for they are the beliefs of everybody – the

<u>only</u> difference is that while most people <u>talk</u> about doing something I cut out the talk and just get the thing <u>done</u>. I have crossed that dividing line and for me there is no turning back. My cause is Freedom – is that really a lost cause? Is it not <u>worth</u> fighting for?

I have studied with a great deal of attention what you said in your letter and I am left with an enormous sadness. I wish at times that I was just an ordinary bloke, devoid of ideals, living for NOW and keeping well clear of danger, the average guy in the street, conventional, etc. And so there is sadness. I have gone through <u>too much</u>, you see, to ever be that kind of a person.

I was very moved to see you say that the bond between us will grow stronger, I hope so very much.

Well, I am thinking of getting married. Her name is Joan Brönnimann and, though she is 14 or 15 years older (chronologically – <u>I'm</u> Eleventy Eight) than me I know we shall be happy. At present she is away in Zürich (her daughter Tamara and son André are studying there) and is visiting Norway next week, but she will be back on June 14th and I'll see her soon after. I know she will say yes if I ask her, but I want to meet André and Tamara first. I think they will be coming to England in July. I'm getting too old now, Fiona, it's time I was settling down and a wife <u>will</u> be a stabilising factor; with that kind of responsibility I won't be able to afford serious trouble. And we'll go a long way. But I'm by no means yet fully decided, there are a lot of factors involved and I have to make absolutely certain it is what we want; I guess next time I see her I will make a decision one way or the other. Oh, well, wish me luck.

I see the Old Vic has closed down this week; another blow to the British traditional theatre. What a state. And they closed with 'The Beggar's Opera' – I wonder, did you decide to attend? I know it's a performance you are very familiar with.

I think it is absolutely wonderful for you to have the children around you as you do, they must be quite a tonic and you'll give them someone to look up to. Keep them smiling and happy and they will do the same for you.

On Medway Wing I have one or two guys that I talk to, one of them is 65 and plays me at Scrabble (beating me every time to be honest), but I like to think I'm helping take his mind off things. The other bloke keeps getting nicked for one thing and another – it's just the way he is. I used to be like him too at the beginning of my sentence, not caring about anything with the life stretch falling away in front of me.

Most cons think people outside don't give a damn about them and really begin to believe that. Consequently they go out of prison cursing the whole of society and generally end up back in the Necropolis as a result. If only more people recognised prisoners as humanoid we might begin to get somewhere, it would lead to a reciprocal awareness and do much to reduce the statistics of crime.

I left my spider behind in Gartree and at the moment I have no pets, I was thinking of getting a budgie and teaching it Russian but I think it would be cruel to keep a budgie in a cell full of Alex's cigarette smoke. Seriously. A lot of cons have budgies yet neglect them in such a way, the poor birds have to suffer and that's something I feel strongly about. Consideration, it doesn't cost anything.

Well, my darling, this letter is coming to an end, the night is closing in and I want this in the post box by first thing tomorrow. I hope I haven't sounded too heavy, when writing to you I try to make a conscious effort not to do so. You need cheering up just as much as I do and I sincerely hope you have raised at least one smile during this letter. Do not worry about me, worry instead about how to make the children happy! Be kind, be tolerant, be yourself.

Stay safe, stay wonderful; be HAPPY in all that you do.

With Deepest Respect,

Your Devoted Friend and Brother,

Alex

Since my last letter on May 7th, my life had changed considerably. Not only was I dating again but also the surge in publicity had resulted in a global contract with the cosmetics company Max Factor, to be the 'face' of their new range and to represent them as an ambassador for their products. I had gone from a very sheltered childhood at home with my parents, straight into a marriage and was now experiencing what it was like to be young, free and single in London. Suddenly, things were looking up.

My next letter to Alex, after a considerable gap, is missing, but I must have mentioned my new job with Max Factor because he replied as follows:

HM Prison Maidstone
Medway Wing
4. 8. 1981

My Dearest Friend

Thanks for your letter! Though short. Wonderful nonetheless!

How are you, my friend (apart, that is, from what I read in the newspapers)? To be sure, from what I see in your letter, fate is being kind to you once more; and no-one deserves it more than yourself! May it always be so. Stay happy and always follow your heart! And … look at this – first, all those submarines; and now an advertising campaign! – for Max Factor – and things are only just starting for you (I can see ahead for <u>years</u>!). One day, all that you seek will be yours. I've also thought about you, it isn't an exaggeration to say that every day I find myself wondering how you are and whether I'd ever hear from you again. I blamed 'The Liquid Cosh' for your silence, thinking it too radical and, perhaps, revealing for you. By hearing from you again you've made me feel one hell of a lot better – Fiona, I'm glad you wrote!!

Next year I get married. We haven't fixed a proper date yet but no doubt we'll arrive at something specific soon. Joan – my fiancée – is a wonderful person and I love her very much. When I get out (how many times have I used those words!) we will live in East Grinstead, which is fairly near to London – though first we shall rent a cottage in The Lakes for a week or two – something I know I'll appreciate more than anything (you know of my love for Cumberland)!

Did you see much of the royal wedding? I thought it was quite an affair – though I couldn't help but remember another much more beautiful, more radiant Princess who once graced the steps of St. Paul's …

I went on a Board the other day – it's a meeting they have every so often where one is confronted with a deputy governor, chaplain, welfare worker, education officer, etc. for the purpose of assessment, or something equally ridiculous – anyway, I was told I would have to remain here for at least another two years. This before I would even be considered for a move towards release. So I was pretty cut-up over that. Still, I'm getting used to this kind of thing. I can't help wondering whether I ever will get out.

I'm presently involved in re-writing my play 'Tempestuous Grows The Don' into a farce, which includes introducing a female role – how do you fancy playing the role of a Mafia Don's daughter?!

Again, it was fantastic to hear from you! I will be writing a more comprehensive letter soon – I have three more people to write to tonight! 'Till then – stay safe, happy and beautiful! As always, my dear Nomad: Your Friend and Brother.

All of My Love, Alex

The summer of 1981 saw me suddenly thrust into the limelight again with the filming of the Max Factor commercial and my face was plastered across giant hoardings. Invitations to the most glamorous parties came thick and fast and the trauma of the events six months previously started to ease. But there was an uncomfortable feeling about all this attention. Did people sense that the vulnerability made me easy prey? Was I being manipulated?

I hadn't written to Alex for a while and I was bemused about how he was going to get married, when the following letter arrived.

West View Gardens
East Grinstead
West Sussex
13th September 1981

Dear Fiona,

I am writing to you on behalf of Alex Alexandrowicz, Maidstone Prison.

Alex has received a document in which the government of the United Kingdom submits its observations regarding an application made by Alex. In this document it states that during the first six months of 1980 he had three visits from his 'prison visitor' and one visit from Miss Fiona Fullerton!

Well, Alex had in fact one visit from Tom his prison visitor and, as you know, you did not visit him then.

Alex would very much appreciate if you could write to him and on a separate piece of paper make a sworn statement 'to verify that you have never been to see him in prison'.

Hoping you will be able to do this and many thanks.

Yours sincerely

Joan Brönnimann

PS On second thoughts! Maybe it would be better if you sent your statement to me, so that I could make extra copies of it to send to Alex, which he will no doubt need. JB.

Of course, two prison visitor passes had been sent to me in early 1980 when I was unable to visit Alex. I sent the statement as requested, hoping it would help.

In October 1981 I was cast in the lead role in the wonderful Stephen Sondheim musical 'Gypsy', playing the American burlesque entertainer Gypsy Rose Lee, who transforms herself from goofy kid to dazzling star. It is still one of my favourite musical roles. We opened at the Leicester Haymarket in December, during the coldest, snowiest winter in years.

Alex, meanwhile, had made sufficient noise to get himself transferred from Maidstone Prison to Lewes Prison in Sussex, in November 1981. He claimed he was being threatened by a group of prisoners at Maidstone.

- 9 -
Letting Go

It would be dishonest if I said that Alex was always at the forefront of my mind at the beginning of 1982, for the show I was in was exhausting and I was also having to return to London, sometimes in the middle of the night, to fulfil Max Factor commitments. 'Gypsy' was lavishly mounted with a view to transferring to the West End, which in the end didn't happen. As a consolation prize, we were all picked up and recast in the Sandy Wilson musical 'The Boyfriend', which toured the Far East and Middle East for 12 weeks. A prize indeed.

I wrote to Alex in March 1982 to tell him that I was off to the Far East again and to apologise if my silence had hurt or worried him. From his reply it seemed he very much regretted trying to end our friendship the previous summer and thought that was why I hadn't been in touch.

HM Prison Lewes
C-Wing
5. 4. 1982

To My Very Dear Friend

Hello, Princess! I guess I could say it's wonderful to hear from you, but 'wonderful' would perhaps be the wrong word to use. Marvellous? Still the wrong word. Somebody's swiped my dictionary. Anyhow, it was good to get your letter! – it made me very happy … I've been following all the press about you and I've been very content that there's been no 'looking back' for you and that what you are doing now is giving you much happiness.

Yes, I've been hoping so much that you would write, and I've thought about you on countless occasions but after the letter I sent to you last summer … I really couldn't turn to anyone else at that time, you see, and I wrote that letter to you five times, tearing it up again and again, before I closed my eyes and let it go. Even so, I knew inside that I was probably doing the wrong thing … I've lived through worse mistakes of my own making but there have been none that I've regretted so much afterwards. Still, what I wrote were the facts as they stood. Sure, I can understand you being a little frightened then; you must believe that I am extremely sorry for whatever distress I caused you, I never meant it to be that way, Fiona. I'm not very proud of myself.

In the event, I went ahead and I managed to obtain limited legal aid from the European Court, but not for the case which I considered the more important (my medical records to be made public – which could have brought about my release) but, rather, a secondary case, which is due to be heard at the Council of Europe later this year.

Of course you haven't hurt me, my dear friend. I was hurt a little. More than a little. Well, to tell the truth, quite a hell of a lot, actually. But there's no one to blame for that but myself. You understand? Self-inflicted. I wanted very much to write, but I didn't think that that would be fair, and so I decided to wait for you to write, in your own time. Perhaps I was wrong. And if that waiting was painful, then don't kid yourself, girl, I deserved it; maybe it will pay in part for my having hurt you! Anyway, Nomad, all I know is it's great to be in touch with you again.

However, yes, my friend, I did follow the successful progress of 'Gypsy' from opening night in November, and I was overjoyed that it did so well, though I was as disappointed as you that the show didn't transfer to the West End! Never mind. Next time, eh?

A friend of mine from Epic House went along with his wife, to see you, and he said they thought you were 'stunning' and the biggest hit at the Leicester Haymarket since a Junkers went down in 1944 – mind you, they got in for free, compliments of Radio Leicester, but for a couple of critics like those – who cares? Most of all, I'm really glad that you found your role, the show and everything concerned with it, such a happy experience. That's all that counts.

I also saw you a few times on television last year, when I was at Maidstone (note my new address), and I thought you looked a million Swiss francs! These were the

Max Factor advertisements. Because I didn't want to miss more than I had to, you were responsible for putting me through such psychological sedatives as 'Crossroads' and 'Emmerdale Farm'; by the time the ads ceased to appear, my brain was sloshing around my head like semolina pudding.

Yes, Fiona, of course I remember your last stay in Hong Kong. Certainly, I have a postcard on the wall, which you sent from there – will you also be staying at the HK Hilton on this occasion? From the list of all the places you're to visit, I can see what you mean when you say this tour will be a long one, by the time you reach Singapore you're going to be exhausted, woman!

Perhaps they will allow you to change from 'The Boyfriend' to 'The Sleeping Beauty' at Kuala Lumpur and Muscat – at least that would get you off your feet! Anyway, do send a postcard or two, will you?

Aye, another year older. Seems like a decade. This time next year I'm hoping to be out, back in the world of liquorice sticks and Rice Krispies. This time, I think I can be a little optimistic, with good reason. It may be earlier. A Petition was finally launched in December, calling either for my release, or a public inquiry, and there's around 250 signatures on it, so far.

Lewes is a very different prison from Maidstone. I've been in 11 different prisons on this sentence, in as many years: and I'm hoping this one will be my last. I have my Review in October and I hope they'll make a decision to release me on the Hostel Scheme – though I won't know either way until around six months after the Review has begun – so I'll know, say, in March, next year.

Will you write again soon? Half a page, or whatever. Doesn't matter.

In the meantime, my dear Fiona, take good care of yourself, lass, and STAY HAPPY! It was really something to hear from you again … Take care. Let me know your progress with 'The Boyfriend'!

As Ever, Your Friend and Brother,
All my love

Alex Xxxx

Once again Alex was being overly optimistic, which can be a symptom of the discretionary lifer. In fact, far from being his 'last prison', he was only at Lewes until February 1983 and spent some of that time on C-Wing. He would spend time in a further *nine* prisons before his eventual release which was still years away. He was unable to settle, to make friends, and continually struggled to conform to the system, which made him 'a problem'. His levels of despair plunged to greater depths as time went by.

Meanwhile, I was touring in 'The Boyfriend', playing to ex-pats all over the Middle East and Far East. Far removed from Alex's ever-more depressing existence, we were having a ball and once again were treated like visiting royalty in Hong Kong, Bangkok and Singapore. In all, there were eight cities on the itinerary, finishing in Muscat, Oman.

Worried about Alex and riddled with guilt that I was not communicating as frequently as before, I wrote him a long, chatty letter. In a previous one I had asked him what he thought about having his letters and poetry published; particularly his poetry, which I thought should have a wider audience. I suggested that a friend of mine, Andy Ward, come to see him to explain the idea and to see what he thought (I was still too anxious about meeting Alex to go myself).

HM Prison Lewes
C- Wing
19. 5. 1982

To My Dearest Friend

Hello, Princess! It won't be very long now until you return from abroad, so here's a couple of lines to say Welcome Back Welcome Back Welcome Back Welcome Back Welcome Back Welcome Back …

There's no way you're going to believe this but it's true! – I've just been to see if I had any mail, and I find I have one from you!! If I didn't believe in superstitious claptrap I'd probably write it off as a coincidence. Make what you will of it … this keeps happening … Anyhow, excuse me for a few minutes while I read your letter!

A 'few minutes' indeed! That is a very beautiful letter I've just read. Six years, is it? Since I first wrote? That's a quarter of your life – and almost a fifth of mine … a long time, in those terms. I do remember my first letter to you … was it over-complimentary? Yes, ma'm. The problem being of course, my not being able to make it over-complimentary enough – I guess I liked you one hell of a lot. There is nothing that I wouldn't do for you. In the context of a brother feeling the same way for a sister, you understand. Kind of. You say I have a gift with words, Princess – but without inspiration there is nothing … One day when people begin to read my work and wonder where my inspiration comes from, only you and I will ever know.

Yes, Andy Ward came down at the beginning of the month and we had a good talk during which he outlined the details of the project, which you mentioned in your last letter. I think it is a good idea so far, Fiona, but there are certain things I want done, which will tie up a few loose ends.

Wow, you're surely not worrying about your age already?? Surely not. 26. Can you tell me if there's something wrong with growing more beautiful, learning more knowledge, acquiring an understanding and a 'feel' for life? Sure, you are growing older, isn't it great? It's the only precise thing we know about our future and there isn't a damn thing we can do to alter it. If we can accept it, that's fine, my friend – if we can't, we're in trouble. The only thing to do with life is <u>live</u> it!

Yes, I'm certain that if I'd been abroad for three months, I too would be glad to be back home again! I don't think you've ever been away for as long as this before, have you? So getting back will be nice! Cheer up, Nomad, it won't be long now. It's true what you say about our letters … today there has been no work for us, so I was faced with a long and boring day when I woke up this morning. Locked in my cell I was wracking my brains to think of something to do – I didn't feel much like writing a letter, really, and then I thought 'well – why not write to Fiona, she'll be coming home soon'. So I began this letter and it cheered me up to be writing to you … just like always, like old times. And I'm glad for that. Six years … !

We've sure come through a lot, haven't we? Since 1976. Incredible. Yes, please <u>do</u> write again when you get back, after you've wound down and settled-in, I'll look forward to that! In the meantime, though, look after yourself, Fiona, and stay safe!

As Ever – Your Friend and Brother

Lots of love

Alex, Xxx

My friend Andy Ward made a transcript of his meeting with Alex and in it he noted that the only time Alex became agitated was when talking about his parents. They discussed his letters to me and he said that he didn't have this kind of relationship with anyone else and that none of the other prisoners knew about it. He told Andy about the night he was arrested and what happened in the days that followed.

> 'The police produced this picture of me with this guy Laptev, I suppose they must have taken it in the park. They asked me what we talked about and wouldn't believe what I told them. They then stripped me and left me in a cell for two days. Then they came back and offered me a deal: if I was charged under the civil offence of helping the Russians—they maintained I had been carrying things for the local KGB people in the North—I would certainly get life and probably never come out. They then said if I pleaded guilty to two criminal charges for offences that had been committed in Preston that night, I'd get off with four years. I was stoned, so I said OK. They wouldn't let me have a solicitor and then I discovered that the two charges I'd pleaded guilty to were GBH and breaking into a house and knifing an old woman. Well I just wouldn't do that, it wasn't and never has been my style.'

Andy described him as 'perfectly sane, very charming and occasionally displaying the same dry humour that appears so often in the letters'. Sadly, the project came to nothing.

During the summer of 1982, I auditioned for the lead role of Guinevere in the Lerner and Loewe musical 'Camelot'. The New York production was transferring to London complete with its star Richard Harris and I was determined to capture the part. I was up against some stiff competition but it would mean the world to me to be starring in a West End musical of this calibre. The director Michael Rudman put me through my paces in four exhausting auditions, singing opera, spouting Shakespeare (which was highly unnecessary) and most of the score. Eventually the part was mine and I was giddily excited. Having always wanted to be like Julie Andrews, here I was playing the same role that had made her name on Broadway in 1960.

Max Factor was thrilled as well and had me appearing at cosmetics counters all over the country. I was also involved in an obsessive relationship, which possibly explains the lack of contact with Alex.

For Alex, life at Lewes was becoming unbearable and he asked to be transferred out. Once again he sought to be on Rule 43.

HM Prison Lewes
Segregation Unit
22. 12. 1982

To My Dear Friend

Thanks for the Christmas card you sent. Is it Christmas, already? I guess the time's going by pretty fast, these Christmases are getting fairly blurred, you just wake up and another one hits you. 1983. Well, I hope this New Year proves to be even happier for you than the last one, if that's possible. I'm glad to see that recently things are going so well for you and that 'Camelot' seems to be extremely successful (But that's only what the Financial Times and Daily Mail says – what do you think?).

Joan has been to see me virtually every fortnight since I left Maidstone in 1981, braving all kinds of weather to make the 6-hour return bus journey … and every time she leaves here to go home alone … well, it's not so good, you know. This Christmas she has gone to Jersey to spend a week with her Mum and her sister's family, so at least I'm not so worried about her being alone at this time of year as I normally would be. I saw her a couple of days ago … she looked well … I'm beginning to understand a lot of things, Fiona, that I've been blind to before.

At the moment the temperature in my cell is very low, but outside the sun is shining brightly and the sky is blue – I wouldn't be surprised if it's like this on Christmas Day, however odd that would seem to be! According to Charles Dickens, it ought to be grey with snowflakes the size of lace curtains gently falling, and deep golden lamplight deepening yet further as the evening grows dark, shining on the faces of carollers and the noses of top-hatted gentry going down with influenza. But it's all changed. Except for the prisons, of course.

At the moment the Parole Board is reviewing my case and I'm hoping for a favourable result, maybe a move to an open prison and a date for when I'm to be released. But, as you know, I've had too many hopes raised and crushed in recent years ever to take them seriously.

So I'm taking each day as it comes, living for now. I've taken up art more seriously now, and I've decided to specialise with railway drawings.

Also I've just taken a City & Guilds exam, subject: Communication Skills. I think I'll work towards a degree, or something, what do you think?

Right now I'm down the block – not because I've been in trouble, but at my own request. I've had enough of prison, all it is is containment; there's no concern for individual needs or any effectual plans for rehabilitation whatsoever. Recently I wrote down in a 35-page account all that I've experienced and witnessed over the past 12 years and when I read through it, it was horrific. I gave it to the governor. Maybe it'll help me to get out, maybe not. Probably it won't, because in these places, horror is normal – can you believe it?

I was talking to one of the prison officials only a week ago and he said it wasn't any more terrible than a soldier fighting in the trenches. I said it's a lousy comparison – at least the soldier knows what he's fighting for, and no matter what he sees, or does, he can excuse his actions on the premise that he's doing what's expected of him, and that he's doing it on behalf of ordinary, honest people. And, he said, well at least you'll get through all right, Alex, you've a good sense of humour, and things will work out fine … well, Fiona, it's come to a hell of a pretty pass when the best advice one can get is to treat life, and one's circumstances, as a joke! As I may have said to you before sometime; 'there's a funny side to everything', but it's no less true that there's a serious side to all things, and once the serious side is avoided so, too, is reality.

So, anyway, I decided to come on Solitary, and at least I can now think. It's much quieter down here than on the wing. I get my newspaper every day, and I have the radio to listen to. I can read a book, or sleep. These things are normal things. There aren't many of them, but it's more than I had on the wing, where I found it next to impossible to do anything. There's no question of my <u>not</u> seeing this sentence through, it's not that I think that for a minute – but I really don't see any purpose to my imprisonment. Hey, that's enough of that. I wanted this letter to be a happy one, and look how it's ended up!

How's your higher register? I heard some creep on the radio saying your voice had a good middle register, but that you could maybe do something about your higher. And that Mr Richard Harris wanted half an hour removed from the show's running time … I guess that was agreed to without a great deal of opposition, huh? Why is the show becoming known as Hamlet?

There was quite a good play on Radio 4 yesterday, which I listened to, Marcel Maurette's 'Anastasia', which I liked – although it was the story of a woman who claimed to be Anastasia, and not of Anastasia herself.

I lost my case at the European Court, but I wasn't too concerned – now that's out of the way I can turn my mind to something else. Like, food … which reminds me, I'm starving!

Thank you again for your Christmas Card – it was a kind thought, and perhaps more than I deserve considering how I've neglected to write you – but I hope you will accept my reasons for that … never forget me, because I'll never forget you, my dear friend, and if it sometimes seems a long time between my letters please believe that I think of you very often and wish you a good, safe and happy time, as I have always done.

Lots of Love,

As Ever – YF&B

Alex Xx

The production of 'Camelot' had not been the success we had hoped for and received savage reviews; it was staggering on playing to half-empty houses (It was known as 'Hamlet' because like Shakespeare's longest play it dragged on too much). The atmosphere backstage was fragile, to say the least, and Richard was proving to be an unpredictable leading man, with alarming mood swings. He wasn't happy with the director so another was summoned. I was taken ill over Christmas and ended up in hospital for five days while they tried to figure out what was wrong with me. Eventually gallstones, the size of pebbles, were diagnosed and I was told to stop eating avocados! My understudy, unusually, was rather relieved when I returned.

One highlight of the run, however, was a visit from Elizabeth Taylor, who came backstage after the show and was ushered reverentially into Richard's suite. She was staggeringly beautiful and doll-like—going through one of her thin phases—and sat down on the sofa proclaiming, 'Darling, I'm paaaaaaarched. Has anyone got any champagne around here?' As Harris was on the wagon, her flunky was dispatched to my dressing-room to get a bottle, which she downed with relish.

The following letter arrived just after Alex's 30th birthday:

Segregation Unit
HM Prison Lewes
Sussex
Sunday 13. 2. 1983

To My Dear Friend …

Hello Princess – just a few lines to ask how you are and to say Happy February! Yesterday was sunny, overnight came snow, today is white – how about one of those smiles of yours to get rid of some of this ice! At the moment it is extremely cold; any minute now a finger will drop off and shatter into a thousand pieces … God knows what it's like outside … the world is a Frigidaire.

I heard you for an hour on Radio 2 last Saturday and you sounded well, played some nice music, cheered me up, and a few million others. I enjoyed it. I heard you were ill at Christmas? Sorry to learn that Fiona and I hope things are okay now. Also it was sad to hear of Mr Harris's condition.

I now have City and Guilds distinction passes in Numeracy and Communication Skills – good, eh? In June, if I'm still in prison (who am I kidding?) I'm to take a Foundation Course with the Open University with a view to studying Philosophy and how to operate an iron lung from the inside.

I've just realised I'm running low on batteries (for the radio – not the pacemaker) so it looks like no more of 'The Archers' for at least another week. Crisis, that's too much.

Well, life goes on. I have a bedspread, which I bought some years ago and it's made of – so the label says –'Acrylic'. Anyway, after I woke up (again!) this morning there was a distinct crackling noise coming from it, as I folded it up. Inadvertently, I touched the iron bedstead and I was thrown about two feet! Static electricity. I'd earthed myself – hell of a shock! Sure, and I've heard of electric blankets but this is ridiculous.

The night draws on. It's dark out there … at least, I suppose beyond the wall it is – there are so many spotlights on inside the nick that it's like Heathrow. I guess it's like that so people don't trip over things while they're escaping.

I'll be leaving this place very soon to go to another – I don't know where but I imagine they'll make it interesting; plenty of gangsters, rapists, murderers and footpads.

Seriously, I have no idea where I will be sent. I'm waiting for an answer from the Parole Review Board which will tell me whether I'll be getting out within the next two years or whether I'll have to wait longer. It means a very great deal to me because if it's the latter, I'll be going on segregation, which means I won't get out at all for many years longer. My own choice. Because although I've held on for 12 years to date I certainly won't get through another two-plus. I'm slipping, mentally, physically and spiritually. To keep myself 'together' I need to be alone – and that means segregation. I also think the book project will help in a positive way. Are you still in favour of the book, Fiona?

All I want to do when I get out is write. Can't be done from in here – wrong kind of atmosphere …

Got to go now. Please write soon. Take good care and keep on smiling.

Lots of Love,

Your Friend and Brother,

Alex

There is a different kind of despair running through this letter and I think it is one of resignation. Alex's Parole Review result was bad news. It made me terribly sad and I responded quickly, but unfortunately Alex was moved to Blundeston Prison, Suffolk in February 1983 and didn't receive my letter. Once again he sought to be segregated but this didn't last long because in August he was moved again.

I wrote to Alex with all the news, including the fact that I was selling my little house in West London and buying an apartment in Knightsbridge, a mere bomb-blast away from Harrods. I was juggling my Max Factor commitments with the show, but after 'Camelot' closed and I had moved into the new flat, it was suggested that I try my luck in Los Angeles. Considering my miserable experiences there with Simon in the 1970s, I'm surprised I even considered it but I needed to escape from the obsessive relationship — So in the autumn of 1983 I packed my bags, rented out the Knightsbridge flat to a charming couple from Chile, and left.

I wrote to Alex and told him that I was going to the US for a couple of years but I didn't hear back from him. Unsurprisingly. With hindsight I realise this was probably not the best timing in the world for him; or for either of us, as it turned out. The communication between us was petering out, partly due to geography but mainly because, I suspect, he was drowning in a hopeless quagmire of depression and despair.

Predictably, I hated every minute in LA and missed my home, friends and family very much indeed. My legs, my hips, my teeth, my hair and my face were discussed and analysed. Every fibre in my body felt insecure. LA does that to you.

In August 1983 Alex was transferred to Bristol Prison and then in May 1985 to Dartmoor, where he railed against the regime there.

> 'I was on Hunger Strike for two months. During that time I smuggled a letter out to the local newspaper, which was published.
>
> Basically I was saying that I was innocent but had already served the sentence of a murderer. If I was being treated as a murderer then I would prefer to be given Capital Punishment and be done with it. There's no doubt this embarrassed the Home Office because, two weeks afterward, they gave in and sent me to Preston, a prison much nearer home.'

Shortly after Alex's transfer to Preston I received the following letter written whilst he was recovering from the effects of the hunger strike and indicative of the way things were deteriorating, despite a long-awaited improvement in his security category. Being closer to home was obviously good for him but he continued to maintain a misplaced optimism about his release.

HM Prison Preston
2 Ribbleton Lane
Preston
Lancashire
Sunday 18. 8. 1985

Hello Fiona,

I'm still your friend. I haven't been very well for some time, in and out of hospital, the world upside down, not much going right; anyhow, I've been trying to get myself sorted out and maybe now I'm getting there.

The doctors said I had anorexia and I've lost two stones in weight since 1982. A lot of the cause has been due to worry over my Dad who's just had another heart attack and the silly sod won't give up drinking or smoking. Next time he's not going to be so lucky.

Well, it's 1985. How are you?

My cellmate is also writing a letter … he can't spell and keeps asking me how to write this word or that and it's playing hell with my concentration. He's serving 20 months, only 22 years old, can't see any future for himself … he says all young people are the same where he comes from, one of the districts of Manchester. I think that's terrible. There ought to be <u>something</u>.

One good thing is that I've been downgraded to Cat-C and now it won't be long before I get out – two, maybe three, years. The prison I'm in now is a lot nearer home and I'm happy about that – I can see a lot more of my family. I've only been here two weeks; before that I was in Dartmoor, which is in the middle of nowhere, all mist, fog, wind and driving rain. Hardly any sun – although this seems to be typical of the weather generally so far this year! Up here it's a bit warmer.

Have you mastered that top register yet?

I must stop eating cheese. If I eat cheese sandwiches after 11 pm, the cheese doesn't agree with me – but it's entitled to its own opinion.

Take good care of yourself.

Love, Alex

The reduction in his security category was extremely good news but he had had a rough time during his stay in Dartmoor. The conditions there were dreadful and, quite rightly, he felt seriously aggrieved at being sent to such a remote place. His hunger strike, which had lasted nearly eight weeks, was to draw attention to his situation.

Who made these decisions to place him with murderers and rapists? Eventually, the authorities had no choice but to move him. I felt terrible that I hadn't been in touch with Alex for so long. Since my move to LA, I had been whizzing back and forth between the UK and the USA and ended up doing several movies abroad. One of them, 'A View to A Kill', was filmed in mid-1984 partly at England's Pinewood Studios and partly in San Francisco, so I ended up being rootless again for a while. In this James Bond movie, which was Roger Moore's final foray as 007, I played a Russian KGB double-agent and former ballerina called Pola Ivanova. The synchronicity of my playing Pola Ivanova, Anastasia Romanov and Lisanka Ilyich, three Russians, could be a coincidence I suppose but, looking back, there is an unavoidable irony given Alex's background.

In early 1985, I spent some time in New York and then filmed a series, 'Shaka Zulu', in South Africa, a country that Alex had previously warned me against visiting. I think he was right to be concerned, but I wasn't black-listed.

When the Bond movie had its Royal Premiere in Leicester Square in July 1985, I was wearing a couture gown that had been designed especially for me by David and Elizabeth Emanuel, plus rather a lot of diamonds, which were on loan. As I didn't have a boyfriend at the time, I was 'fixed up' with Sir Gordon White (then chairman of the Hanson Trust) as an escort. When it was all over, I went home alone and slept with the borrowed diamonds under my pillow. A promotional tour followed, with trips to Australia, Europe and South America; I was living up to my nickname of 'Nomad'.

Nineteen-eight-six, my 30th year, began with the filming of various TV movies, when I was suddenly offered the female lead role in a six-part television series called 'The Charmer', starring Nigel Havers as conman, seducer and murderer Ralph Gorse. London Weekend Television were pinning their hopes on this being their flagship series for 1987. Set in the 1930s, filming took six months on location around England and then in the LWT studios.

Alex was still in Preston Prison and his relationship with Joan had ended amicably. He had then started a special friendship with a young girl, K, who had written to him and subsequently visited him. In February 1987, he was moved, again, this time to Stocken Prison in Leicestershire.

The Night Sky of My Soul

Victoria Rd
Stechford
Birmingham
9th July 1987

Dear Fiona,

Alex has given me your letters to look after in safekeeping. However, since I wish to go travelling, things may get lost in transit, so for your own peace of mind Alex has asked me to contact you so that I may return them. I would hate to have to destroy them and I can bring them down to you in London if you like or give them to your agent.

Whenever's convenient Fiona. I'm sure you'd rather have your letters back.

Alex is OK and he sends his love and hopes that you are continuing to meet success, as I do too.

We still don't know his release date and sometimes he gets very depressed. He's got a stomach ulcer now, which isn't being helped either. It's been difficult seeing Alex on a regular basis over the past couple of months but things are getting better.

With lots of love, peace and cosmic wisdom.

K

This letter from 'K', Alex's girlfriend, arrived out of the blue and a meeting with my agent was arranged so that she could return my letters. I was pleased to have them back but also slightly bemused, even if (with the benefit of hindsight) it would never have been possible to write this book without them. But at the time, could it have been a subtle, subliminal way of keeping open a line of communication between Alex and myself? After filming a couple of American mini-series, the summer of 1987 was taken up with promotional work for 'The Charmer' which had been filmed in the previous year for LWT and was due to start airing nationwide that autumn. An appearance at the Cannes TV Festival was followed by endless rounds of interviews, photo-sessions, talk shows and shoots for magazines. My personal life was a mess and in an interview with the *Daily Mirror*, I happened to mention my friendship with Alex, and my guilt at not having been in touch with him. In fact I didn't know where he was until I received the following letter.

Segregation Unit.
HM Prison Stocken
Stretton
Nr Oakham
Leicestershire
10. 10. 1987

Hello Fiona,

Remember the Catherine Cookson poem 'Life Comes in Like the Tide'? It's kept me going. How about you? Never say die. I saw the article in the Mirror yesterday. Came as a bit of a shock. Why go to such lengths to get in touch?

Are you in need of an old friend – life can't be that bad? Better people than myself around. By authorised definition. If all this sounds inane so far, you'd be right to think so; it's difficult for me to write properly at the moment because such a lot needs to be said, or maybe it doesn't – you see?

Too many scars in the night sky of my soul.

Despair. Confusion. Cynicism.

At the moment, my thoughts are scrambled, hard to concentrate. Don't be concerned; you have found me in the centre of a quagmire; tomorrow, next week, whenever, but soon, I'll reach the boundaries and haul myself out – just one of those things, happens to us all, God love us. Maybe the article in the Mirror helps. No. It does. Take care my friend.

With Love and Peace, Ever Your Friend,

Alex X

PS Are your parents well? Please give them my love. And Sunday? Woof. Hope I'll hear from you soon.

HAPPY BIRTHDAY FIONA – THINKING OF YOU.

On receiving this heart-rending note, I was wracked with the thought that my selfishness in not communicating that year (or indeed the year before) had contributed to his feeling of utter despair. He was still in solitary confinement. I wrote to him immediately. That letter is missing although I have Alex's reply in which he tries to take responsibility for our lack of communication and explains why he got K to return my letters to me.

Segregation Unit
HM Prison Stocken
22. 10. 1987

My Dear Friend,

It was a big relief to receive your letter today. I admit to having been more than a little worried and it's good to know now that you're okay; in addition to this you've put my mind at rest regarding the article in the Mirror. I know you lost track of where I was, this was intentional on my part, rightly or wrongly, because I thought things had begun to come together for you in good, positive ways and I had no business writing largely depressive letters, which would be likely to interfere with your happiness.

You must have known how much I respected you as a person, the best friend I ever had (forgive the past tense, unintentional) but I felt it was wrong to burden you with my own black cynicism and despair. I had to get out of it but I could only do it on my own, by myself, in my own way.

Throughout the years that followed I have seen, via the media, how your career has progressed and that you appeared to be happy, which has given me much happiness.

Your letters mean a very great deal to me Fiona, but I decided long ago that they had to be kept safe. I've been moved to a lot of prisons and, in transit, possessions can become misplaced. I gave them to Joan to look after them for me. Later, I was beginning a relationship with an arts student, K, who agreed to take over the safekeeping of the letters. I decided the best thing was for you to have them back. It always played on my mind that if anything happened to me they might end up with the wrong sort of person.

In addition, reading one's own letters written when one was younger can be a fascinating and enlightening experience. Do not think, please, that I want their return to you for any reason other than this. They must get back to you.

I met K about two years ago. We exchanged a couple of letters and she came to see me and we fell in love. She never failed to come to see me on visiting days, hitch-hiking hundreds of miles each time. Ah, I loved K. Still do. She was at university then but things changed after she graduated. My deep love for her became my own undoing and our ultimate break-up. We used to discuss the more profound aspects of life and all things great and small. But two people. One separated from the other.

I should have seen the end coming this summer when she said, 'Alex, if we ever do split, I want us to stay friends.' The idea seemed so utterly appalling I couldn't begin to understand what she was saying.

You and I have something special, but strictly platonic. With K it was molten fire and I gave her my mind, my spirit and greater than these, my love. Which leaves me empty, an abyss. Because K has gone her own way now.

When you love someone so completely, Fiona, when they hit you with 'goodbye' suddenly, it seems so great a betrayal – or is it just me? So I cannot continue as 'friends' with K. Fiona, tell me, am I being unreasonable or do you understand how I'm hurting?

There is, of course, so much about her I don't know, because I've never been with her 'out there'. But nothing can be weirder than a relationship with a guy who lives his life in a box.

I'll tell you what's got me through these years, Fiona. You know some of the places I've been in. I'd lie on my bed in the cell and just think of the awful situation I was in and Fiona, it's amazing how close one can come to real despair.

I'd say to myself, well, you're locked in here and it's a fact they have your body but they sure as hell ain't got what's inside you, your mind, your spirit …

And, well, this made it easier for me. Do you understand?

But as I said in my last letter, I'm pulling out of that quagmire now.

Ah, Fiona, I'm sorry to bend your ears with all this woe but it's been good to get it off my chest, so thanks for that. I'm not feeling so down now.

Poor little Sunday. I was sorry to hear that he has died.

Keep smiling and do take care.

With Love and Peace.

Alex

Now it was my turn to console Alex over his broken heart, just as he had provided such wise counsel for me six years earlier. I was devastated that he should have put so much trust in a young student with her whole life ahead of her and a penchant for travelling. Had the realist in him completely departed?

I told him that my letters had been returned safely (and he was right, reading them was an enlightening experience) and I gave him news of my current activities, such as appearing on Terry Wogan's TV talk show and on 'Aspel and Co' with Michael Aspel to promote 'The Charmer', and I told him that I was currently dating a man called M who was good fun. I was also disappointed that a movie I was due to start in Africa, about an elephant, had just been cancelled.

I enquired as to whether he was still writing poetry, and whether the 'CANTEEN 1st STOCKEN' stamps in the corners of his letters meant that he was working in the prison kitchens! I soon received the following reply bringing me up to date with what had happened to Alex since our correspondence was interrupted.

HM Prison Stocken
25. 11. 1987

Dearest Fiona,

Many thanks for your letter today. I am really glad you got the letters back safely. Maybe I misjudged K but only time will tell.

I won't say I'm sorry that you're not going to Africa after all for now the chances of your being eaten by a lion or swallowed whole by a crocodile are greatly reduced. Not to mention the fact that you won't be away for three months. For how can Christmas be celebrated properly without perfidious Albion's white and frozen shores?

My handwriting isn't up to much today; in fact I've been feeling low due to not enough sleep last night.

The 'CANTEEN' stamp in the top corner means this letter was purchased in the canteen (the name we use for prison shop) – my dear friend, I could never stoop so low as to dish out the spuds and I wish to keep my friends, so I could not put prison spuds on anyone's plate. I have compassion. For people. You see.

Ah, so you have to put up with Wogan, have you? The wit and the blarney you'll be in for, so you will. Seriously, I'd give anything to watch but there's no TV in the part of the prison I'm in, so you see, it's the kind of luck I have.

One day you must visit. Tell me something Fiona, how do you feel about that these days? Would you? Visit? The years seem to be passing by so quickly (in retrospect), maybe as we get older it would not be such a bad thing. As friends. To meet. It is not difficult. I do not presume, navaesta (princess).

Well, you ask how I am. I have not changed, essentially. Ideas and outlooks perhaps, physically yes, now there is grey in my hair and I have progressed to the grand old age of 34. Alas, this takes little account of prison years which, should they be considered, would place me at around eleventy-six. I admit I do not feel so young but I feel full of what I have learned over these years, to the extent that I now understand all things.

Yes, I'm still writing, my friend, when I can. I am studying to prepare for an Arts Foundation course with the Open University, which begins next January. At the end of this month I'm having a poem published in a theatre programme and I'm being paid the princely sum of ten pounds! Good, eh?

I remember I used to send many poems to you in the 1970s. Do you still have any of them? Could you make me a copy of 'Getting Through the Night'? Those poems belong to you – I really should have made written copies for future reference.

Three or four years ago I became an associate member of the Guild of Railway Artists and I draw railway scenes and steam locomotives but I always give them away instead of selling them. Whenever I get out, I want to go professional and really create, with access to materials not allowed in prison. 'The Realm of the Last Inch'. I take that very seriously!

I want to live to see you at the very top of your profession, Fiona. I know you're going to get there. How about theatre? Do you work only in film and television now?

Forget about sending me anything, it's kind of you to offer but your own good friendship is more than enough. I'm off to bed now, so take care.

Love and Peace,

Alex X

So, what calumny and circumstance brought Alex to this place? Was he the architect of his own misfortune or were there darker forces at work? I will never know, but what I do know is that every time I thought of him, a tsunami of sadness engulfed me.

It was as if a light had gone out in my life. This wonderful friend, who had been so kind to me, was receding into a black hole, into the abyss, and I was so wrapped up in my own life that I couldn't even find the time to visit him. Or maybe there was more to it than that. I remember being torn about whether to go to see him or whether this might make things worse. Several friends advised against it, for all sorts of reasons, and I recall being not a little afraid of going inside a prison, of meeting him and of the possible consequences . . .

At what point should Alex have given in to the authorities and sacrificed his principles in the interests of getting out of prison? There is only so much pain, betrayal, injustice and horror that one person can take and stay sane.

At the beginning of 1988, I started filming a P D James TV series 'A Taste For Death' playing a very nasty piece of work, which I relished. This was followed by a glamorous promotional trip for the re-opening of the Mamounia Hotel in Marrakech, with a group of international stars. There are few perks to being a 'celebrity' and this was supposed to be one of them. Unfortunately, because I was due to start rehearsals for 'The Royal Baccarat Scandal', playing a Victorian aristocrat, I was forbidden from acquiring a suntan and had to skulk everywhere covered up to my chin, wearing a large hat! Suddenly, another letter arrived.

HM Prison Stocken
Saturday 6. 5. 1988

My Dear Friend,

Please accept my apology for not writing earlier. I do believe my last few letters to you haven't been very positive in their construction, but sometimes it's difficult to write when there are so many negative aspects influencing one's life. I usually make an extra effort to sort these out before turning my mind to more central matters such as writing to a friend.

I guess I haven't had a very high opinion of myself of late and of course the spin-off from this is a feeling that ergo others must share similar opinions. Anyhow, there's always a dawn at the end of a night, and a new day – and I am beginning to sort myself out and rid myself of the dark pessimism that's been so prevalent up until now.

Today has been a wonderful warm one, with the sun shining throughout – the first real foretaste of the summer to come – I do hope that wherever you are you also have found this day pleasing and bright. I know that you adore the sun.

This year has been a very hectic one so far. At the beginning of it I decided on the positive approach and I began to take up poetry more seriously. My poem 'Return of the Purple Haze' was published and I have since written a sequel 'Escape From the Purple Haze' which I will enclose with this letter. I have also written the first chapter of a book – some 7,500 words – and I am busily studying for an undergraduate place at university for when I get out. It's immensely interesting.

The disciplines involved are History, Literature, Music, Philosophy, Art History, Religion, Culture and Social History. At present I'm reading Ernst Gombrich's 'Art and Illusion'. Fascinating stuff.

K still writes and visits. I think we've said things to hurt each other but we're learning about one another, so instead of growing apart, we're becoming more tolerant of each other and more sensitive to each other's feelings.

Incidentally – this may surprise you – I have become a Quaker, a member of the Society of Friends. Wonderful. I have never felt such a true belonging to any other Christian faith and I'm so glad I have found where I truly belong Fiona, so distant now from the Parkhurst Bolshevik, no? C'est la vie. How strange life is.

I must close now, sometimes my moods and feelings, my outlook, becomes less than what is expected – this is purely the effects of frustration and, sometimes, being alone as a prisoner. Please take this into consideration. Write soon.

Kindest regards to your Mum and Dad.
Take care my friend.

Das Vidaniya!

Alex

Escape From the Purple Haze

Mirage
Image
Imagine
Wild ebony shadows converging
Into a single night where terror boils
(An acidic sea within the living flesh)
Flight!
Blind
Total
The Purple Tendrils reveal Revelation's purpose
Running feet echo as heartbeats crash
And pain pursues, overtakes and holds

Survive!

Resist!

Escape!

To live, and so escape, Strength is all

And Strength is lost—what hope? And yet...

There is yet one blow, one last resource.

And so it is

Your Self is immortal and secure

Within the limits of limitless wisdom

Within the apex of your mind—expand!

From impulse to the outer reaches—expand!

Along the essence, which is truth in you—expand!

A circle is divided into nine equal parts

Six points are connected by a Figure,

Symmetrical in relation to the diameter that passes

Through the uppermost point of the circumference's

divisions

More than this:

The uppermost points of the divisions

Is the apex of an equilateral triangle

Linking together the points of the divisions

Which do not enter into the original Figure's

construction...

Those who knew perceived such significance

That they elected to keep the knowledge of it

Secret!

There, within the reaches of the Purple Haze

Assailed by every sense of forces dark and foul

Describe the diagram with what strength remains

If only by the use of one finger in the dust

For it is the Philosopher's Stone of alchemy and

Is itself that perpetual motion that Man has sought

(But discovered not) since ancient antiquity.

Seek! But seek not outside yourself

For the Answers lay as scattered Gems

Within the garden of your Soul
The keys are found in what is not told
The Spell is invoked.
The Purple Haze is left behind.

Alex 1980

This was the last letter and poem I ever received from Alex and in his final paragraph I could feel him slipping away. His grammar and syntax changed as tiredness, medication and desolation overwhelmed him. By his own admission, life had become so bleak that he felt he could no longer write to me.

After 17 years, why wouldn't they let him go? He had been kept in isolation for much of the last few years so he wasn't causing any trouble. But no-one was fighting his corner. Not yet. Alex was often in my thoughts. I did write back, voicing my concerns about him, giving him news of what I was doing at the time, but sadly I wasn't to hear from him again.

In the summer of 1988 I started rehearsals for 'The Royal Baccarat Scandal' at Chichester Festival Theatre, playing the lead role opposite Keith Michell, which eventually transferred to the West End. My life was becoming ever more tumultuous, with a busy career and social life, a move into a new home in Chelsea and an on-off relationship that was becoming increasingly exhausting.

Later, in August 1988 Alex finally got his wish and, despite the fact that he was still protesting his innocence, was moved to Grendon Prison, where they operate a very different regime to other prisons, based on therapy and cohesion.

David Wilson, who was a governor at Grendon at that time, notes that:

'After a period of assessment, Alex was located on D-Wing, where the wing therapist was the head of the prison's Psychology Department, Dr Eric Cullen. He was fortunate in this allocation, for in Cullen he found a passionate advocate of his case, and someone who was to become a lifelong friend … Gradually Alex began to participate in the life of the wing, eventually becoming wing chairman, and started to take part in therapy groups.'

It was at Grendon that Alex met up again with his old friend Andy from Parkhurst, who had been severely beaten up there. By this time Andy was acutely psychiatrically ill. He spotted Alex one morning from his cell window and called out 'Alex, touch that tree for me.' Alex was to write:

> 'There were some small trees growing in front of the building. The sun was blazing down and the leaves on the trees were green. I reached out and touched one for him. I could only stay briefly, so I gave him a wave.
>
> A few days later Andy spotted me walking by and shouted a greeting. This time he didn't seem so easy within himself and just as I was about to go he said, with immeasurable sadness, and with each word drawn out: "I want someone to hold."
>
> Andy later attacked a member of staff, resulting in him being transferred back to the place he dreaded the most—Parkhurst—where he cut his throat. I hope I'll be able to touch a hell of a lot of trees for him.'

During his time at Grendon, Alex was downgraded to Category-D. In November 1990, he was transferred to Leyhill, an open prison in Gloucestershire. He absconded three weeks later.

It was a calculated risk, but while Alex was on the run he made contact with several newspapers, including *The Guardian*, which ran a story about his case and *The Observer*, where the journalist John Merritt wrote a piece under the headline: 'Burglar Jailed for Life May be Victim of Spy Hunt Gaffe'. Granada Television also subsequently made a documentary about his long-term incarceration called, 'The Curious Case of Alex'.

During his time on the run, several people provided him with a safe house until he returned voluntarily, turning himself in to HM Prison Service at Grendon Prison in February 1991, displaying great dignity and strength of character.

Obviously, the Home Office took a dim view of Alex absconding and refused to let him stay at Grendon, moving him first to the former Oxford Prison and then to Acklington Prison in Northumberland. Finally, he was transferred to Littlehey Prison in Cambridgeshire in June 1991.

During this time, people who had heard about 'The Curious Case of Alex'—and his Kafkaesque nightmare as he railed against the system—began to ask why he had been kept in prison so long. They included criminologists, penal reformers, film-makers, doctors, prison governors and others who believed something had gone wrong and that questions needed to be answered. On one occasion a benefit concert was held in Manchester at which those lending their support included many popular personalities and comedians of the day. Dr Cullen, who worked with Alex at Grendon, proved to be a tenacious ally. He worked tirelessly for his release, including appearing as a witness at Alex's Discretionary Lifer Panel hearing at Littlehey Prison on June 22nd 1993. He testified that Alex was well overdue for release and that he posed no threat to society. It had been a long, hard struggle, but at the end of Alex's arduous journey through the penal system, the panel — after just 30-minutes deliberation — came to the conclusion that there simply wasn't any reason NOT to release him.

Alex was freed on 2nd July 1993, less than two weeks later. He received a discharge grant of £17 but no further assistance or support from the Prison Service. Unfortunately I was on holiday in Portugal at the time and, despite the huge amount of press coverage, was unaware of his release.

I have often wondered, had I known, whether I would have gone to him.

The media circus surrounding Alex soon died down. He had friends and supporters but he was completely institutionalised and, after 22 years of incarceration, it is beyond my comprehension how he coped with adjusting to real life. With freedom, he floundered. The Probation Service initially provided excellent support and a network of friends and campaigners kept him going in the short term. Soon they helped him move into a tiny council flat in Milton Keynes, but despite being with a lady for the first five years, relationships were difficult to sustain and the very fabric of daily life sometimes overwhelming for him.

Alex maintains that people who have committed serious offences can accept their punishment as deserved; that imprisonment is a consequence of their actions and they can therefore, at least, rationalise their situation. This does not apply to the *falsely* accused and the *wrongfully* imprisoned.

For the whole of the time he was held behind bars he considered himself to have been kidnapped and that what was being done to him was illegal. That was how he rationalised his situation and why he found it impossible to conform. He grew further and further apart from his family, until prison was his home and the world outside but a memory. With one exception:

'Becoming friends with Fiona was a turning point. She was an antidote to the shadows and brutality and kicked my soul back into place; she freed my emotions and suddenly I could laugh, worry, empathise, be happy, and be sad … In a very real way she released my senses and my feelings and struck a blow against those who had taken my life away from me. A candle was lit and the flame was never to go out.

My earliest poems were written for Fiona because she gave me inspiration and spiritual encouragement in the early years of my imprisonment, providing me with a lifeline into normality. She was the antidote to the oppressiveness blanketing of my soul; if it were not for her, I doubt I would be here today.'

By the end of 1993 I was having serious misgivings about my career. For some reason I was unhappy and restless and realised that I was unfulfilled. The clock was ticking. In 1994, after a harrowing stint in 'Death and the Maiden', a play about a female political prisoner in Chile who was beaten and raped, I was cast as Eliza Dolittle in 'Pygmalion' at Chichester Festival Theatre. To play Eliza had been a lifetime's ambition. During the run I met a businessman called Neil Shackell and found in him a kindred spirit, someone who could see past the façade I had been trying to maintain. That autumn he asked me to marry him but I had agreed to a three-month tour of Somerset Maugham's comedy 'The Constant Wife'. In December 1994, I married Neil and settled into a life of domestic bliss. Having acquired a beautiful young son by my husband's late wife, I made a life-changing decision to give up acting — and the following year we had a daughter. I never stepped onto a stage again.

I often spoke of Alex to my husband and wondered where he was and how he was coping. I was told that he had been released in 1993, but the years seemed to gallop past and I never actively tried to find him. Alex, for his part, kept a respectful distance and didn't make contact with me, although he says he tried to do so, unsuccessfully, on two occasions.

- Epilogue -

2011

Let us have compassion for those under chastisement. Alas, who are we ourselves?
Who am I and who are you? Whence do we come and is it quite certain that we
did nothing before we were born? This earth is not without some resemblance to
a gaol. Who knows but that man is a victim of divine justice? Look closely at life.
It is so constituted that one senses punishment everywhere.

Victor Hugo

That day in February 2011 when I discovered Alex's letters in a box at home
was not, to all intents and purposes, an unusual day. It began much like any
other. But how often do we, on reaching a certain age, feel that we would
simply ADORE something extraordinary to happen? Just then, a fat pigeon
fell down the chimney and created havoc in the office. Luckily, there wasn't
much soot but an awful lot of twigs and debris. I spent the next hour clear-
ing up the mess, vacuuming around the boxes in the process.

Eventually I got down to the task in hand, as I explained in the *Prologue*,
which was to find a certain document amongst some old archive material,
when I stumbled upon Alex's correspondence, poems and stamps. So something extraordinary *had* happened. Over the next 24 hours, having re-read
most of the letters, I became consumed by the need to know whether Alex
was still alive and if he was alright. Inexplicably, I was stricken with grief
and guilt, much to the consternation of my family. So I had to find him.

The internet seemed to have thousands of references to Alex Alexandrowicz, which was heartening: newspaper articles, television programmes, the
book he wrote with David Wilson and, indeed, there he was on Facebook!

I thought it would be easy. However, all the trails went cold. His personal website had not been updated for several years and neither had his social networking links which had been abandoned in 2009.

I contacted his publisher, Bryan Gibson, his doctor and greatest campaigner, Dr Eric Cullen and David Wilson (no longer Alex's prison governor but by then a Professor of Criminology). They all told me the same thing; that they had lost all contact with Alex and that he had somehow 'disappeared'. There was even talk that he may have returned to Russia or Ukraine although someone did say he'd heard Alex was working with the homeless and living rough.

I checked the register for deaths and even contacted the Prison Service, in case he was back inside (God forbid!). Nothing. I emailed people with tenuous links to Alex but it seemed that I would have to face up to the fact that I might never, ever find him.

Frustrated, I spoke to the Probation Service in Milton Keynes, where he was last known to have been living, thinking he might still be there (he would be under their supervision as an ex-life sentence prisoner), but strangely even they came back negative. I scoured the electoral register in various places, including Nelson, his hometown, and Milton Keynes, but he had slipped under the radar. Thinking he might have returned to his home county, I called the *Lancashire Telegraph* and spoke to a journalist about my search. He ran a story under the headline:

'Former Bond Girl Searches for Cold War Spy Suspect'.

The media pricked up its ears and soon I was appearing on TV and radio telling my story about Alex's mysterious disappearance and appealing for help to find him. Maybe someone, somewhere, knew where he was?

Eventually, a national newspaper called to offer help in exchange for an interview about our friendship. I agreed and to my astonishment they found him the next day, still living in the same flat in Milton Keynes that he had inhabited for 13 years. Having become a recluse, he had lost all contact with the outside world.

Two days later, on Friday 20th May 2011, in the bright sunshine of a Buckinghamshire garden, Alex walked unsteadily towards me and held out his hand. Ever the gentleman, he didn't presume to give me a hug. I threw my arms around him. He looked wonderful and *exactly* how I had imagined him to be. A tall, proud and upright man with a full head of hair, which he wears slicked back in true Slavic style, and a full, white beard. With his piercing blue eyes and high cheekbones, he looked every inch the Russian aristocrat.

We talked quietly for two hours on our own and what was immediately apparent was how comfortable we were in each other's company. It was as if the intervening years had evaporated and I had found a long-lost brother. He struck me as frail and in poor health, which, after years of hunger strikes and taking powerful medication, is hardly surprising. He is in constant pain from his kidneys but his wit and dry humour is still intact and, remarkably, his eyes often twinkle.

Since our initial meeting, the bond between us has grown ever stronger. With extraordinary foresight, everything he wrote in his letters about friends and friendship has come true. With my husband Neil's blessing, Alex and I now meet every week and speak constantly.

Our first venture out together was to the Ashmolean Museum in Oxford, where Alex explained the finer details in certain paintings. This was followed by a visit to the Bodleian Library. With blissful irony, Oxford Prison (where he was once briefly incarcerated) is now a luxury hotel called *Malmaison*, with guests staying in the converted cells! Not knowing how he would feel about seeing the place I tried to steer him in the other direction, but he wanted to go inside. Once there, the plush interior seemed to scream at me. He wanted to show me his cell.

'Oh, they've got carpet now,' was all he said.

Our next outing was to a steam railway museum where Alex could name all of the different types of engine, from his time as an artist of locomotives. He would chat knowledgeably and happily to me but then become withdrawn in the presence of strangers. Over the ensuing months I have seen this improve and he now interacts more readily.

I was quite unprepared for just how institutionalised someone who has spent a long time in prison can be. Even after 18 years of freedom, Alex can still be floored by a simple task, such as ordering fish and chips in a pub, so I have assumed the role of introducing him to some of the more normal, mundane activities in life, which most of us perform unthinkingly. He doesn't drive but enjoys going on journeys and walks, and the simple pleasure of sitting in a field, chatting about life, while a red kite hovers above, takes on a different meaning with Alex.

We talk easily, but he just says, 'We've known each other a long time Fiona. We have a history.'

He has talked about his childhood and how his father died shortly after he came out of prison. His mother never forgave him for remaining loyal to his father and for arranging the funeral and, sadly, he hasn't seen her since. His sister, Susan, moved abroad whilst he was in prison. He has no close friends anymore, although shortly after his release he had a girlfriend for five years.

For a while, Alex used his incapacity benefit to subsidise a service enabling people to get bus timetable information on their mobile phones, which he ran from his flat, until the council objected and closed it down. He also did a high-profile walk from Manchester to the House of Commons in 1994, to protest about changes to prison law. In Milton Keynes, after his relationship failed, he became close to another family, becoming godfather to the youngest, but they moved away and he has lost contact. This is a source of enormous regret, as they were the only family he had for a while. This was when the shutters came down and he withdrew from society completely.

His knowledge, however, is tremendous and we have interesting discussions, with me taking on the role of pupil once again. There is no question that he is an intelligent man. Was this Alex's problem inside? Was he cleverer than the people trying to restrain him? Was he too articulate?

After years in a darkened flat in Milton Keynes, which he would often refer to, accidentally as his 'cell', his rehabilitation had to be gradual, but I became anxious that his living conditions were threatening his health. For years, he had been without heating or hot water and his bronchitis was worsening. I rang the council (something he wouldn't do for himself) and they fixed the heating the same day. The neighbourhood was also proving a challenge because, being on life licence, he could not risk trouble or he might be recalled to prison. Unfortunately, trouble was on his doorstep and he was unable to deal with it.

Eventually after a stint in hospital, he said he wanted to move, so after much form-filling and the kind of bureaucracy that Alex abhors, I managed to relocate him, with the help of the local council, to a sunny flat with a pleasant view, in a place that is proving much better for his health.

So now Alex is a part of my family. I finally have the brother I always wanted. It just took me a while to find him.

Alex has such a gentle soul and I feel extraordinarily protective of him. But above all, I burn with anger that this great, proud man should have battled, *for almost his entire life,* for justice.

However, far more mysterious is the feeling between us that we are old souls in a modern world, who have known each other before. And there is a pervading sense of relief that, at last, we have found each other.

Index

SIR WILLIAM GARROW
His Life, Times and Fight for Justice
John Hostettler and Richard Braby
Foreword Geoffrey Robertson QC

The true story of the central character in the BBC prime-time drama 'Garrow's Law'.

Written by historian and biographer John Hostettler and family storyteller Richard Braby (a descendent of Garrow).

'A blockbuster of a book' *Phillip Taylor*

'A delight' *Internet Law Book Reviews*

www.**WatersidePress.co.uk/SWG**

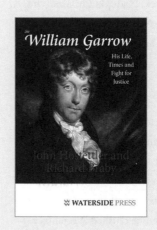

Extent	352 pages
Format	Paperback
Published	January 2011
ISBN	978-1-904380-69-6

THE CURIOUS MR HOWARD
Legendary Prison Reformer
Tessa West, Foreword by Clive Stafford-Smith

'A riveting account' *The Guardian*

'A wonderful book'
Times Literary Supplement

'Impeccably researched and
fascinating' *The Howard Journal*

'A brilliant book' *Nick Hardwick*

www.**WatersidePress.co.uk/CMH**

Extent	384 pages
Format	Hardback
Published	May 2011
ISBN	978-1-904380-73-3

THE LONGEST INJUSTICE
The Strange Story of Alex Alexandrowicz
Alex Alexandrowicz and David Wilson

Read Alex Alexandrowicz's own story including more from his '**Prison Chronicles**'.

'Challenges the very fabric of our understanding of the legal and penal processes in the UK'
Internet Law Book Reviews

www.**WatersidePress.co.uk/Alex**

Extent	160 pages
Format	Paperback
Published	July 1999
ISBN	978-1-872870-45-8

07788 470097.